Praise for
Software Engineering with Microsoft Visual Studio Team System

W9-BLK-118

"Fascinating! This book is packed with details about VSTS' capabilities, and the reason behind why these capabilities were included in the VSTS product—information that only an internal team member could provide. Perhaps more importantly, each technical capability or how-to instruction is encased in the explanation of why the functionality is critical to you. The book discards the pitfalls within processes of the past while amplifying the sweet spots within those same processes. In so doing, it defines the methodology direction of the future and identifies the metrics for refining and customizing that methodology within your own projects."
    —Mark Michaelis, author of *Essential C# 2.0*

"This book is a must read for anyone hoping to embrace Visual Studio Team System and Microsoft Solutions Framework 4.0 as intended by their creators. One of its key themes is 'agility with accountability.' It explains the paradigm shift to a value-up project approach, and describes how Team System enables this shift. The many examples of how this approach was applied to the development of VSTS bring the message to life on a meaningful scale."
    —Aaron Kowall, EDS Applications Portfolio Development,
    Innovation Engineering

"Sam Guckenheimer ushers in the era of trustworthy transparency that will revolutionize the way we manage software development projects. Don't just buy Visual Studio Team System; learn how to use it to drive change and reap the rewards. Sam shows you how."
    —David J. Anderson, author of *Agile Management for Software Engineering*

"In 250 pages, Sam has captured the essence of Visual Studio Team System. If you are involved in the process of making software or managing software projects—as a developer, tester, project manager, architect, or CIO—you'll want a copy for everyone on your team. The book both makes modern software engineering practices approachable, and does so with clear examples of how to implement them with Team System tools. Unlike previous books on software methodology, this one does not shy away from putting the principles into practice. Whether you already have VSTS, are considering it, or just want to improve your software productivity and business alignment, you'll find this full of insight. The book is enjoyable, approachable, and easy to read in a weekend."
    —Rick LaPlante, general manager, Visual Studio Team System, Microsoft

"Sam Guckenheimer has been one of the intellectual powerhouses and mentors for the software testing community for years. It is a pleasure to see a book from him at last, especially one that illustrates his vision as well as this one does."
> —Cem Kaner, J.D., Ph.D., professor of software engineering,
> Florida Institute of Technology; lead author of *Lessons Learned in Software Testing* and *Testing Computer Software*

"In *Software Engineering with Microsoft Visual Studio Team System*, Sam Guckenheimer captures the gestalt of Team System and the emerging software process paradigm of value-up. Measuring the value delivered, instead of the long-held paradigm of measuring work accomplished, is core to Team System's design and implementation. As a result, you will find that the unprecedented project transparency Team System provides improves team interaction and project predictability. Moreover, it does so without burdening team members with time-robbing overhead. You must read this book to appreciate fully the vision behind Team System and the virtuous cycle of value-up software development it makes possible."
> —Rob Caron, content architect, Microsoft; author of *Team System Nexus*

"Sam Guckenheimer is a technical diplomat. In a world where the guerilla forces of agile methods are aligned against the armored legions of CMMI, Sam provides a path for coexistence. This is first and foremost a book about software engineering. In discussing flash points such as planning, documentation, governance, auditability, and organization, Sam presents the case for both agile and more formal practices, as well as describing the optimal conditions for each. Even though the material is presented in the context of VSTS, the guidance is universal. Sam writes to each of the roles on a project, providing them with sound advice regardless of the 'weight' they have chosen for their practices. The material is current and timely, with discussions of service oriented architectures, Test-Driven Development, and design techniques developed in the user interface community. Sam's book is a Very Superior Text on Software."
> —Dr. Bill Curtis, chief process officer, Borland Software Corporation;
> lead author of *People Capability Maturity Model*

"Sam Guckenheimer is a true advocate for the user. Buoyed by Team System, a platform that provides process in a way that is automated by tools, managed by metrics, and nearly transparent to the user, he presents an approach to software engineering that is practical and achievable without ignoring the fact that we have hard problems to solve."
> —James Behling, Accenture Delivery Methods lead architect, Accenture

"Sam Guckenheimer and I have always walked a common road to improving support between development and operations teams. Sam's book delivers an easy to understand, process-centered approach to the best practices of software development embodied in MSF and delivered through Visual Studio Team System. The 'waterfall' is a failure, but Sam's book can guide you through the use of Visual Studio Team System to rapid development with just enough process to get the job done."

—Brian White, senior director of product management, iConclude, Inc., author of *Software Configuration Management Strategies and Rational ClearCase: A Practical Introduction*

"Transparency is a critical element in today's agile environment. Sam was and still is instrumental in creating the overall architecture that provides the level of integration and transparency in Team System necessary to scale agile projects to larger teams. This transparency, if used in an environment fostering trust and personal safety, can create more productive development teams while propagating the discipline of agile methods. Reporting information such as velocity becomes effortless. Now the entire software development team, including business analysts, architects, and testers, can join in the agile process."

—Granville "Randy" Miller, co-author of *A Practical Guide to eXtreme Programming and Advanced Use Case Modeling*

"Can you imagine having a Business Process Re-engineering (BPR) tool for software engineering (SE)? A tool that could actually help the IT industry get leaner? This is what this book is all about! It's an eye opener: a door to a new era of SE. The question at stake in this book is simple: Could MSFT VSTS empower our IT industry to become more of a science and less of an art that it has been up to now? Sam Guckenheimer explains not only why this could be the case, but also gives many tips on how an entire SE team could evolve to be more productive and efficient, without manual overhead."

—Francis T. Delgado, senior program manager, Avanade, Inc.

Software Engineering with Microsoft Visual Studio Team System

Microsoft .NET Development Series

John Montgomery, *Series Advisor*
Don Box, *Series Advisor*
Martin Heller, *Series Editor*

The Microsoft .NET Development Series is supported and developed by the leaders and experts of Microsoft development technologies including Microsoft architects. The books in this series provide a core resource of information and understanding every developer needs in order to write effective applications and managed code. Learn from the leaders how to maximize your use of the .NET Framework and its programming languages.

Titles in the Series

Brad Abrams, *.NET Framework Standard Library Annotated Reference Volume 1: Base Class Library and Extended Numerics Library*, 0-321-15489-4

Brad Abrams and Tamara Abrams, *.NET Framework Standard Library Annotated Reference, Volume 2: Networking Library, Reflection Library, and XML Library*, 0-321-19445-4

Keith Ballinger, *.NET Web Services: Architecture and Implementation*, 0-321-11359-4

Bob Beauchemin and Dan Sullivan, *A Developer's Guide to SQL Server 2005*, 0-321-38218-8

Bob Beauchemin, Niels Berglund, Dan Sullivan, *A First Look at SQL Server 2005 for Developers*, 0-321-18059-3

Don Box with Chris Sells, *Essential .NET, Volume 1: The Common Language Runtime*, 0-201-73411-7

Keith Brown, *The .NET Developer's Guide to Windows Security*, 0-321-22835-9

Eric Carter and Eric Lippert, *Visual Studio Tools for Office: Using C# with Excel, Word, Outlook, and InfoPath*, 0-321-33488-4

Eric Carter and Eric Lippert, *Visual Studio Tools for Office: Using Visual Basic 2005 with Excel, Word, Outlook, and InfoPath*, 0-321-41175-7

Mahesh Chand, *Graphics Programming with GDI+*, 0-321-16077-0

Krzysztof Cwalina and Brad Abrams, *Framework Design Guidelines: Conventions, Idioms, and Patterns for Reusable .NET Libraries*, 0-321-24675-6

Len Fenster, *Effective Use of Microsoft Enterprise Library: Building Blocks for Creating Enterprise Applications and Services*, 0-321-33421-3

Sam Guckenheimer and Juan J. Perez, *Software Engineering with Microsoft Visual Studio Team System*, 0-321-27872-0

Anders Hejlsberg, Scott Wiltamuth, Peter Golde, *The C# Programming Language*, Second Edition, 0-321-33443-4

Alex Homer, Dave Sussman, Mark Fussell, *ADO.NET and System.Xml v. 2.0—The Beta Version*, 0-321-24712-4

Alex Homer and Dave Sussman, *ASP.NET 2.0 Illustrated*, 0-321-41834-4

Alex Homer, Dave Sussman, Rob Howard, *ASP.NET v. 2.0—The Beta Version*, 0-321-25727-8

Joe Kaplan and Ryan Dunn, *The .NET Developer's Guide to Directory Services Programming*, 0-321-35017-0

Mark Michaelis, *Essential C# 2.0*, 0-321-15077-5

James S. Miller and Susann Ragsdale, *The Common Language Infrastructure Annotated Standard*, 0-321-15493-2

Christian Nagel, *Enterprise Services with the .NET Framework: Developing Distributed Business Solutions with .NET Enterprise Services*, 0-321-24673-X

Brian Noyes, *Data Binding with Windows Forms 2.0: Programming Smart Client Data Applications with .NET*, 0-321-26892-X

Fritz Onion, *Essential ASP.NET with Examples in C#*, 0-201-76040-1

Fritz Onion, *Essential ASP.NET with Examples in Visual Basic .NET*, 0-201-76039-8

Ted Pattison and Dr. Joe Hummel, *Building Applications and Components with Visual Basic .NET*, 0-201-73495-8

Dr. Neil Roodyn, *eXtreme .NET: Introducing eXtreme Programming Techniques to .NET Developers*, 0-321-30363-6

Chris Sells and Michael Weinhardt, *Windows Forms 2.0 Programming*, 0-321-26796-6

Chris Sells, *Windows Forms Programming in C#*, 0-321-11620-8

Chris Sells and Justin Gehtland, *Windows Forms Programming in Visual Basic .NET*, 0-321-12519-3

Guy Smith-Ferrier, *.NET Internationalization: The Developer's Guide to Building Global Windows and Web Applications*, 0-321-34138-4

Paul Vick, *The Visual Basic .NET Programming Language*, 0-321-16951-4

Damien Watkins, Mark Hammond, Brad Abrams, *Programming in the .NET Environment*, 0-201-77018-0

Shawn Wildermuth, *Pragmatic ADO.NET: Data Access for the Internet World*, 0-201-74568-2

Paul Yao and David Durant, *.NET Compact Framework Programming with C#*, 0-321-17403-8

Paul Yao and David Durant, *.NET Compact Framework Programming with Visual Basic .NET*, 0-321-17404-6

For more information go to www.awprofessional.com/msdotnetseries/

Software Engineering with Microsoft Visual Studio Team System

■ Sam Guckenheimer
with Juan J. Perez

✦Addison-Wesley

Upper Saddle River, NJ • Boston • Indianapolis • San Francisco
New York • Toronto • Montreal • London • Munich • Paris • Madrid
Cape Town • Sydney • Tokyo • Singapore • Mexico City

The publisher offers excellent discounts on this book when ordered in quantity for bulk purchases or special sales, which may include electronic versions and/or custom covers and content particular to your business, training goals, marketing focus, and branding interests. For more information, please contact:

> U. S. Corporate and Government Sales
> (800) 382-3419
> corpsales@pearsontechgroup.com

For sales outside the U. S., please contact:

> International Sales
> international@pearsoned.com

Visit us on the Web: www.awprofessional.com

This Book Is Safari Enabled

Safari BOOKS ONLINE ENABLED The Safari® Enabled icon on the cover of your favorite technology book means the book is available through Safari Bookshelf. When you buy this book, you get free access to the online edition for 45 days. Safari Bookshelf is an electronic reference library that lets you easily search thousands of technical books, find code samples, download chapters, and access technical information whenever and wherever you need it. To gain 45-day Safari Enabled access to this book:

- Go to http://www.awprofessional.com/safarienabled
- Complete the brief registration form
- Enter the coupon code 9WFX-DMEE-QD7K-SWE8-6R1Y

If you have difficulty registering on Safari Bookshelf or accessing the online edition, please e-mail customer-service@safaribooksonline.com.

Library of Congress Catalog Number:
Guckenheimer, Sam, 1956-
  Software engineering with Visual studio team system / Sam Guckenheimer, Juan J. Perez.
    p. cm.
  ISBN 0-321-27872-0 (pbk. : alk. paper)
1. Microsoft Visual studio. 2. Software engineering. 3. Microsoft .NET Framework. I. Perez, Juan J. II. Title.
  QA76.758.G82 2006
  005.1--dc22
                                2006004369

ISBN 0-321-27872-0

Text printed in the United States on recycled paper at R. R. Donnelley in Crawfordsville, Indiana.

Fifth Printing, October 2007

*To my wife, Monica, whose support
made this book possible.*

Contents

CHAPTER 6   **Development**

About the Author

Sam Guckenheimer has 25 years of experience as architect, developer, tester, product manager, project manager, and general manager in the software industry in the U.S. and Europe. Currently, Sam is the group product planner for Microsoft Visual Studio Team System. In this capacity, he acts as chief customer advocate, responsible for the end-to-end external design of the next releases of these products. Prior to joining Microsoft in 2003, Sam was director of Product Line Strategy at Rational Software Corporation, now the Rational Division of IBM. He holds five patents on software life-cycle tools. A frequent speaker at industry conferences, Sam is a Phi Beta Kappa graduate of Harvard University.

Sam lives in the Puget Sound area with his wife and three of his four children.

Foreword

For almost ten years I've been encouraging Sam Guckenheimer to write a book about software engineering. "Oh no, I'm not ready," was the invariable reply.

With the release of Visual Studio Team System, Sam no longer had an excuse: he really *had* to explain his ideas about software engineering to help people make sense of the product that embodies them. It's great to see that turn into a book that puts equal weight on practicum and theory, rather than a book-length product advertisement or a vague discussion of the philosophy of software engineering. I like the concrete examples here: they make the concepts come alive.

One key concept in this book is that of value-up processes. Sam believes that we are facing a huge paradigm shift in the way we approach software, which rings true. The work-down paradigm has led to a number of problems with the software development process and ultimately to a high rate of failed projects. Whether the value-up paradigm will solve the problems without creating new ones, of course, remains to be seen.

In the past, the practice of software metrics has not kept up with its potential, largely because of the high cost of collecting data. As Sam explains in this book, instrumenting daily activities to allow painless data collection opens up a new set of opportunities for meaningful metrics. Sam hasn't stopped there; he has applied some of the more interesting techniques from lean project management to demonstrate how to troubleshoot software projects on a daily basis. That also enables the reliable application of value-up processes.

For almost a decade, a number of ideas have percolated in the various areas of software engineering: in programming, user experience, testing, and architecture. Sam has pulled the best of these together to apply across the entire software lifecycle.

I trust that you'll enjoy them as much as I have.

Ivar Jacobson, Ph.D.
Ivar Jacobson Consulting LLC

Preface

Why I Wrote This Book

I joined Microsoft in 2003 to work on Visual Studio Team System (VSTS), the new product line that was just released at the end of 2005. As the group product planner, I have played chief customer advocate, a role that I have loved. I have been in the IT industry for twenty-some years, spending most of my career as a tester, project manager, analyst, and developer.

As a tester, I've always understood the theoretical value of advanced developer practices, such as unit testing, code coverage, static analysis, and memory and performance profiling. At the same time, I never understood how anyone had the patience to learn the obscure tools that you needed to follow the right practices.

As a project manager, I was always troubled that the only decent data we could get was about bugs. Driving a project from bug data alone is like driving a car with your eyes closed and only turning the wheel when you hit something. You really want to see the right indicators that you are on course, not just feel the bumps when you stray off it. Here too, I always understood the value of metrics, such as code coverage and project velocity, but I never understood how anyone could realistically collect all that stuff.

As an analyst, I fell in love with modeling. I think visually, and I found graphical models compelling ways to document and communicate. But the models always got out of date as soon as it came time to implement anything. And the models just didn't handle the key concerns of developers, testers, and operations.

And in all these cases, I was frustrated by how hard it was to connect the dots for the whole team. I loved the idea in Scrum (one of the agile processes) of a "single product backlog"—one place where you could see all the work—but the tools people could actually use would fragment the work every which way. What do these requirements have to do with those tasks, and the model elements here, and the tests over there? And where's the source code in that mix?

From a historical perspective, I think IT turned the corner when it stopped trying to automate manual processes and instead asked the question, "With automation, how can we reengineer our core business processes?" That's when IT started to deliver real business value.

They say the cobbler's children go shoeless. That's true for IT, too. While we've been busy automating other business processes, we've largely neglected our own. Virtually all tools targeted for IT professionals and teams seem to still be automating the old manual processes. Those processes required high overhead before automation, and with automation, they still have high overhead. How many times have you gone to a one-hour project meeting where the first ninety minutes were an argument about whose numbers were right?

Now, with Visual Studio Team System, we are seriously asking, "With automation, how can we reengineer our core IT processes? How can we remove the overhead from following good process? How can we make all these different roles individually more productive while integrating them as a high-performance team?"

Who Should Read This Book

This book is written for a software team that is considering running a software project using VSTS. This book is about the why, not the *how*.[1] What are the guiding ideas behind VSTS? Why are certain ideas presented in certain ways? For example, why are so many things called work items? What does the metrics warehouse measure? Why would you use those particular reports?

It has been my experience time and time again that knowledgeable, skillful, experienced people bring uneven starting assumptions to software projects. What appear to be self-evident truths to one person are folk myths to another, and one person's common wisdom is another's discovery. This issue is exacerbated by a natural emphasis on functional roles, which are often baked into career ladders. I certainly believe that there are expert developers, expert testers, expert architects, expert business analysts, and expert project managers, but delivering customer value requires collaboration across all disciplines. Attempts to optimize one special role in isolation from the others do not necessarily improve the delivery of results as the customer sees them.

One way of solving the discrepancies has been to have an onsite coach who can lead the team through a consistent set of processes. Coaches are great, but not everyone has the luxury of working with one. So, because I cannot ship you an on-demand coach, I've written this book.

This is *not* a step-by-step tutorial in the sense of a user manual that tells you where to click in what sequence. Plenty of good documentation on those topics is available with VSTS, and I reference it where appropriate. Rather, this book offers a framework for thinking about software projects in a way that can be directly tooled by VSTS. Indeed, we built VSTS to run software projects this way.

This book is also not a survey of software engineering literature. Dozens, perhaps hundreds, of books have been written about software engineering in the last forty years. I do not recap them here, and I do not cover all the material that they do. I expect the criticism from many experts that some of my arguments go without saying nowadays. Unfortunately, as Freud pointed out, what goes without saying is often *not* said at all. As a result, differences in team members' assumptions are not exposed until the wrong argument happens. So if you want to fault me for stating too many obvious things, I'm guilty as charged.

I present enough Team System theory and practice examples to describe a realistic process for most mainstream IT projects and teams. It may not be formal enough for avionics software that requires FAA approval; it may not be loose enough for a three-person team co-located in a garage.

How to Read This Book

VSTS includes process guidance called Microsoft Solutions Framework (MSF), which includes the central concept of a *team model* based on a team of peers. The team model allows for different scales of specialization. MSF defines seven constituencies, or points of view, that must be represented on a successful project, and it includes recommendations for scaling up and down. I call out these points of view throughout the book with icons that look like this:

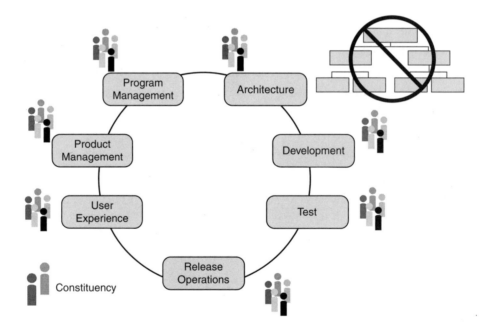

Figure P.1   Microsoft Solutions Framework introduces a model of a team of peers, anchored in seven viewpoints that need to be represented for a successful project. MSF for CMMI Process Improvement specializes the seven into eighteen, whereas MSF for Agile Software Development realizes the seven with six roles, clustering product management and user experience, and offers guidelines to reduce the list to three.

This book is written for the team as a whole. It presents information in a style that will help all team members get a sense of each other's viewpoint. However, role-specific sections are called out so that you can focus on or skim over portions as needed for your specific roles. I've tried to keep the topics at a level that is engaging to all team members and not arcane for any. (For some, this choice may reinforce the criticism of simplicity.) In this age of specialization, I think it is important to have at least this level of contract with and expectations of your colleagues in other specialties. If you're in a hurry, you can use the constituency icons as a guide to the role-related topics that interest you most.

Pointers to Documentation

As I said, this is not a how-to book. Where details of VSTS or its documentation are appropriate, you will see a pointer to it, like this example:

Microsoft Developer Network Subscription (MSDN)

Every VSTS includes a subscription to Microsoft Developer Network. Start at http://msdn.microsoft.com/teamsystem and follow the links for Reference → Product Documentation. There may be a number of terms for which you want to check the usage. To look them up, please consult the MSDN topic:

Development Tools and Technologies

Visual Studio Team System

Visual Studio Team System Glossary

I made this choice because I assume that most of the time that you are reading this book, you are not sitting in front of a computer, and occasionally you will want to go back and try something hands-on. When you're just reading, you can skip these pointers.

Other People's Ideas

My goal in this book is to introduce the ideas behind VSTS, not to claim the ideas as original. VSTS was designed from the ground up to enable different processes to be applied to fit different organizations and projects. VSTS, and correspondingly this book, make liberal use of good practices that have been developed by the software community. Where possible, I've tried to capture relevant sources in endnotes. If you're not interested in the references, you don't need to read the endnotes.

Enough About VSTS to Get You Started

Reviewers of early drafts of this book complained that I did not explain clearly enough what is in VSTS, so I'm putting a product introduction in the following sidebar, straight from a Microsoft Web page. There are currently four VSTS client products, and there may be more in the future, but I do not distinguish them because the value is in the Team Suite. Of course, Microsoft lets you buy the functionality à la carte, but I'm going to keep things simple.

So when I write about "VSTS" or "Team System," assume that I am writing about the Team Suite.

Part of VSTS is Microsoft Solutions Framework (MSF), shown as the "Process Guidance" box in Figure P.2. MSF comes in two forms out of the box and can be customized into countless variations. The two standard ones are

- MSF for Agile Software Development
- MSF for CMMI Process Improvement

I'll describe these in a little more depth later, but basically, if your organization is new to software process, start with MSF for Agile Software Development. If you need more formality due to geographic distribution, process improvement programs, compliance audits, or the desire for CMMI appraisal, then you should consider MSF for CMMI Process Improvement.

Unless it's necessary to distinguish these variants, I will I stick to concepts that are common to both.

Introducing Visual Studio 2005 Team System

From Microsoft's Marketing Department

Visual Studio 2005 Team Edition for Software Developers provides advanced development tools that enable teams to build reliable, mission-critical services and applications.

Visual Studio 2005 Team Edition for Software Architects provides visual designers that enable architects, operations managers, and developers to design service-oriented solutions that can be validated against their operational environments.

Visual Studio 2005 Team Edition for Software Testers provides advanced load testing tools that enable teams to verify the performance of applications prior to deployment.

Visual Studio 2005 Team Suite combines each of these products into a comprehensive lifecycle management tool which addresses the needs of multifunctional roles in an organization.

All these products are supported by **Visual Studio 2005 Team Foundation Server,** an extensible team collaboration server that enables all members of the extended IT team to effortlessly manage and track the progress and health of projects.

Figure P.2   Visual Studio 2005 Team System is comprised of four client products and one server product.

Disclaimer

Finally, I need to be clear that the views in this book are my own and not necessarily those of Microsoft Corporation. Although I am a Microsoft employee, I am writing on my own behalf, and not for the company. Don't blame Microsoft for the opinions I express and the errors I make here (unless you want to tell them they made a bad hire), but blame me instead. You can flame me on my blog directly at http://blogs.mircosoft.com/sam/.

Endnotes

1. For a how-to book, see Will Stott and James Newkirk, *Visual Studio Team System—Better Software Development for Agile Teams* (Boston, MA: Addison-Wesley, 2006).

Acknowledgments

There are several people whose prodding distinctly helped me write this book. Let me start by acknowledging my editor, Karen Gettman, who was willing to consider a first-time author with a vision and proposal. Ivar Jacobson and Cem Kaner have separately been important mentors, who have encouraged me to write for many years.

Next is Rick LaPlante, who is still my boss at my day job. Rick took a bet on me when he hired me as group product planner for Visual Studio Team System, and he has been a completely supportive manager. Beyond Rick are a couple hundred colleagues who have made VSTS the product that it is. Every contact with them has been and continues to be an intellectual charge.

As you will see, I rely very heavily on the work of Granville ("Randy") Miller and David J. Anderson, who created MSF for Agile Software Development and MSF for CMMI Process Improvement. We had endless debates and discoveries in creating the instances of MSF v4, and that learning has shaped what you read here in a major way.

Juan J. Perez, my coauthor, and Kim Tapia St. Amant of Personify Design made the rich examples and illustrations here possible. Working with them has been a great pleasure.

Finally, I am indebted to a large number of reviewers, including Jeff Beehler, James Behling, Charlie Bess, Rossen Blagoev, Rob Caron, Wendy Chun, Kevin P. Davis, Cristof Falk, Linda Fernandez, Ken Garove, Bill Gibson, Martin Heller, Bijan Javidi, Yulin Jin, Cem Kaner, Chris Kinsman, Aaron Kowall, Clementino Mendonca, Thomas Murphy, Gary Pollice,

Tomas Restrepo, Johanna Rothman, Joel Semeniuk, Will Stott, Dan Sullivan, David Trowbridge, Mike Turner, Kumar Vadaparty, and Peter Williams. Kim Boedigheimer, Ben Lawson, and Michael Thurston of Addison-Wesley were extremely helpful in the endgame. Without the advice and suggestions of all these reviewers, this book would have been a small fraction of what it became.

Sam Guckenheimer
Redmond, WA
January 2006

1

A Value-Up Paradigm

"A theory should be as simple as possible, but no simpler."
—Albert Einstein

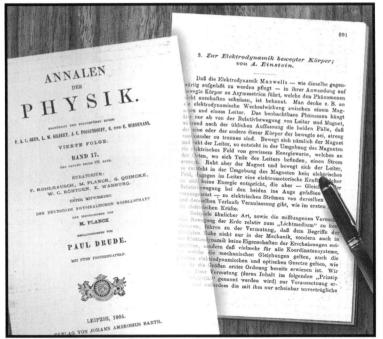

Permissions granted by the Hebrew University of Jerusalem, Israel.

Figure 1.1   Einstein's Theory of Special Relativity was the focal point of a paradigm shift in our understanding of physics. It capped forty years of debate on the most vexing technical challenges of his day—how to synchronize clocks and how to accurately draw maps over long distances.

1

A Paradigm Shift

Paradigm shifts come in fits and starts, as old theories can no longer explain the world as observed.[1] A poster child for the scientific paradigm shift is Albert Einstein's Theory of Special Relativity, published in 1905. Einstein's work reduced Newtonian mechanics to a special case, settled forty years of debate on the nature of time and synchronicity, and set the agenda for much of science, technology, and world affairs of the twentieth century.

According to a posthumous legend many of us learned in school, Einstein was a solitary theoretician whose day job reviewing patent applications was a mere distraction from his passionate pursuit of physics. Yet this popular view of Einstein is misguided. In fact, the majority of patent applications that Einstein reviewed concerned the very physics problem that fascinated him—how to synchronize time over distance for multiple practical purposes, such as creating railroad schedules, maritime charts, and accurate territorial maps in an age of colonial expansion. Indeed, the synchronization of time was a great technological problem of the age, for which special relativity became a mathematical solution, capping decades of debate.

Einstein was not the only person to solve the mathematical problem in 1905—the far more prominent Henri Poincaré produced an alternative that has long since been forgotten.[2] Why is Einstein's solution the one taught in every physics class today? Poincaré's calculations relied on the "ether," a supposed medium of space that had pervaded nineteenth-century physics. Einstein's Special Relativity, on the other hand, used much simpler calculations that required no ether. This was the first notable example of the principle attributed to Einstein, also posthumously, that "a theory should be as simple as possible, but no simpler."

Three Forces to Reconcile

A shift similar to the contrasting views of physics 100 years ago has been occurring today in software development. On a weekend in 2001, seventeen software luminaries convened to discuss "lightweight methods." At the end of the weekend, they launched the Agile Alliance, initially charged around the *Agile Manifesto*.[3] Initially, it was a rallying cry for those who saw contemporary software processes as similar to the "ether" of nineteenth-century physics—an unnecessary complexity and an impediment to productivity. Five years later, "agility" is mainstream. Every industry analyst advocates it, every business executive espouses it, and everyone tries to get more of it.

At the same time, two external economic factors came into play. One is global competition. The convergence of economic liberalization, increased communications bandwidth, and a highly skilled labor force in emerging markets made the outsourcing of software development to lower-wage countries (especially India) profitable.[4] The Indian consultancies, in turn, needed to guarantee their quality to American and European customers. Many latched onto Capability Maturity Model Integration (CMMI) from the Software Engineering Institute at Carnegie Mellon University.[5] CMMI epitomized the heavyweight processes against which the agilists rebelled, and it was considered too expensive to be practical outside of the defense industry. The offshorers, with their cost advantage, did not mind the expense and could turn the credential of a CMMI appraisal into a competitive advantage.

The second economic factor is increased attention to regulatory compliance after the lax business practices of the 1990s. In the United States, the Sarbanes-Oxley Act of 2002 (SOX) epitomizes this emphasis by holding business executives criminally liable for financial misrepresentations. This means that software and systems that process financial information are subject to a level of scrutiny and audit much greater than previously known.

These forces—agility, outsourcing/offshoring, and compliance—cannot be resolved without a paradigm shift in the way we approach the software lifecycle. The modern economics require agility with accountability. Closing the gap requires a new approach, both to process itself and to its tooling.

What Software Is Worth Building?

To overcome the gap, you must recognize that software engineering is not like other engineering. When you build a bridge, road, or house, for example, you can safely study hundreds of very similar examples. Indeed, most of the time, economics dictate that you build the current one almost exactly like the last to take the risk out of the project.

With software, if someone has built a system just like you need, or close to what you need, then chances are you can license it commercially (or even find it as freeware). No sane business is going to spend money on building software that it can buy more economically. With thousands of software products available for commercial license, it is almost always cheaper to buy. Because the decision to build software must be based on sound return on investment and risk analysis, the software projects that get built will almost invariably be those that are *not* available commercially.

This business context has a profound effect on the nature of software projects. It means that software projects that are easy and low risk, because they've been done before, don't get funded. The only new software development projects undertaken are those that haven't been done before or those whose predecessors are not publicly available. This business reality, more than any other factor, is what makes software development so hard and risky, which makes attention to process so important.[6]

Contrasting Paradigms

The inherent uncertainty in software projects makes it difficult to estimate tasks correctly, which creates a high variance in the accuracy of the estimates. A common misconception is that the variance is acceptable because the positive and negative variations average out. However, because software projects are long chains of dependent events, the variation itself accumulates in the form of downstream delays.[7]

Unfortunately, most accepted project management wisdom comes from the world of roads and bridges. In that world, design risks are low, design cost is small relative to build cost, and the opportunity to deliver incremental value is rare. (You can't drive across a half-finished bridge!) With this style of project management, you determine an engineering design early, carefully decompose the design into implementation tasks, schedule and resource the tasks according to their dependencies and resource availability, and monitor the project by checking off tasks as completed (or tracking percentages completed). For simplicity, I'll call this style of project management the *work-down* approach because it is easily envisioned as burning down a list of tasks.

The work-down approach succeeds for engineering projects with low risk, low variance, and well-understood design. Many IT projects, for example, are customizations of commercial-off-the-shelf software (COTS), such as enterprise resource planning systems. Often, the development is a small part of the project relative to the business analysis, project management, and testing. Typically, these projects have lower variability than new development projects, so the wisdom of roads and bridges works better for them than for new development.

Since 1992,[8] there has been a growing challenge to the work-down wisdom about software process. No single term has captured the emerging paradigm, but for simplicity, I'll call this the *value-up* approach. And as happens with new paradigms, the value-up view has appeared in fits and starts (see Figure 1.2).

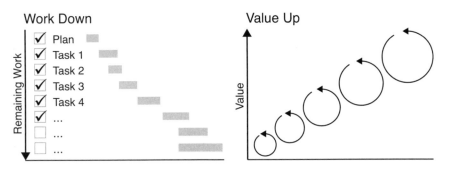

Figure 1.2   The attitudinal difference between work-down and value-up is in the primary measurement. Work-down treats the project as a fixed stock of tasks at some cost that need completion and measures the expenditure against those tasks. Value-up measures value delivered at each point in time and treats the inputs as variable flows rather than a fixed stock.

An example of the value-up school is the agile project management manifesto Declaration of Interdependence.[9] It states six principles that characterize value-up:

- We increase return on investment by making continuous flow of value our focus.
- We deliver reliable results by engaging customers in frequent interactions and shared ownership.
- We expect uncertainty and manage for it through iterations, anticipation, and adaptation.

- We unleash creativity and innovation by recognizing that individuals are the ultimate source of value, and creating an environment where they can make a difference.
- We boost performance through group accountability for results and shared responsibility for team effectiveness.
- We improve effectiveness and reliability through situationally specific strategies, processes, and practices.

Behind these principles is a significantly different point of view about practices between the work-down and value-up mindsets. Table 1.1 below summarizes the differences.

Table 1.1   Attitudinal Differences Between Work-Down and Value-Up Paradigms

Core Assumption	Work-Down Attitude	Value-Up Attitude
Planning and change process	Planning and design are the most important activities to get right. You need to do these initially, establish accountability to plan, monitor against the plan, and carefully prevent change from creeping in.	Change happens; embrace it. Planning and design will continue through the project. Therefore, you should invest in just enough planning and design to understand risk and to manage the next small increment.
Primary measurement	Task completion. Because we know the steps to achieve the end goal, we can measure every intermediate deliverable and compute earned value running as the percentage of hours planned to be spent by now versus the hours planned to be spent to completion.	Only deliverables that the customer values (working software, completed documentation, etc.) count. You need to measure the flow of the work streams by managing queues that deliver customer value and treat all interim measures skeptically.

Core Assumption	Work-Down Attitude	Value-Up Attitude
Definition of quality	Conformance to specification. That's why you need to get the specs right at the beginning.	Value to the customer. This perception can (and probably will) change. The customer might not be able to articulate how to deliver the value until working software is initially delivered. Therefore, keep options open, optimize for continual delivery, and don't specify too much too soon.
Acceptance of variance	Tasks can be identified and estimated in a deterministic way. You don't need to pay attention to variance.	Variance is part of all process flows, natural and man-made. To achieve predictability, you need to understand and reduce the variance.
Intermediate work products	Documents, models, and other intermediate artifacts are necessary to decompose the design and plan tasks, and they provide the necessary way to measure intermediate progress.	Intermediate documentation should minimize the uncertainty and variation in order to improve flow. Beyond that, they are unnecessary.
Troubleshooting approach	The constraints of time, resource, functionality, and quality determine what you can achieve. If you adjust one, you need to adjust the others. Control change carefully to make sure that there are no unmanaged changes to the plan.	The constraints may or may not be related to time, resource, functionality, or quality. Instead, identify the primary bottleneck in the flow of value, work it until it is no longer the primary one, and then attack the next one. Keep reducing variance to ensure smoother flow.
Approach to trust	People need to be monitored and compared to standards. Management should use incentives to reward individuals for their performance relative to the plan.	Pride of workmanship and teamwork are more effective motivators than individual incentives. Trustworthy transparency, where all team members can see the overall team's performance data, works better than management directives.

Attention to Flow

Central to the value-up paradigm is an emphasis on *flow*. There are two discrete meanings of flow, and both are significant in planning software projects.

First, flow is the human experience of performing expertly, as Mihaly Csikszentmihalyi explains in *Flow: The Psychology of Optimal Experience*:

> We have seen how people describe the common characteristics of optimal experience: a sense that one's skills are adequate to cope with the challenges at hand, in a goal-directed, rule-bound action system that provides clear clues as to how well one is performing. Concentration is so intense that there is no attention left over to think about anything irrelevant, or to worry about problems. Self-consciousness disappears, and the sense of time becomes distorted. An activity that produces such experiences is so gratifying that people are willing to do it for its own sake, with little concern for what they will get out of it, even when it is difficult, or dangerous.[10]

This meaning of flow is cited heavily by advocates of eXtreme Programming (XP) and other practices that focus on individual performance.

The second meaning of flow is the flow of customer value as the primary measure of the system of delivery. David J. Anderson summarizes this view in *Agile Management for Software Engineering*:

> Flow means that there is a steady movement of value through the system. Client-valued functionality is moving regularly through the stages of transformation—and the steady arrival of throughput—with working code being delivered.[11]

In this paradigm, you do not measure planned tasks completed as the primary indicator of progress; you count units of value delivered. Your rates of progress in throughput of delivered value and stage of completion at the units of value are the indicators that you use for planning and measurement.

Correspondingly, the flow-of-value approach forces you to understand the constraints that restrict the flow. You tune the end-to-end flow by identifying the most severe bottleneck or inefficiency your process, fixing it, and then tackling the next most severe one. As Anderson explains:

The development manager must ensure the flow of value through the transformation processes in the system. He is responsible for the rate of production output from the system and the time it takes to process a single idea through the system. To understand how to improve the rate of production and reduce the lead time, the development manager needs to understand how the system works, be able to identify the constraints, and make appropriate decisions to protect, exploit, subordinate, and elevate the system processes.[12]

A flow-based approach to planning and project management requires keeping intermediate work-in-process to a minimum, as shown in Figure 1.3. This mitigates the risk of late discovery of problems and unexpected bubbles of required rework.

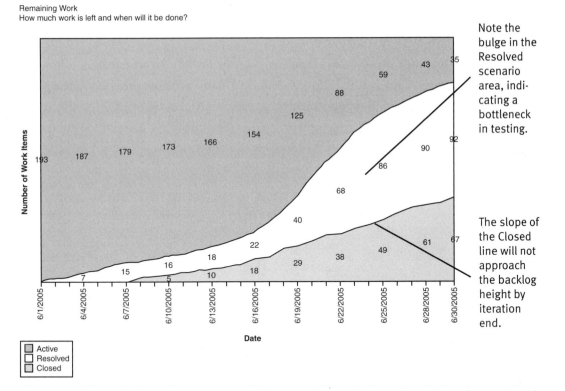

Remaining Work
How much work is left and when will it be done?

Note the bulge in the Resolved scenario area, indicating a bottleneck in testing.

The slope of the Closed line will not approach the backlog height by iteration end.

Figure 1.3   Measuring flow of scenario completion on a daily basis shows the rhythm of progress and quickly identifies bottlenecks that can be addressed as they arise.

Figure 1.3 shows how the continuous measurement of flow can illuminate bottlenecks as they are forming. Planned work for the iteration is progressing well through development (Active turning to Resolved), but is increasingly getting stuck in testing (Resolved to Closed). This accumulates as the bulge of work-in-process in the middle band. If you tracked development only (the reduction in Active work items), you would expect completion of the work by the expected end date; but because of the bottleneck, you can see that the slope of the Closed triangle is not steep enough to finish the work on time. This lets you drill into the bottleneck and determine whether the problem is inadequate testing resources or poor quality of work from development.

Contrast to Work-Down

An icon of the work-down paradigm is the widely taught "iron triangle" view of project management. This is the notion that there are only three variables that a project manager can work with: time, resources (of which people are by far the most important), and functionality. If you acknowledge quality as a fourth dimension (which most people do now), then you have a tetrahedron, as shown in Figure 1.4.

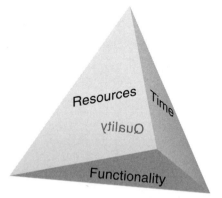

Figure 1.4   The "iron triangle" (or tetrahedron) treats a project as a fixed stock of work, in classic work-down terms. To stretch one face of the tetrahedron, you need to stretch the others.

In *Rapid Development*, Steve McConnell summarizes the iron triangle as follows:

> To keep the triangle balanced, you have to balance schedule, cost, and product. If you want to load up the product corner of the triangle, you also have to load up cost or schedule or both. The same goes for the other combinations. If you want to change one of the corners of the triangle, you have to change at least one of the others to keep it in balance.[13]

According to this view, a project manager has an initial stock of resources and time. Any change to functionality or quality requires a corresponding increase in time or resources. You cannot stretch one face without stretching the others because they are all connected.

Although widely practiced, this paradigm does not work well. Just as Newtonian physics is now known to be a special case, the iron triangle is a special case that assumes the process is flowing smoothly to begin with. In other words, it assumes that resource productivity is quite uniformly distributed, that there is little variance in the effectiveness of task completion, and that no spare capacity exists throughout the system. These conditions exist sometimes, notably on low-risk projects. Unfortunately, for the types of software projects usually undertaken, they are often untrue.

Many users of agile methods have demonstrated experiences that pleasantly contradict to this viewpoint. For example, in many cases, if you improve qualities of service, such as reliability, you can *shorten* time. Significant improvements in flow are possible within the existing resources and time.[14]

Transparency

It's no secret that most software projects are late, both in the execution and in the discovery that they are late.[15] This phenomenon has many consequences, which are discussed in almost every chapter of this book. One of the consequences is a vicious cycle of groupthink and denial that undermines effective flow. Late delivery leads to requests for replanning, which lead to pressure for ever more optimistic estimates, which lead to more late delivery, and so on. And most participants in these projects plan optimistically, replan, and replan further but with little visibility into the effects. Of course, the all-too-frequent result is a death march.

This is not because people can't plan or manage their time. The problem is more commonly the disparity among priorities and expectations of different team members. Most approaches to software engineering have lots of places to track the work—spreadsheets, Microsoft Project Plans, requirements databases, bug databases, test management systems, triage meeting notes, and so on. When the information is scattered this way, it is pretty hard to get a whole picture of the project—you need to look in too many sources, and it's hard to balance all the information into one schedule. And when there are so many sources, the information you find is often obsolete when you find it.

Things don't need to be that way. Some community projects post their development schedules on the Web, effectively making individual contributors create expectations among their community peers about their tasks. Making all the work in a project visible can create a virtuous cycle. Of course, this assumes that the project is structured iteratively, the scheduling and estimation are made at the right granularity, and triage is effective at keeping the work item priorities in line with the available resources in the iteration.

SCRUM, one of the agile processes, championed the idea of a transparently visible product backlog, as shown in Figure 1.5. Here's how the founders of SCRUM, Ken Schwaber and Mike Beedle, define the product backlog:

> Product Backlog is an evolving, prioritized queue of business and technical functionality that needs to be developed into a system. The Product Backlog represents everything that anyone interested in the product or process has thought is needed or would be a good idea in the product. It is a list of all features, functions, technologies, enhancements and bug fixes that constitute the changes that will be made to the product for future releases. Anything that represents work to be done on the product is included in Product Backlog.[16]

This transparency is enormously effective for multiple reasons. It creates a "single set of books," or in other words, a unique, maintained source of information on the work completed and remaining. Combined with flow measurement, as shown in Figure 1.3, it creates trust among the team because everyone sees the same data and plan. And finally, it creates a virtuous cycle between team responsibility and individual accountability. After all, an individual is most likely to complete a task when he or she knows exactly who is expecting it to be done.[17]

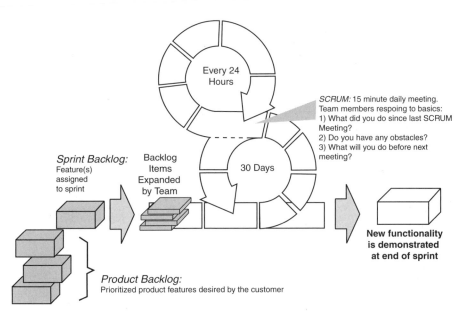

Figure 1.5 The central graphic of the SCRUM methodology is a great illustration of flow in the management sense. Not surprisingly, SCRUM pioneered the concept of a single product backlog as a management technique.

One Work Item Database

Visual Studio Team System (VSTS) takes the idea of a transparent product backlog even further (see Figure 1.6). Team System uses a common product backlog to track all planned, active, and completed work for the team and a history of the majority of actions taken and decisions made regarding that work. It calls these units "work items" and lets the user view and edit them in a database view inside Visual Studio, in Microsoft Excel, and in Microsoft Project, all the while synchronizing them to a common database.

One database behind the common, familiar tools defragments the information. Instead of cutting and pasting among randomly distributed artifacts, project managers, business analysts, developers, and testers all see the same work, whether planned in advance or scheduled on the fly, and whether from well-understood requirements or discovered while fixing a bug (see Figure 1.7). And unlike separate project tracking tools and techniques, much of the data collection in VSTS is automatic.

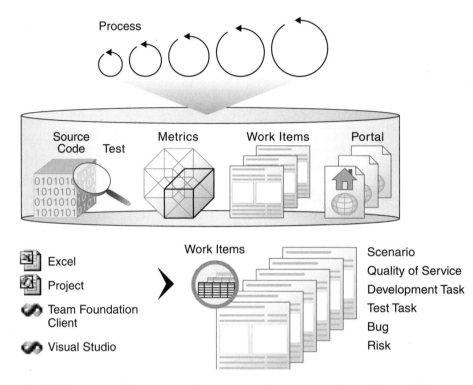

Figure 1.6   VSTS enacts and instruments the process, tying source code, testing, work items, and metrics together. Work items include all the work that needs to be tracked on a project, such
as scenarios, quality of service requirements, development tasks, test tasks, bugs, and
risks. These can be viewed and edited in the Team Explorer, Visual Studio, Microsoft Excel,
or Microsoft Project.

Because VSTS uses a common database to track work items, it exposes them not
just in Team Explorer but also in Microsoft Excel (see Figures 1.8 and 1.9). The use
of Excel and Project is convenient but not necessary. All the functionality is available
through the Team Explorer, which is the client for Team Foundation. If you're using
any Visual Studio Team System client edition or Visual Studio Professional, then the
Team Explorer appears as a set of windows inside the development environment.

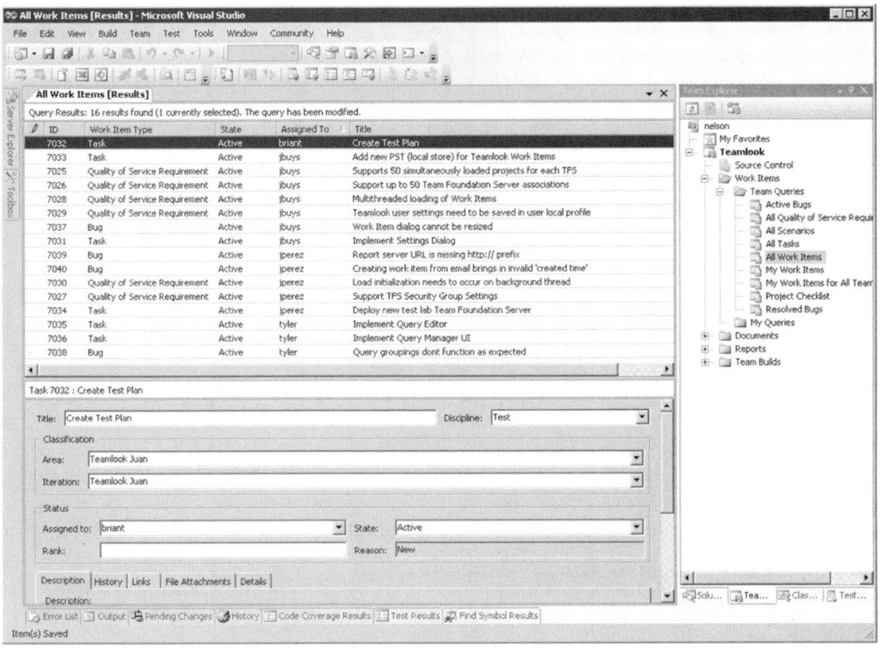

Figure 1.7   This is an example of the work items as they appear either in the Team Explorer of VSTS or in Visual Studio. Note that tasks, requirements, and bugs can all be viewed in one place.

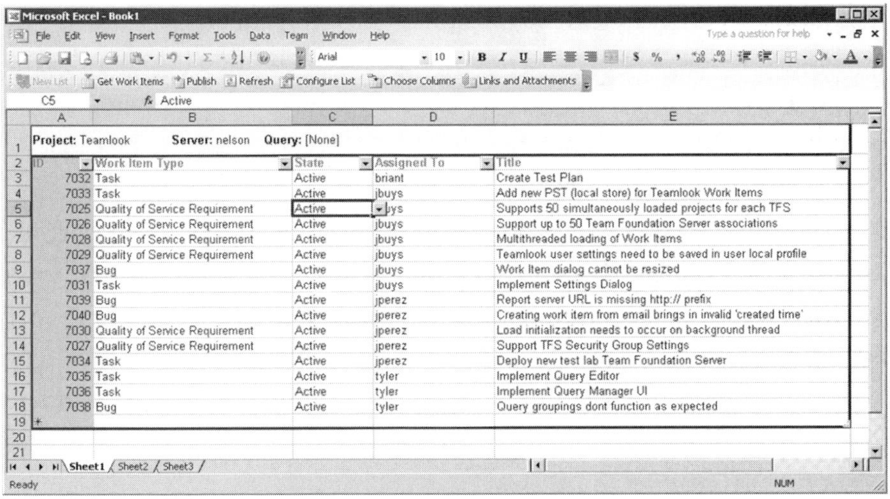

Figure 1.8   With VSTS, the same data can be viewed and edited in Microsoft Excel. The work items, regardless of type, are stored in the same Team Foundation database.

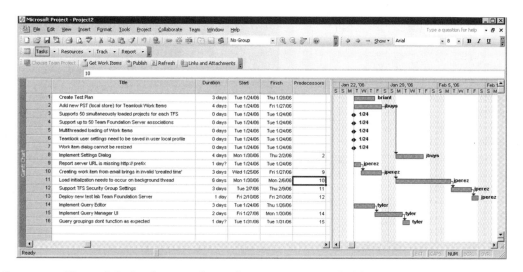

Figure 1.9   Microsoft Project lets you plan and manage some or all of the work items with full round tripping to the Team Foundation database.

Offline Editing, Management, and "What-Ifs" of Work Items

For these tasks, use Excel or Project. Your files are stored locally on your client machine while you work. The changes are written back in Team Foundation when you next synchronize with the database, and any potential merge conflicts are highlighted at that time. On the other hand, when you use Team Explorer, changes are saved to the database during the session.

The extensibility of Team System makes it possible for Microsoft partners to add functionality. For example, Personify Design Teamlook[18] provides team members a view of their Team Projects on multiple Team Foundation Servers from within Microsoft Office Outlook. Team Foundation Server extensibility enables Teamlook to track work items with full accountability in the familiar communications tool, Outlook (see Figure 1.10).

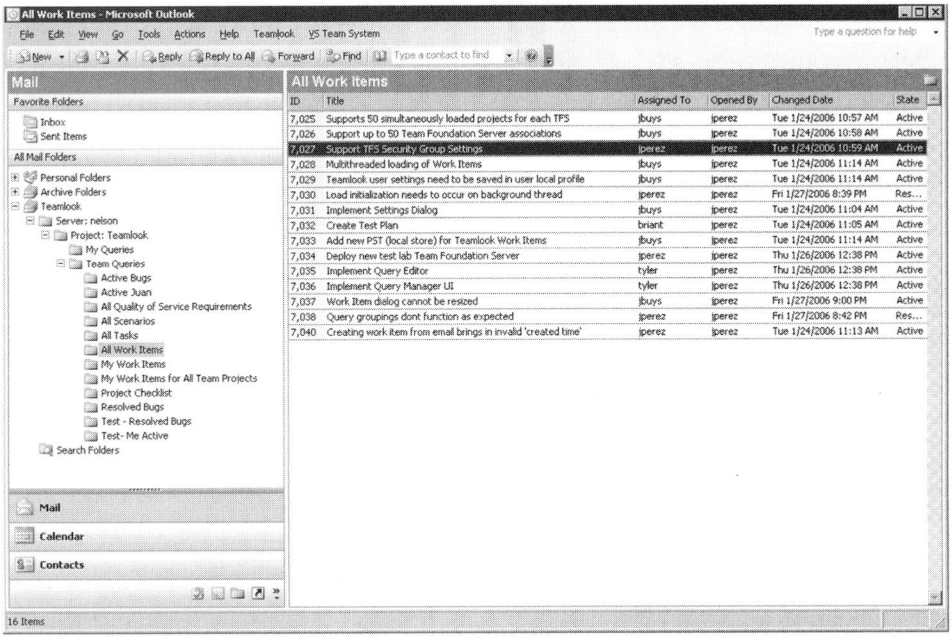

Figure 1.10   With Teamlook from Personify Design, you can also use Outlook as a client for the Team Foundation server.

Instrument Daily Activities

The transparent backlog relies on accurate data to be useful. Often, collecting the data becomes a major activity in itself that relies on willing compliance of large numbers of participants. This disciplined attention to the bookkeeping is rarely sustained in practice, especially during periods of intense activity.

The irony is that the vast majority of the data that a team needs is directly correlated to other actions that are already managed by software. Developers check in code, builds parse that code, testers write and run tests, and all their activities are tracked somewhere—in Project, Excel, the bug database, or timesheets. What if you could gather all that data automatically, correlate it, and use it to measure the process?

Team System takes that approach. It instruments the daily activities of the team members to collect process data with no overhead. For example, every time a developer checks updated code into version control, work items are updated to reflect the tasks and scenarios updated by this code. The relationships are captured in a "changeset," and when the next build runs, it identifies the change sets included and updates work items again with the build number. When tests execute, they use the same build number. Then test results, code changes, and work items are all correlated automatically by Team System (see Figure 1.11).

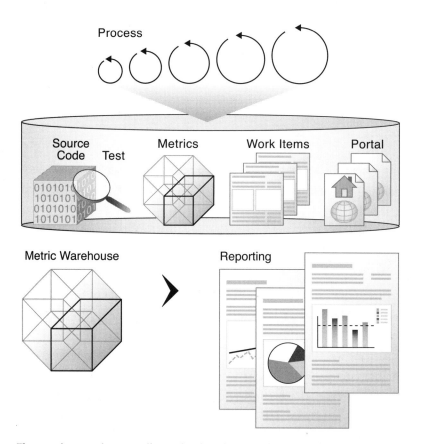

Figure 1.11 The metrics warehouse collects the data from all the actions on the project to provide reports that correlate the different sources and dimensions of data.

In addition to keeping the backlog current and visible, this automatic data collection populates a data warehouse with metrics that reveal trends and comparisons of quality from many dimensions on a daily basis. Just like a data warehouse that provides business intelligence on functions such as a sales or production process, this one provides intelligence on the software development process.

Simple Observations

With this data warehouse, basic questions become easy to answer: Is the project coming in on time, or how far off is it? How much has the plan changed? Who's over or under and needs to have work rebalanced? What rates should we use to estimate remaining work? How effective are our tests? Most project managers would love to answer these basic questions with hard data. When the data collection is automated, the answers become straightforward.

Project "Smells"

More significantly, most project managers would love to find blind spots—places where data indicates a likely problem. It is now common to talk about "smells" for suspicious areas of code.[19] Problems for the project as a whole also appear often as hard-to-pin-down smells, which are not well exposed by existing metrics. I'll cover smells in some detail in Chapter 9, "Troubleshooting the Project," but for now I'll share a common example. Imagine a graph that shows you these bug and test pass rates (see Figure 1.12).

Based on Figure 1.12, what would you conclude? Probably that the Instore Pickup Kiosk code is in great shape, so you should look for problems elsewhere.

At the same time, there's a danger of relying on too few metrics. Consider the graph in Figure 1.13, which overlays code churn (the number of lines added, modified, and deleted) and code coverage from testing (the percentage of code lines or blocks exercised during testing) on the same axes.

Suddenly the picture is reversed. There's really high code churn in Instore Pickup Kiosk, and the code is not being covered by the tests that supposedly exercise that component. This picture reveals that we may have stale tests that aren't exercising the new functionality. Could that be why they're passing and not covering the actual code in this component?

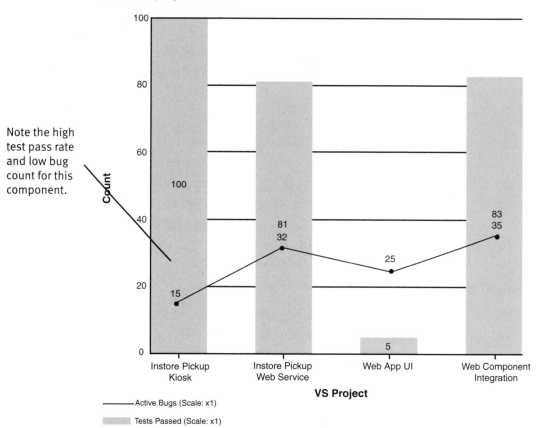

Figure 1.12   The X-axis identifies different components of your project; the bars show you the test pass rate for each component, while the points and line show the active bug count.

Multidimensional Metrics and Smells

The ability to see more dimensions of the project data is a direct benefit of the metrics warehouse, which collects and correlates data from daily activities. It provides a quantitative, visual tool to pursue the smells. In this way, you can achieve the visibility level needed for the strictest compliance reporting while working in an agile manner and having the same visibility into a remote project, even outsourced, that you would have in a local one.

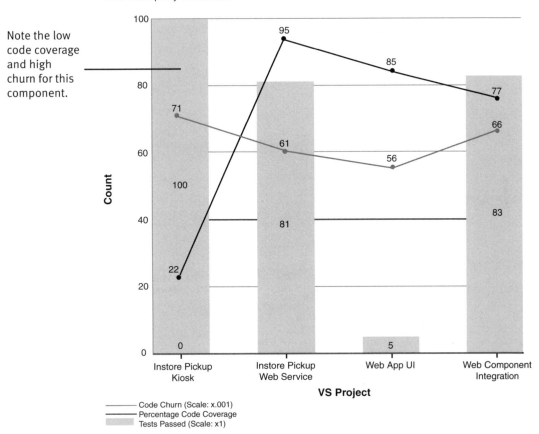

Quality Indicators
What is the quality of software?

Note the low code coverage and high churn for this component.

Figure 1.13 Overlaying code coverage and code churn for the components provides a very different perspective on the data.

Fit the Process to the Project

Instrumenting daily activities and automatically collecting data make it much easier to follow a consistent software process. Team System automates the process guidance and instruments the process so that most of the overhead associated with process and most of the resistance to compliance are eliminated.

However, this quickly exposes a valid concern, which is that no one process fits all software projects, even within one organization. Regulatory environment, business risk, business upside, technology risk, team skills, geographic distribution, and project size all play a role in determining the right fit of a process to a project.

Team System takes the diversity of process into account, enabling the project team to choose or adapt its methodology for contextual realities. When you start a team project in VSTS, you pick a process template, as shown in Figure 1.14. In effect, you can choose and customize the process further for each project, determining not only guidance but also workflow, policies, templates, reports, and permissions.

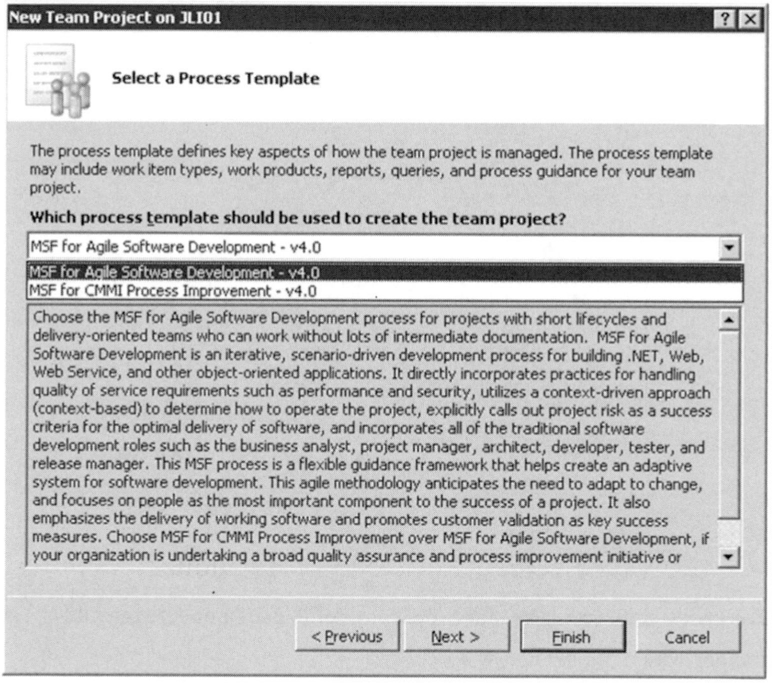

Figure 1.14   When you start a Team Project, your first choice is which "Process Template" to apply for the project. The Process Template defines the process guidance web site, the work item types and their workflow, starter work items, the security groups and permissions, and reports and templates for work products.

Summary

In practice, most software processes require manual enactment, where collecting data and tracking progress are expensive. Up front, such processes need lots of documentation, training, and management, and they have high operating and maintenance costs. Most significantly, the process artifacts and effort do not contribute in any direct way to the delivery of customer value. Project managers can often spend 40 hours a week cutting and pasting to report status.

This constraint has left process as an exercise for managers, specialist Program Management Offices, and skilled practitioners, who sometimes define metrics and activities quite divorced from the interests of the practitioners or the tools used to implement them. The dominant paradigm in this world has been the work-down view, where software engineering is a deterministic exercise, similar to other engineering pursuits.

In contrast, the business forces driving software engineering today require a different paradigm. In keeping with the dictum "As simple as possible, but *no* simpler," a team today needs to embrace the paradigm of customer value, change, variance, and situationally specific actions as a part of everyday practice. This is equally true whether projects are in-house or outsourced and whether they are local or geographically distributed. Managing such a process usually requires a value-up approach instead.

Typically, the value-up approach requires tooling. Collecting, maintaining, and reporting the data without overhead is simply not practical otherwise. In situations where regulatory compliance and audit are required, the tooling is necessary to provide the change management and audit trails. Team System is designed from the ground up to support the value-up approach in an auditable way. The rest of this book describes the use of Team System to support this paradigm.

Endnotes

1. Thomas Kuhn, *The Structure of Scientific Revolutions* (University of Chicago Press, 1962).
2. Peter Galison, *Einstein's Clocks, Poincaré's Maps* (New York: Norton, 2003), 40.
3. www.agilemanifesto.org
4. See Thomas L. Friedman, *The World Is Flat: A Brief History of the Twenty-First Century* (New York: Farrar, Strauss & Giroux, 2005) for a discussion of the enabling trends.

5. http://www.sei.cmu.edu/cmmi/

6. There are other arguments as well, such as the design complexity of software relative to most engineering pursuits. See, for example, Boris Beizer, "Software Is Different," in *Software Quality Professional I:1* (American Society for Quality, December 1998).

7. The negative consequence of the interplay of variation and dependent events is central to the Theory of Constraints. For example, see Eliyahu M. Goldratt, *The Goal* (North River Press, 1986).

8. The first major work to highlight what I call the value-up approach is Gerald M. Weinberg, *Quality Software Management, Volume I: Systems Thinking* (New York: Dorset House, 1992).

9. The Agile Project Manifesto is available at http://www.pmdoi.org/. It is another example of the value-up approach.

10. Mihaly Csikszentmihalyi, *Flow: The Psychology of Optimal Experience* (New York: HarperCollins, 1990), 71.

11. David J. Anderson, *Agile Management for Software Engineering: Applying the Theory of Constraints for Business Results* (Upper Saddle River, NJ: Prentice Hall, 2004), 77.

12. Ibid., 77.

13. Steve McConnell, *Rapid Development* (Redmond, WA: Microsoft Press, 1996), 126.

14. For a more detailed discussion of this subject, using the nomenclature of the Theory of Constraints, see David J. Anderson and Dragos Dumitriu, "From Worst to Best in 9 Months: Implementing a Drum-Buffer-Rope Solution in Microsoft's IT Department," presented at the TOCICO Conference, November 2005, available at http://www.agilemanagement.net/Articles/Papers/From_Worst_to_Best_in_9_Months_Final_1_2.pdf.

15. The Standish Group (www.standishgroup.com) publishes a biennial survey called "The Chaos Report." According to the 2004 data, 71% of projects were late, over budget, and/or canceled.

16. Ken Schwaber and Mike Beedle, *Agile Software Development with SCRUM* (Upper Saddle River, NJ: Prentice Hall, 2001), 32–3.

17. Bellotti, V., Dalal, B., Good, N., Bobrow, D. G., and Ducheneaut, N., "What a to-do: studies of task management towards the design of a personal task list manager. " ACM Conference on Human Factors in Computing Systems (CHI2004); 2004 April 24–29; Vienna; Austria. NY: ACM; 2004; 735–742.

18. http://www.personifydesign.com/

19. Originally used for code in Martin Fowler, *Refactoring: Improving the Design of Existing Code* (Reading, MA: Addison-Wesley, 1999), 75.

2.

Value-Up Processes

Program Manager
Project Manager

"One methodology cannot possibly be the "right" one, but . . . there is an appropriate, different way of working for each project and project team."[1]
—Alistair Cockburn

Figure 2.1   The rhythm of a crew rowing in unison is a perfect example of flow in both the human and management senses. Individuals experience the elation of performing optimally, and the coordinated teamwork enables the system as a whole (here, the boat) to achieve its optimum performance.

In the last chapter, I argued the importance of the value-up paradigm. In this chapter, I cover the next level of detail—the characteristics of such processes, the "situationally specific" contexts to consider, and the examples that you can apply.

> **Software Process Options in VSTS**
>
> Two processes are shipped with VSTS, both of which are variants of Microsoft Solutions Framework (MSF):
>
> - MSF for Agile Software Development
> - MSF for CMMI Process Improvement
>
> You can download and preview these from http://msdn.microsoft.com/msf/. This web page also includes links to the many processes that partner companies deliver for VSTS, including SCRUM, FDD, and EUP. You can also tailor your own process templates from the MSF ones.

Microsoft Solutions Framework

Dozens of documented software processes exist.[2] Over the last thirty years, most of these have come from the work-down paradigm, and they have spawned extensive amounts of documentation to cover all possible situations and contingencies.[3] Managers have wanted to play it safe without understanding the corresponding drain on productivity. Unfortunately, the idea has backfired. When teams don't know what they can safely do without, they include everything in their planning and execution process. Barry Boehm and Richard Turner have described the problem well:

> **Build Your Method Up, Don't Tailor It Down**
>
> Plan-driven methods have had a tradition of developing all-inclusive methods that can be tailored down to fit a particular situation. Experts can do this, but nonexperts tend to play it safe and use the whole thing, often at considerable unnecessary expense. Agilists offer a better approach of starting with relatively minimal sets of practices and only adding extras where they can be clearly justified by cost-benefit.[4]

Similarly, most processes and tools have not allowed adequately for appropriate diversity among projects and have forced a "one size fits all" approach on their teams. In contrast, VSTS is a collaboration and development environment that allows a process per project. VSTS also assumes that a team will "stretch the process to fit"—that is, to take a small core of values and practices and to add more as necessary. This approach has been much more successful, as the previous quote notes.

Inside Team System are two fully enacted process instances, both based on a common core called Microsoft Solutions Framework (MSF):

- **MSF for Agile Software Development.** A lightweight process that adheres to the principles of the Agile Alliance.[5] Choose the MSF Agile process for projects with short lifecycles and results-oriented teams who can work without lots of intermediate documentation. The MSF Agile process is a flexible guidance framework that helps create an adaptive system for software development. It anticipates the need to adapt to change, emphasizes the delivery of working software, and promotes customer validation as key success measures.

- **MSF for CMMI Process Improvement.** A process designed to facilitate CMMI Level 3 as defined by the Software Engineering Institute.[6] This extends MSF Agile with more formal planning, more documentation and work products, more sign-off gates, and more time tracking. MSF for CMMI clearly maps its practices to the Practice Areas and Goals in order to assist organizations that are using the CMMI as the basis for their process improvement or that are seeking CMMI appraisal. However, unlike previous attempts at CMMI processes, MSF uses the value-up paradigm to enable a low-overhead, agile instantiation of the CMMI framework.[7]

Both instances of MSF are value-up processes. In both cases, MSF harvests proven practices from Microsoft, its customers, and industry expertise. The primary differences between the two are the level of approval formality, the level of accounting for effort spent, and the depth of metrics used. For example, MSF for CMMI Process Improvement considers the appraiser or auditor as an explicit role and provides activities and reports that the auditor can use to assess process compliance. In its agile sibling, compliance is not a consideration.

In both the agile and CMMI instances, MSF's smooth integration in Team System supports rapid iterative development with continuous learning and refinement. The common work item database and metrics warehouse answer questions on project health in near real time, and the coupling of process guidance to tools makes it possible to see the right guidance in the context of the tools and act on it as you need it.

Iteration

MSF is an iterative and incremental process. For more than twenty years, the software engineering community has understood the need for iterative development. This is the generally defined as the "software development technique in which requirements definition, design, implementation and testing occur in an overlapping, iterative (rather than sequential) manner, resulting in incremental completion of the overall software product."[8]

Iterative development arose as an antidote to sequential "waterfall" development. Fred Brooks, whose *Mythical Man Month* is still among the world's most widely admired software engineering books, sums up the waterfall experience as follows:

> The basic fallacy of the waterfall model is that it assumes a project goes through the process once, that the architecture is excellent and easy to use, the implementation design is sound, and the realization is fixable as testing proceeds. Another way of saying it is that the waterfall model assumes the mistakes will all be in the realization, and thus that their repair can be smoothly interspersed with component and system testing.[9]

Why Iterate?

There are many highly compelling arguments for iterative development:

1. **Risk management.** The desired result is unknowable in advance. To manage risks, you must prove or disprove your requirements and design assumptions by incrementally implementing target system elements, starting with the highest-risk elements.

2. **Economics.** In an uncertain business climate, it is important to review priorities frequently and treat investments as though they were financial options. The more flexibility gained through early payoff and frequent checkpoints, the more valuable the options become.[10]

3. **Focus.** People can only retain so much in their brains. By batching work into small iterations, all the team players focus more closely on the work at

hand—business analysts can do a better job with requirements, architects with design, developers with code, and so on.

4. **Motivation.** The most energizing phenomenon on a software team is seeing early releases perform (or be demo'd) in action. No amount of spec review can substitute for the value of working bits.

5. **Control theory.** Small iterations enable you to reduce the margin of error in your estimates and provide fast feedback about the accuracy of your project plans.

6. **Stakeholder involvement.** Stakeholders (customers, users, management) see results quickly and become more engaged in the project, offering more time, insight, and funding.

7. **Continuous learning.** The entire team learns from each iteration, improving the accuracy, quality, and suitability of the finished product.

A simple summary of all this wisdom is that "Incrementalism is a good idea for all projects . . . and a must when risks are high."[11]

Nonetheless, iterative development struggles to be adopted in many IT organizations. In practice, iterative development requires that the team and its project managers have a total view of the work to be done and the ability to monitor and prioritize frequently at short iteration boundaries. This frequent updating requires a readily visible backlog, preferably with automated data collection, such as the VSTS work item database provides.

In the value-up view of iterative development, there are many cycles in which activities overlap in parallel. The primary planning cycle is the "iteration." An iteration is the fixed number of weeks, sometimes called a "time box," used to schedule a task set. Use iterations as the interval in which to schedule intended scenarios, measure the flow of value, assess the actual process, examine bottlenecks, and make adjustments (see Figure 2.2). In the chapters on development and testing, I'll cover the finer-grained cycles of the check-in and daily build, which are often called "increments" and which naturally drive the iteration.[12]

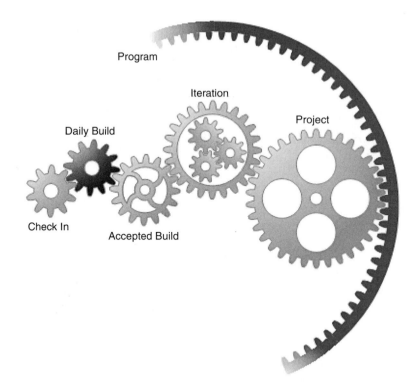

Figure 2.2　Software projects proceed on many interlocking cycles, ranging from the code-edit-test-debug-check in cycle, measured in minutes, to the iteration of a few weeks, to a program that might span years. If the cycles connect, the process as a whole can be understood.

Length

In practice, the length of iterations varies from project to project, usually two to six weeks. Again, the iteration determines the size of the batch that you use for measuring a chunk of deliverable customer value, such as scenarios and quality of service (QoS) requirements. You need to keep the batch size as small as possible while meeting this objective, as David Anderson explains in *Agile Management for Software Engineering*:

> Small batch sizes are essential for flow! Small batch sizes are also essential for quality. In software development human nature creates a tendency for engineers to be less exacting and pay less attention to detail when considering larger batches. For example, when code reviews are performed on small batches, the code review takes only a short time to

prepare and a short time to conduct. Because there is only a small amount of code to review, the reviewers tend to pay it greater attention and spot a greater number of errors than they would on a larger batch of code. It is therefore better to spend 4 hours per week doing code reviews than 2 days at the end of each month or, even worse, one week at the end of each quarter. A large batch makes code reviewing a chore. Small batches keep it light. The result is higher quality. Higher quality leads directly to more production. . . . Reducing batch sizes improves ROI![13]

Different Horizons, Different Granularity

One of the benefits of using iterations is that it provides clear levels of granularity in planning. You can plan tasks to one-day detail for the current iteration while maintaining a rough candidate list of scenarios and QoS requirements for future iterations. In other words, you only try to go into detail for the current iteration. (By the way, the person who should plan and estimate the detailed tasks is the one who is going to do them.) Not only does this keep the team focused on a manageable set of work items, but it also gives the maximum benefit from the experience of actual completion of delivered value when planning the next set.

Apply common sense to the depth of planning and prioritization. Obviously, you want to mitigate major risks early, so you will prioritize architectural decisions into early iterations, even if they are incomplete from the standpoint of visible customer value.

Prioritization

There are two complementary ways to plan work: by priority and by stack rank. VSTS supports both. Ranking by priority involves rating the candidate scenarios and QoS into broad buckets, such as Must have (1), Should have (2), Could have (3), and Won't have (4). This scheme is mnemonically referred to as MoSCoW.[14]

MoSCoW and similar priority schemes work well for large numbers of small candidates, such as bugs, or scenarios under consideration for future iterations, where it is not worth spending the time to examine each item individually.

Stack ranking, on the other hand, is the practice of assigning cardinal ranks to a set of requirements to give them a unique order (see Figure 2.3). Stack ranking is well

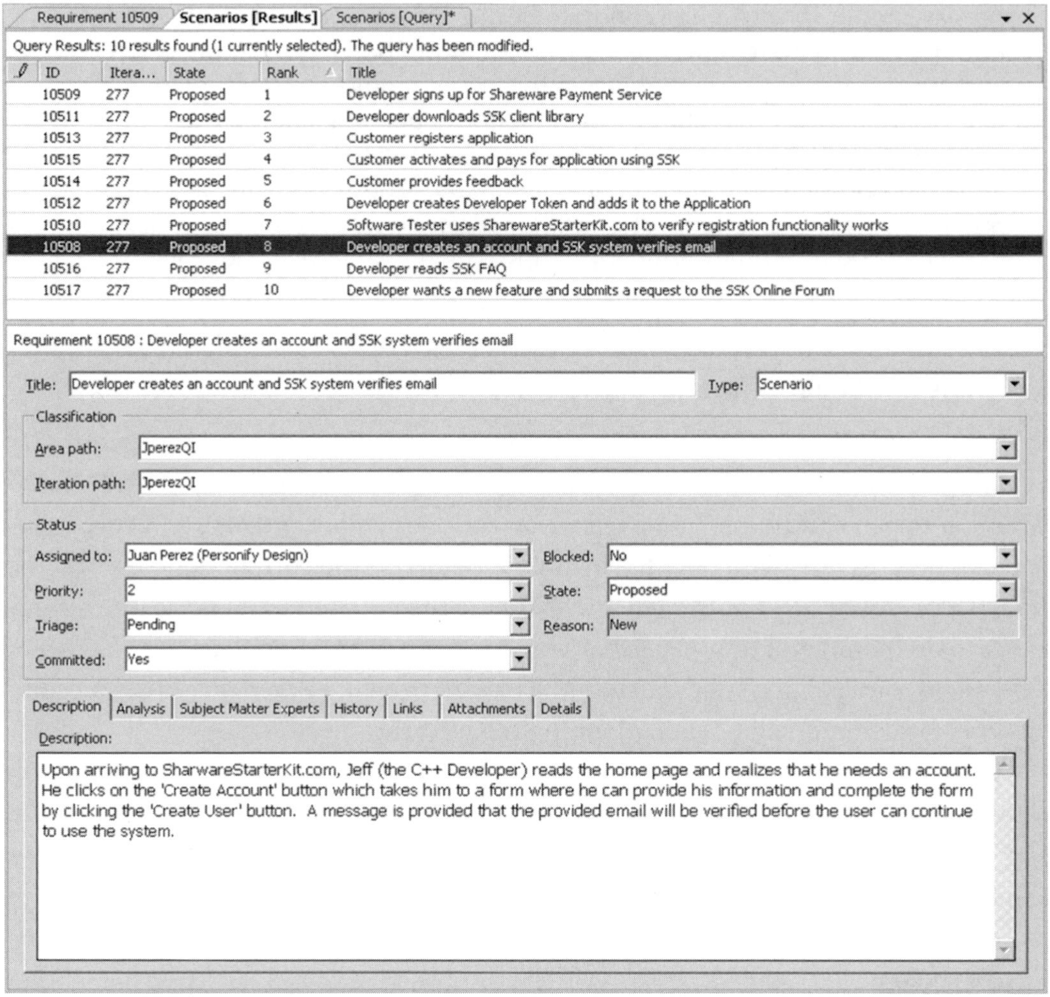

Figure 2.3   In MSF, scenarios are stack ranked, as shown on this work item form. Here the scenarios are shown in the Team Explorer of VSTS.

suited to planning scenarios and QoS for near-term iterations. Stack ranking mitigates two risks. One is that you simply end up with too many "Must haves." The other is that your estimates of effort are wrong. If you tackle scenarios and QoS according to a linear rank order, then you know what's next, regardless of whether your planned work fits your available time. In fact, it helps you improve your estimates. DeMarco and Lister describe this effect well:

Rank-ordering for all functions and features is the cure for two ugly project maladies: The first is the assumption that all parts of the product are equally important. This fiction is preserved on many projects because it assures that no one has to confront the stakeholders who have added their favorite bells and whistles as a price for their cooperation. The same fiction facilitates the second malady, piling on, in which features are added with the intention of overloading the project and making it fail, a favorite tactic of those who oppose the project in the first place but find it convenient to present themselves as enthusiastic project champions rather than as project adversaries.[15]

Adapting Process

Iterations also give you a boundary at which to make process changes. You can tune based on experience, and you can adjust for context. For example, you might increase the check-in requirements for code review as your project approaches production and use VSTS check-in policies and check-in notes to enforce these requirements. Alistair Cockburn has been one of the clearest proponents of adapting process:

> There is one more device to mention in the design of methodologies. That is to adjust the methodology on the fly. Once we understand that every project deserves its own methodology, then it becomes clear that whatever we suggest to start with is the optimal methodology for *some other* project. This is where incremental delivery plays a large role.
>
> If we interview the project team between, and in the middle of, increments, we can take their most recent experiences into account. In the first increment, the mid-increment tune-up address the question, "Can we deliver?" Every other interview addresses, "Can we deliver more easily or better?"[16]

The process review at the end of an iteration is called a *retrospective*, a term with better implications than the alternative *post-mortem*.

Retrospectives and Lessons Learned

Both instances of MSF provide guidance on retrospectives.

MSF for CMMI Process Improvement captures the information in a Lessons Learned document to facilitate continuous improvement.

Risk Management

The risks projects face differ considerably. Traditional risk management tends to be event-driven, in the form of "What if X were to happen?" MSF complements event-driven risk management with a constituency-based approach, in which there are seven points of view that need to be represented in a project to prevent blind spots.

In some cases, for example, technology is new and needs to be proven before being adopted. Sometimes extreme QoS issues must be addressed, such as huge scalability or throughput. At other times, there are significant issues due to the assembly of a new team with unknown skills and communication styles. VSTS, in turn, tracks risks directly in the work item database so that the project team can take them on directly.

Viewpoints of Risk: Advocacy Groups

This is the description of Advocacy Groups in the Team Model of MSF (both instances).

Program Management Advocates for Solution Delivery

The focus of program management is to meet the goal of delivering the solution within project constraints. This group ensures that the right solution is delivered at the right time and that all stakeholders' expectations are understood, managed, and met throughout the project.

Architecture Advocates for the System in the Large

This includes the services, technology, and standards with which the solution will interoperate, the infrastructure in which it will be deployed, its place in the business or product family, and its roadmap of future versions. The architecture group has to ensure that the deployed solution meets all qualities of service as well as the business objectives and is viable in the long term.

Development Advocates for the Technical Solution

In addition to being the primary solution builders, development is responsible for thoughtful technical decisions, clean design, good bottom-up estimates, and high-quality maintainable code and unit tests.

Test Advocates for Solution Quality from the Customer Perspective

Test anticipates, looks for, and reports on any issues that diminish the solution quality in the eyes of the users or customers.

Release/Operations Advocates for the Smooth Delivery and Deployment of the Solution into the Appropriate Infrastructure

This group ensures timely readiness and compatibility of the infrastructure for the solution.

User Experience Advocates for the Most Effective Solution in the Eyes of the Intended Users

User experience must understand the user's context as a whole, appreciate any subtleties of their needs, and ensure that the whole team is conscious of usability from their eyes.

Product Management Advocates for the Customer Business

Product management has to understand, communicate, and ensure success from the standpoint of the economic customer requesting the solution.

Looking at risk from the standpoint of constituencies changes the approach to mitigation in a very healthy way. For example, all projects face a risk of poorly understood user requirements. Paying attention to user experience and QoS as central concerns encourages ongoing usability research, storyboarding, prototyping, and usability labs. The event-driven version of this approach might be construed as a risk that the customer will refuse acceptance and therefore that requirements need to be overly documented and signed off to enforce a contract. One approach embraces necessary change, whereas the other tries to prevent it. The constituency-based approach follows the value-up paradigm, whereas the event-driven one, when used in isolation, follows the work-down paradigm.

Fit the Process to the Project

The Agile Project Management Declaration of Interdependence speaks of "situationally specific strategies" as a recognition that the process needs to fit the project. VSTS uses the mechanism of process templates to implement this principle. But what contextual differences should you consider in determining what is right for your project?

Some of the considerations are external business factors; others have to do with issues internal to your organization. Even if only certain stakeholders will choose the process, every team member should understand the rationale of the choice and the value of any practice that the process prescribes. If the value can't be identified, it is very unlikely that it can be realized. Sometimes the purpose may not be intuitive, such as certain legal requirements, but if understood can still be achieved.

The primary dimensions in which contexts differ are as follows:

- Adaptive Versus Plan-Driven
- Tacit Knowledge Versus Required Documentation
- Implicit Versus Explicit Sign-Off Gates and Governance Model
- Level of Auditability and Regulatory Concerns
- Prescribed Organization Versus Self-Organization
- One Project at a Time Versus Many Projects at Once
- Geographic Distribution
- Contractual Obligations

The next sections describe each of these considerations.

Adaptive Versus Plan-Driven

To what extent does your project need to pin down and design all of its functionality in advance, or conversely, to what extent can the functionality and design evolve over the course of the project? There are advantages and disadvantages to both approaches. The primary benefit of a plan-driven approach is stability. If you are assembling a system that has many parts that are being discretely delivered, obviously interfaces need to be very stable to allow integrations from the contributing teams. (Consider a car, a web portal hosting products from many sellers, or a payment clearing system.) Of course, the main drawback to a plan-driven approach is that you often have to make the most important decisions when you know the least.

On the other hand, if your project needs to be highly responsive to competitive business pressure, usability, or technical learning achieved during the project, you can't pin the design down tightly in advance. (Consider consumer devices and commercial web sites.) The main risk with the adaptive approach is that you discover design issues that force significant rework or change of project scope.

Adaptive or Plan-Driven

- MSF for Agile Software Development is more adaptive.
- MSF for CMMI Process Improvement can be more plan-driven.

Required Documentation Versus Tacit Knowledge

A huge difference in practice is the amount of documentation used in different processes. For this process discussion, I intend "writing documentation" to mean preparing any artifacts—specifications, visual models, meeting minutes, presentations, and so on—not directly related to the executable code, data, and tests of the software being built. I am *not* including the help files, manuals, training, and other materials that are clearly part of the product value being delivered to the end user or customer. Nor am I discounting the importance of the educational materials.

Any documentation that you write should have a clear purpose. Usually the purpose concerns contract, consensus, architecture, approval, audit, delegation, or work tracking. Sometimes the documentation is not the most effective way to achieve the intended goal. For example, when you have a small, cohesive, collocated team with strong domain knowledge, it may be easy to reach and maintain consensus. You may need little more than a vision statement, a scenario list, and frequent face-to-face communication with the customer and with each other. (This is part of the eXtreme Programming model.)

On the other hand, when part of your team is twelve time zones away, domain knowledge varies, and many stakeholders need to review designs, much more explicit documentation is needed. (And of geographic necessity, many discussions must be electronic rather than face-to-face.)

The key point here is to write the documentation for its audience and to its purpose and then to *stop* writing. After the documentation serves its purpose, more effort on it is waste. Instead, channel the time and resources into work products that bring value to the customer directly. If you later discover that your documentation is inadequate for its purpose, update it then. In other words, "fix it when it hurts."[17]

Tacit Knowledge or Documentation

- MSF for Agile Software Development relies on tacit knowledge more heavily.
- MSF for CMMI Process Improvement requires more explicit documentation.

Implicit Versus Explicit Sign-Off
Gates and Governance Model

Appropriately, business stakeholders usually require points of sign-off. Typically, these gates release funding and are, at least implicitly, points at which a project can be canceled. When development is performed by outside companies or consultants, contractual formality usually prescribes these checkpoints.

Often, setting expectations and communicating with the stakeholders is a major part of the project manager's responsibility. For correct communication, perhaps the most important issue is whether the sign-offs are based on time (how far did we get in the allotted time?) or functionality (how long did it take us to implement the functionality for this milestone?).

This alignment of IT with the business stakeholders is the domain of IT governance. In MSF, unlike other processes, the governance model is separated from the operational process. Governance concerns the alignment of the project with its customers, whereas the operational activities are managed in much finer-grained iterations (see Figure 2.4). Note that the alignment checkpoints do not preclude any work from being started earlier, but they do enable the delivery team and its customer to pass an agreement milestone without a need to revisit the earlier track.

Governance Checkpoints

- MSF for CMMI Process Improvement has explicit governance checkpoints that are organized at the end of each *track*.
- MSF for Agile Software Development relies on a less formal model.

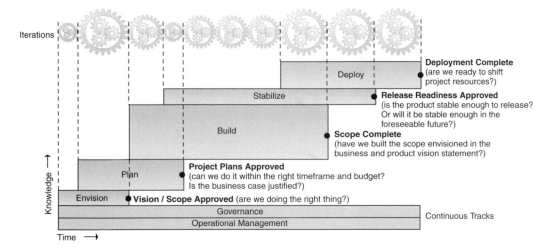

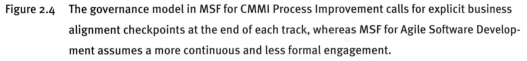

Figure 2.4   The governance model in MSF for CMMI Process Improvement calls for explicit business alignment checkpoints at the end of each track, whereas MSF for Agile Software Development assumes a more continuous and less formal engagement.

VSTS provides a web-hosted project portal, based on Windows SharePoint Services, to make the project more transparent to all the stakeholders outside the immediate project team (see Figure 2.5). Of course, access to the portal can be controlled by permission and policy.

Auditability and Regulatory Concerns

Related to sign-off gates is the need to satisfy actual or potential auditors. In many industries, the risk of litigation (over product safety, customer privacy, business practices, and so on) drives the creation of certain documentation to prove the suitability of the development process. At the top of the list for all publicly traded U.S. companies is Sarbanes-Oxley (SOX) compliance, which requires executive oversight of corporate finance and accordingly all IT development projects that concern money or resources.

Sometimes these auditors are the well-known industry regulators, such as the FDA (pharmaceuticals and medical equipment), SEC (securities), FAA (avionics), or their counterparts in the European Union and other countries. Usually, these regulators have very specific rules of compliance.

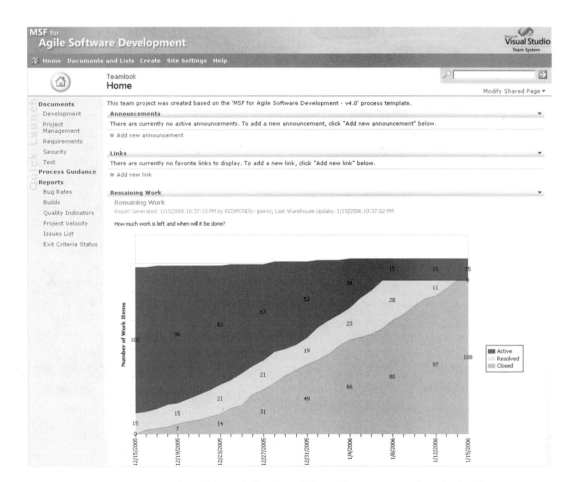

Figure 2.5   The project portal provides a daily view of the project status so that checkpoints can act to confirm decisions rather than to compile newly available information.

Audit and Appraisal

- MSF for CMMI Process Improvement defines an Auditor role and has explicit activities, work products, and reports that gather evidence for the audit.

- MSF for Agile Software Development also keeps a full audit trail of changes but does not prescribe the gathering of evidence for an audit.

Prescribed Versus Self-Organization

High-performance teams tend to be self-directed teams of peers that take advantage of the diverse personal strengths of their members. Such teams strive to organize themselves with flexible roles and enable individuals to pick their own tasks. They follow the principle that "responsibility cannot be assigned; it can only be accepted."[18]

In other organizations, this ideal is less practical. People have to assume roles that are assigned. Often a good coach may have a better idea than the players of their capabilities and developmental opportunities. Central assignment may also be necessary to take advantage of specialist skills or to balance resources. This constraint becomes another factor in determining the right process.

In either case, it is important to recognize the distinction between *roles* on a project and *job descriptions*. MSF makes a point of describing roles, which consist of related activities that require similar skills, and of emphasizing that one person can fill multiple roles. Most career ladders have conditioned people to think in terms of job descriptions. This is an unpleasant dichotomy. When staffing your project, think about the skills your team offers and then make sure that the roles can be covered, but don't be slavish about partitioning roles according to job titles.

Specificity of Roles

- MSF for CMMI Process Improvement assumes a more prescribed organization and defines up to eighteen roles.
- MSF for Agile Software Development defines six roles and can be scaled down to three.

One Project at a Time Versus Many Projects at Once

One of the most valuable planning actions is to ensure that your team members can focus on the project at hand without other commitments that drain their time and attention. Twenty years ago, Gerald Weinberg proposed a rule of thumb to compute the waste caused by project switching, shown in Table 2.1.[19]

Table 2.1 Waste Caused by Project Switching

Number of Simultaneous Projects	Percent of Working Time Available per Project	Loss to Context Switching
1	100%	0%
2	40%	20%
3	20%	40%
4	10%	60%
5	5%	75%

In situations of context switching, you need to perform much more careful tracking, including effort planned and spent, so that you can correlate results by project.

A related issue is the extent to which team members need to track their hours on a project and use those numbers for estimation and actual work completion. If your team members are dedicated to your project, then you ought to be able to use calendar time as effectively as hours of effort to estimate and track task completion. However, if their time is split between multiple projects, then you need to account for multitasking.

This issue adds a subtle complexity to many metrics concerning estimation and completion of effort. Not only are they harder to track and report, but also the question of estimating and tracking overhead for task switching becomes an issue.

In many organizations, however, it is a fact of life that individuals have to work on multiple projects, and VSTS makes this possible. VSTS keeps all the relevant projects on a Team Foundation Server and displays the active ones you have chosen on the Team Explorer (see Figure 2.6).

For Detailed Instructions on Setting Up VSTS for Multiple Projects, See This MSDN Section

Development Tools and Technologies
   Visual Studio Team System
      Team Foundation
         Team Foundation Project Leads
            Creating and Managing Team Projects

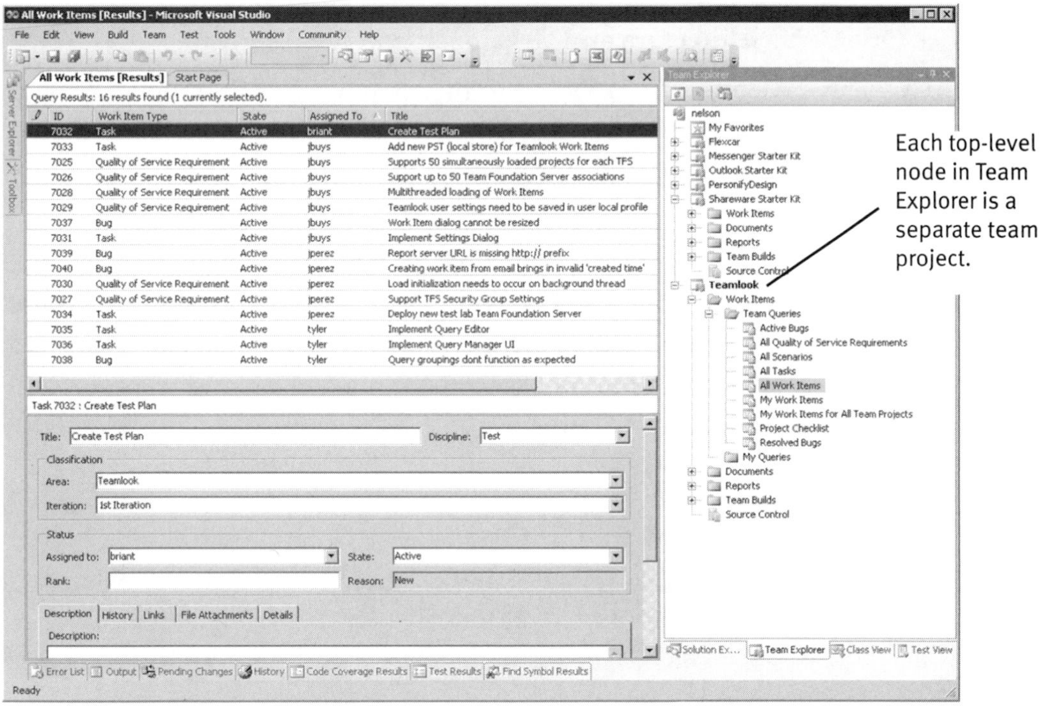

Each top-level node in Team Explorer is a separate team project.

Figure 2.6   VSTS makes it possible to switch context between multiple projects (such as new development and maintenance) directly in the development environment. The bookkeeping of code versions, tests, documents, and work items is handled automatically. Although this approach does not remove the cognitive load, it does eliminate many errors that are caused by the mechanical complexity of handling multiple projects.

Geographic and Organizational Boundaries

Teams are often distributed geographically, sometimes around the world. The VSTS team, for example, was distributed in Redmond, Raleigh, Copenhagen, Hyderabad, and Beijing. When you have to work across locations and time zones, you typically need to rely on explicit documentation over tacit knowledge and must be more of a prescribed organization than a self-organizing team. It is important to have clear technical boundaries and interfaces between the local teams and leave decisions within the boundaries of the teams.

Service Oriented Architecture and Organizational Boundaries

Service Oriented Architecture is a great technical model for designing a system so that different services can be implemented by teams in different locations. See Chapter 5, "Architectural Design."

A very large amount of IT work is outsourced, that is, contracted with a separate company. The outsourcer might be local or on the other side of the planet. These cases obviously require business contracts, which tend to specify deliverables in high detail. Clearly, these cases also require explicit documentation and a more plan-driven than adaptive approach.

Explicit Documentation

MSF for CMMI Process Improvement requires more explicit documentation and provides a more plan-driven approach.

Summary

Chapter 1, "A Value-Up Paradigm," argued the importance of the value-up paradigm. This chapter addressed the issues of choosing and applying a suitable process in the value-up context.

In VSTS, the two processes delivered by Microsoft are MSF for Agile Software Development and MSF for CMMI Process Improvement. Both are value-up processes, relying on iterative development, iterative prioritization, continuous improvement, constituency-based risk management, and situationally specific adaptation of the process to the project.

MSF for CMMI Process Improvement stretches the practices of its more agile cousin to fit contexts that require a more explicit governance model, documentation, prescribed organization, and auditability. It supports appraisal to CMMI Level 3, but more importantly, it provides a low-overhead, agile model of CMMI.

Endnotes

1. Alistair Cockburn coined the phrase "Stretch to Fit" in his Crystal family of methodologies and largely pioneered this discussion of context with his paper "A Methodology Per Project," available at http://alistair.cockburn.us/crystal/articles/mpp/methodologyperproject.html.

2. For a comparison of thirteen published processes, see Barry Boehm and Richard Turner, *Balancing Agility with Discipline: A Guide for the Perplexed* (Boston: Addison-Wesley, 2004), 168–194.

3. As Kent Beck pithily put it: "All methodologies are based on fear." Kent Beck, *Extreme Programming Explained: Embrace Change, First Edition* (Boston: Addison-Wesley, 2000), 165.

4. Barry Boehm and Richard Turner, *Balancing Agility with Discipline: A Guide for the Perplexed* (Boston: Addison-Wesley, 2004), 152.

5. www.agilealliance.org

6. www.sei.cmu.edu

7. See David J Anderson, "Stretching Agile to fite CMMI Level 3," presented at the Agile Conference, Denver 2005, available from http://www.agilemanagement.net/Articles/Papers/StretchingAgiletoFitCMMIL.html.

8. [IEEE Std 610.12-1990], 39.

9. Frederick P. Brooks, Jr., *The Mythical Man-Month: Essays on Software Engineering, Twentieth Anniversary Edition* (Reading, MA: Addison-Wesley, 1995), 266.

10. http://www.csc.ncsu.edu/faculty/xie/realoptionse.htm

11. Tom DeMarco and Timothy Lister, *Waltzing with Bears: Managing Risk on Software Projects* (New York: Dorset House, 2003), 137.

12. The convention of "iteration" for the planning cycle and "increment" for the coding/testing one is common. See, for example, Alistair Cockburn's discussion at http://saloon.javaranch.com/cgi-bin/ubb/ultimatebb.cgi?ubb=get_topic&f=42&t=000161.

13. Anderson 2004, op. cit., 89.

14. MoSCoW scheduling is a technique of the DSDM methodology. For more on this, see http://www.dsdm.org.

15. DeMarco and Lister, op. cit., 130.

16. Cockburn, op. cit.

17. Scott W. Ambler and Ron Jeffries, *Agile Modeling: Effective Practices for Extreme Programming and the Unified Process* (New York: Wiley, 2002).

18. Kent Beck with Cynthia Andres, *Extreme Programming Explained: Embrace Change, Second Edition* (Boston: Addison-Wesley, 2005), 34.

19. Gerald M. Weinberg, *Quality Software Management: Systems Thinking* (New York: Dorset House, 1992), 284.

3

Requirements

Business Analyst
Product Manager
User Experience

"The single hardest part of building a software system is deciding precisely what to build."[1]

—Frederick Brooks, *Mythical Man-Month*

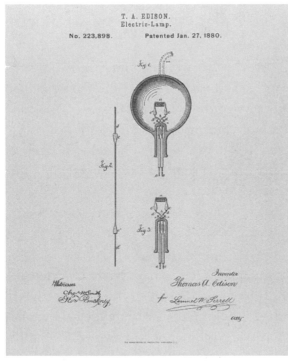

United States Patent and Trademark Office

Figure 3.1

Edison patented the light bulb in 1880, but it is still being improved today.

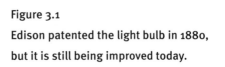

In the previous chapter, I discussed the choice of software process and the contextual issues that would favor one process over another. Regardless of your process choice, you need to start by envisioning your solution requirements. Usually, this responsibility is led by a business analyst or product manager, and in pure XP, it is done by an onsite customer. Obviously, you have to do much of the solution definition before you start your project. You won't get funding, recruit team members, or identify the rest of work until you know what you're trying to do.

> **Vision Statement, Personas, Scenarios, and Quality of Service Requirements**
>
> In VSTS, the vision statement and personas are captured in documents accessible from the Team Explorer and Project Portal. Scenarios and quality of service requirements are work items, and they are tracked and maintained like other work items in the work item database.
>
> There are only minor differences between MSF for Agile Software Development and MSF for CMMI Process Improvement with regard to envisioning, mostly in the details of their work item type definitions.

MSF defines requirements primarily as *scenarios* and *qualities of service (QoS)*. VSTS uses specific work item types to capture and track these requirements so that they show up in the project backlog, ranked as an ordinary part of the work. You continue to refine your requirements throughout your project as you learn from each iteration. Because these requirements are work items, when you make changes to them, a full audit is captured automatically, and the changes flow directly into the metrics warehouse.

What's Your Vision?

Every project should have a vision that every stakeholder can understand. Often the vision statement is the first step in getting a project funded. Even when it's not, treating the vision as the motivation for funding is helpful in clarifying the core values of the project. Certainly it should capture why a customer or end user will want the solution that the project implements.

The shorter the vision statement is, the better it is. A vision statement can be one sentence long, or one paragraph, or longer only if needed. It should speak to the end user in the language of the user's domain. A sign of a successful vision statement is that everyone on the project team can recite it from memory and connect their daily work to it.

Strategic Projects

Projects can be strategic or adaptive. Strategic projects represent significant investments, based on a plan to improve significantly over their predecessors. For example, when startup companies form around a new product idea, or when new business units are launched, the rationale is typically a bold strategic vision.

A useful format for thinking about the key values of such a strategic project, and hence the vision statement, is the "elevator pitch."[2] It's called an elevator pitch because you can recite it to a prospective customer or investor in the brief duration of an elevator ride. It's useful because it captures the vision crisply enough that the customer or investor can remember it from that short encounter. Geoffrey Moore invented a succinct form for the evaluator pitch.

Table 3.1 Elevator Pitch

For	(target customer personas in identified segment only)
Who are dissatisfied with	(the current . . . alternative)
Our solution is a	(new product category)
That provides	(key problem-solving capability)
Unlike	(the product alternative)
We have assembled	(key scenarios and QoS for your solution)

Adaptive Projects

On the other hand, most IT projects are more adaptive. They tackle incremental changes to existing systems. It is often easiest and most appropriate to describe the vision in terms of business process changes. In these cases, if a business process model or description is available, it is probably the best starting point. Use the as-is model as the current alternative and the proposed one as the solution.

Business Process Models

In the current MSF process templates, there are work products for the vision statement, scenarios, and qualities of service. However, currently there are no direct activities for business process modeling. If you need to define a business process model, VSTS does include Microsoft Visio with useful stencils for diagramming business process flow.

When to Detail Requirements

"Analysis paralysis" is a common condemnation of stalled projects. This complaint reflects the experience that trying too hard to pin down project requirements early can prevent any forward movement. This can be a significant risk in envisioning. There are two factors to keep in mind to mediate this risk: the shelf life of requirements and the audience for them.

Requirements Are Perishable

One of the great insights of the value-up paradigm is that requirements have a limited shelf life, for four reasons:

- **The business environment or problem space changes.** Competitors, regulators, customers, users, technology, and management all have a way of altering the assumptions on which your requirements are based. If you let too much time lapse between the definition of requirements and their implementation, you risk discovering that you need to redefine the requirements to reflect a changed problem.

- **The knowledge behind the requirements becomes stale.** When an analyst or team is capturing requirements, knowledge of the requirements is at its peak. The process of communicating their meanings, exploring their implications, and understanding their gaps should happen then. Documentation might capture some of this information for intermediate purposes such as contractual signoff, but ultimately what matters is the implementation. The more closely you couple the implementation to the requirements definition, the less you allow that knowledge to decay.

- **There is a psychological limit to the number of requirements that a team can meaningfully consider in detail at one time.** The smaller you make the batch of requirements, the more attention you get to quality design and implementation. Conversely, the larger you allow the requirements scope of an iteration to grow, the more you risk confusion and carelessness.

- **The implementation of one iteration's requirements influences the detailed design of the requirements of the next iteration**. Design doesn't happen in a vacuum. What you learn from one iteration enables you to complete the design for the next.

In the discussion about capturing requirements that follows, I risk encouraging you to do too much too early. I don't mean to. Think coarse and understandable initially, sufficient to prioritize requirements into iterations. The detailed requirements and design can follow.

Who Cares About Requirements

For most projects, the requirements that matter are the ones that the team members and stakeholders understand. On a successful project, they all understand the same requirements; on an unsuccessful one, they have divergent expectations (see Figure 3.2).

This tension between specificity and understandability is an inherently hard issue. The most precise requirements are not necessarily the most intelligible, as illustrated in Figure 3.2. A mathematical formulation or an executable test might be much harder to understand than a more commonplace picture with a prose description.

It is important to think of requirements at multiple levels of granularity. For broad communication, prioritization, and costing to a rough order of magnitude, you need a coarse understanding that is easy to grasp. On the other hand, for implementation of a requirement within the current iteration, you need a much more detailed specification. Indeed, if you practice test-driven development (see Chapter 6, "Development"), the ultimate detailed requirement definition is the executable test.

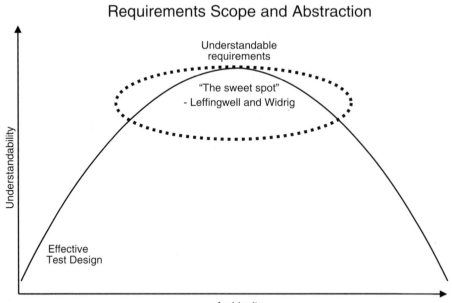

Dean Leffingwell and Don Widrig, *Managing Software Requirements* (Boston, MA: Addison-Wesley, 2000), 273

Figure 3.2 **The X-axis shows the degree of ambiguity (opposite of specificity) in the requirements documents; the Y-axis shows the resulting understandability.**

Think about the audience for your requirements work. The audience will largely determine the breadth and precision you need to apply in specifying requirements. At one end of the scale, in eXtreme Programming, you may have a small, collocated team and an onsite customer. You note future requirements on a 3″ × 5″ card or as the title on a work item, and you move on until it is time to implement. When it is time to do a requirement, within the same session you discuss the requirement with the customer and write the test that validates it, just before implementation.[3]

At the other extreme, your requirements specification may be subject to regulatory approval, audit, or competitive bidding. At this end, you may want every detail spelled out so that every subsequent change can be individually costed and submitted for approval.[4]

MSF recommends that you plan and detail requirements for one iteration at a time. Effectively, the iteration becomes a batch of requirements that progress through realization. For most projects, this is a balanced medium that maximizes communication, keeps requirements fresh, avoids wasted work, and keeps the focus on the delivery of customer value.

Personas and Scenarios

In a value-up paradigm, quality is measured as value to the customer. When you don't have a live customer on site, or your customers can't be represented by a single individual, personas and scenarios are the tools you use to understand and communicate that value.

Start with Personas

To get clear goals for a project, you need to know the intended users. Start with recognizable, realistic, appealing *personas*. By now, personas have become commonplace in usability engineering literature, but before the term *personas* became popular there, the technique had been identified as a means of product definition in market research. Moore described the technique well:

> The place most . . . marketing segmentation gets into trouble is at the beginning, when they focus on a target market or target segment instead of on a target customer . . . We need something that feels a lot more like real people . . . Then, once we have their images in mind, we can let them guide us to developing a truly responsive approach to their needs.[5]

In turn, personas are the intended users who are accomplishing the scenarios. For projects with identified users, who are paying customers, you can name the personas for representative actual users. For a broad market product, your personas will probably be composite fictional characters, who don't betray any personal information. (Note that there are other stakeholders, such as the users' boss, who may be funding the project but are at least one step removed from the personal experience of the users.) Alan Cooper has described the characteristics of good personas:

Personas are user models that are represented as specific, individual humans. They are not actual people, but are synthesized directly from observations of real people. One of the key elements that allow personas to be successful as user models is that they are personifications (Constantine and Lockwood, 2000). They are represented as specific individuals. This is appropriate and effective because of the unique aspects of personas as user models: They engage the empathy of the development team towards the human target of the design. Empathy is critical for the designers, who will be making their decisions for design frameworks and details based on both the cognitive and emotional dimensions of the persona, as typified by the persona's goals.[6]

Good personas are memorable, three-dimensional, and sufficiently well described to be decisive when they need to be. If you were making a movie, personas would be the profiles you would give to the casting agent. They describe the categories of users not just in terms of job titles and functions but also in terms of personality, work or usage environment, education, computer experience, and any other characteristics that make the imagined person come to life. Assign each persona a name and attach a picture so that it is memorable. Some teams in Microsoft put posters on the wall and hand out fridge magnets to reinforce the presence of the personas.[7]

Personas can also be useful for describing adversaries. For example, if security and privacy are a concern, then you probably want to profile the hacker who tries to break into your system. The vandal who tries indiscriminately to bring down your web site is different from the thief who tries to steal your identity without detection. With disfavored personas, everyone can be made conscious of anti-scenarios—things that must be prevented.

Scenarios

In MSF, *scenarios* are the primary form of functional requirements. By "scenario," MSF means the single interaction *path* that a *user* (or group of collaborating users, represented by *personas*) performs to *achieve* a known *goal.* The goal is the key here, and it needs to be stated in the user's language, such as *Place an order.* As your solution definition evolves, you will evolve the scenario into a specific sequence of steps with sample data, but the goal of the scenario should not change.

There are many reasons to use scenarios to define your solution:

- Scenarios communicate tangible customer value in the language of the customer in a form that can be validated by customers. Particularly useful are questions in the form of "What if you could [accomplish goal] like [this scenario]?" You can use these questions in focus groups, customer meetings, and usability labs. As the solution evolves, scenarios naturally turn into prototypes and working functionality.
- Scenarios enable the team to plan and measure the flow of customer value. This enables the creation of a progressive measurement of readiness and gives the team a natural unit of scoping.
- Scenarios unite the narrow and extended teams. All stakeholders understand scenarios in the same way so that differences in assumptions can be exposed, biases overcome, and requirements discussions made tangible.

A key is to state goals in the language and context of the user. The goal—such as *Place an order* or *Return goods*—defines the scenario, even though the steps to accomplish it may change. Even though you may be much more familiar with the language of possible solutions than with the customers' problems, and even though you may know one particular subset of users better than the others, you need to stick to the users' language. Alan Cooper describes this well:

> Goals are not the same as tasks. A goal is an end condition, whereas a task is an intermediate step that helps to reach a goal. Goals motivate people to perform tasks . . . Goals are driven by human motivations, which change very slowly, if at all, over time.[8]

Often, the goals are chosen to address *pain points*, that is, issues that the user faces with current alternatives, which the new solution is intended to solve. When this is true, you should capture the pain points with the goals. At other times, the goals are intended to capture exciters—be sure to tag these as well so that you can test how much delight the scenario actually brings.

Research Techniques

We find the personas by observing target users, preferably in their own environment. Several techniques can be applied—two widely used ones are focus groups and contextual inquiries. For all these techniques, it is important to select a representative sample of your users. A good rule of thumb is not to be swayed heavily by users who are too novice or too expert and instead to look for intermediates who represent the bulk of your target population for most of your solution's life.[9]

Focus groups are essentially directed discussions with a group of carefully chosen interview subjects with a skilled facilitator. When conducted professionally, focus groups usually are closed sessions with observers sequestered behind a one-way mirror (or on the end of a video feed). Open focus groups work too, where observers sit in the back of the room, provided that they sit quietly and let the discussion unfold without interjection.

Focus groups are undoubtedly useful, especially when you are gathering issues expansively. At the same time, you need to be very careful to distinguish between what people *say* and what they *do*. There are many foibles that make the distinction important: wishful thinking, overloaded terminology, desires to impress, and human difficulty at self-observation, to name a few.

People often describe their (or their colleagues') behavior differently from how an outside observer would. *Contextual inquiry* is a technique that attempts to overcome this problem by directly observing users in their own environment when they are doing their everyday tasks.[10]

Contextual inquiry is a technique borrowed from anthropology. The observer watches, occasionally asks open-ended journalistic questions (*Who, What, When, Where, Why, How*), does not try to bias the user's activities, and does not try to offer solutions. It is important to understand pain points and opportunities—where the user is annoyed, where things can be made better, what would make a big difference. If possible, gather relevant documents and other work products and take pictures of the user's environment, especially reference material posted on the wall.

My favorite anecdote to illustrate the problem of self-reporting comes from a customer visit to a major bank in 2003 when Microsoft was trying to define Visual Studio Team System requirements. In a morning meeting, which was run as an open focus group, the Microsoft team asked about development practices, especially unit testing. They were told that unit testing was a universal practice among the bank's developers and indeed was a requirement before checking in code.

One of the Microsoft usability engineers spent that afternoon with one of the developers in his cube. (That's why it's called a *contextual* interview.) The developer went through several coding tasks and checked code in several times. After a couple hours, the usability engineer asked, "I've seen you do several check-ins, and I'm wondering, do you do unit testing, too?" "Of course," came the reply, "I press F5 before checking in—that's unit testing." (In case you're not familiar with Visual Studio, F5 is the compilation key and has nothing to do with testing.) The reported practice of unit testing was simply not found in practice. In designing VSTS, we interpreted this discrepancy as an opportunity to make unit testing easy and practical for developers in organizations like this. (See Chapter 6, "Development.")

One user does not make a persona, and you must repeat the observation until you feel that you have clear patterns of behavior that you can distill into a persona description.

Get Specific Early

When you have defined personas, you can describe the scenarios for the specific personas. Scenarios, too, were first identified as a market research technique. Again, Geoffrey Moore:

> [Characterizing scenarios] is not a formal segmentation survey—they take too long, and their output is too dry. Instead, it is a tapping into the fund of anecdotes that actually carries business knowledge in our culture. Like much that is anecdotal, these scenarios will incorporate fictions, falsehoods, prejudices, and the like. Nonetheless, they are by far the most useful and most accurate form of data to work with at this stage in the segmentation process.[11]

Start with the scenario goal. Then break down the goal into a list of steps, at whatever granularity is most understandable. Use action verbs to enumerate the steps. Keep the scenarios in your user's language, not in the language of your implementation. In other words, scenarios should be described first from the problem space, not the solution space.

Don't try to detail the alternate and exception paths initially—that usually hampers understandability and quickly becomes too complicated to manage—but record just their names as other scenarios and save them for future iterations.

When you are comfortable with the sequence, you can add the second part to the step definition, that is, how the intended solution responds. You now have a list in the form of *Persona-Does-Step, Solution-Shows-Result*. Tag the steps that will elicit a *"Wow!"* from your user. (These are the *exciters,* which are discussed later in this chapter.)

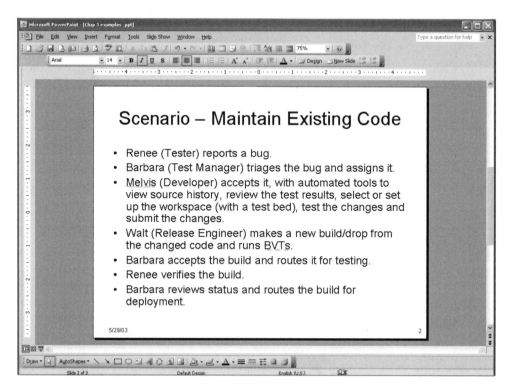

Figure 3.3   When we were developing VSTS, we used high-level scenarios to envision the product
scope. This is a very early example. Over time, the lines of this slide became scenario work
items in our work item database, and we used this as the primary list to drive execution
and testing.

Storyboards

Although scenarios start as goals and then evolve into lists of steps, they don't stop
there. When you are comfortable that the steps and their *sequence* define the experience you want, elaborate them into wireframes, storyboards, prototypes, and working iterations. Although the goal of each scenario should remain constant, the details
and steps may evolve and change with every iteration.

Wireframes and storyboards are often essential to communicate the flow of interaction effectively, especially when you have rich data and state in the solution being
designed. Microsoft Visio provides a stencil for drawing wireframes of user interfaces. For each task, with a title in the form of "Persona does step," draw a wireframe. Sequence the wireframes together, paying attention to the flow and data, and

you have a storyboard. This can be a cut-and-paste of the Visio screens into Power-Point. If you need to distribute the storyboard, you can easily make a narrated movie of it using Producer for PowerPoint or by recording a LiveMeeting.

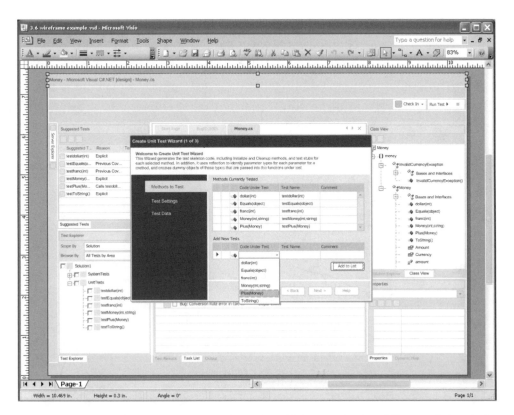

Figure 3.4   This is a very early Visio wireframe from the initial scenarios for VSTS. Not all the windows shown were implemented, and not all the windows implemented were designed as envisioned in the wireframe. Three successive rounds of testing in usability labs and subsequent revisions were needed before users could achieve the intended goal effectively.

Breadth of Scenarios

It is useful to think of the end-to-end story that your solution needs to tell and to line up the scenarios accordingly. This story should start with the customer deploying your solution and run through the customer realizing the value. This is equally useful whether you are building an internal, bespoke solution or a commercial product.

If you take this approach, you must deal with both the issues of discoverability—how first-time users find the necessary features—and the longitudinal issues—how intermediate users, as they become more experienced, become productive.

How many scenarios do you need? Typically, you should have enough scenarios to define the major flows of the target system and few enough to be easy to remember.

Your scenarios should be sufficient to cover the end-to-end flows of the solution without gaps and without unnecessary duplication. This means that your scenarios probably need to decompose into intermediate activities, which in turn contain the steps.

If you are creating a multiperson scenario, then it is useful to draw a flow with swimlanes to show who does what before whom.

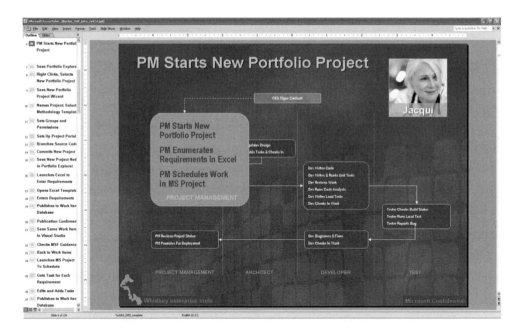

Figure 3.5   This PowerPoint slide is an illustration of the scenarios in an end-to-end story. This particular slide was used in the definition of scenarios for VSTS.

Customer Validation

A key benefit of scenarios and iterations is that you have many opportunities for customers to review your solution as it evolves and to validate or correct your course before you incur expensive rework. Depending on the business circumstances, you might want up to three kinds of signoff you want to see for your solution. *Users* (or their advocates) need to confirm that the solution lets them productively accomplish their goal. *Economic buyers*, sometimes the users' boss, sometimes called business decision makers, need to see that the financial value is being realized from the project. *Technical evaluators* need to see that the implementation is following the necessary architecture to fit into the required constraints of the customer organization. Sometimes these roles are collapsed, but often they are not. Scenarios are useful in communicating progress to all three groups.

Early in a project, this validation can be done in focus groups or interviews with scenarios as lists and then as wireframes. Storyboards and live functionality, as it becomes available, can also be tested in a usability lab.

Figure 3.6   This is a frame from the streaming video of a usability lab. The bulk of the image is the computer screen as the user sees it. The user is superimposed in the lower right so that observers can watch and listen to the user working through the lab assignments.

Usability labs are settings in which a target user is given a set of goals to accomplish without coaching in a setting that is as realistic as possible. At Microsoft, we have rooms permanently outfitted with one-way mirrors and video recording, which enable spectators to watch behind the glass or over streaming video. Although this setup is convenient, it is not necessary. All you need is a basic video camera on a tripod or a service such as Microsoft LiveMeeting with a webcam and desktop recording.

The three keys to making a usability lab effective are as follows:

- Create a trusting atmosphere in which the user knows that the software is being tested, not the user.
- Have the user think out loud continually so that you can hear the unfiltered internal monologue.
- Don't "lead the witness"—that is, don't interfere with the user's exploration and discovery of the software under test.

Usability labs, like focus groups and contextual interviews, are ways to challenge your assumptions regularly. Remember that requirements are perishable and that you need to revisit user expectations and satisfaction with the path that your solution is taking.

Evolving Scenarios

How do you know when you've defined your scenarios well enough? When the team has a common picture of what to build and test in the next iteration. There are three reasonable ways to test whether the scenarios communicate well enough:

- Customers can review the scenarios and provide meaningful feedback on suitability for achieving the goal, (in)completeness of steps, and relevance of the data.
- Testers can understand the sequence sufficiently to define tests, both positive and negative. They can identify how to test the sequence, what data is necessary, and what variations need to be explored.
- The development or architecture team can design the services, components, or features necessary to deliver the flow by identifying the necessary interactions, interfaces, and dependencies.

On the other hand, if you discover that your scenarios don't capture the intended functionality sufficiently for these stakeholders, you can add more detail or extend the scenarios further.

Demos of newly implemented scenarios during or at the end of an iteration are very motivating. They can energize the team, create valuable peer interaction, and if customers are available, generate great dialog and enthusiasm.

As iterations progress, you should add scenarios. In early iterations, you typically focus on satisfiers and exciters, whereas in later iterations, you should ensure the absence of dissatisfiers. This approach naturally leads you to scenarios that explore alternate flows through the solution. The next chapter shows examples of turning scenario completion into a scorecard for tracking velocity and progress.

Personas and Scenarios and Their Alternatives

Although MSF uses personas and scenarios to capture the vision of users and their requirements, there are alternative terms and techniques used by other processes.

Actors and Use Cases

If you are familiar with methodologies such as Rational Unified Process, you probably know the terms "actor" and "use case,"[12] and you might be wondering whether persona and scenario mean the same thing. MSF intentionally distinguishes scenarios from use cases with different terms because MSF advocates capturing a level of specificity that is not ordinarily captured in use cases. Scenarios and use cases start similarly, but they evolve very differently.

One of the MSF mindsets is *Get Specific Early*. For example, give a persona a picture, a name, and a biography instead of using a stick figure with an anonymous role name. You might have several personas for different demographics, whereas in use case analysis, you would have just one actor. The personas described as movie characters will be much more memorable and much easier to discuss when you envision your intended system behavior.

Similarly to personas, make scenarios specific. Include wireframes or sketches for screens and show the specific flow of data from one screen to the next. In use case analysis, this specificity is usually deferred to the step of designing a "realization." Don't defer it—test the intent with the specifics of the example immediately.

Also, unlike with use cases, don't get bogged down in alternative flows until you need them. Your goal is to deliver working software as quickly as possible and to learn from it. If you deliver a working flow, you will know much more about what the alternatives should be than if you try to define them all in the abstract. The single flow of a scenario is easier to schedule, monitor, and revise.

User Stories

If you are familiar with eXtreme Programming, then you know about user stories.[13] In XP, user stories are equivalent to the *goals* of scenarios that I described earlier—one sentence statements of intent written on 3" × 5" cards. XP does not elaborate the scenarios but requires that an onsite customer be available to describe the intended flow at the time of implementation. This is a good process if you have an onsite customer, a collocated team, no need to explore alternative designs, and no requirement that others sign off on designs.

Unfortunately, many teams need more explicit communication and signoff and cannot rely on a single onsite customer. In those cases, elaborating user stories into scenarios can be really helpful. Scenarios are also typically larger than user stories, especially when conceived around end-to-end value.

Exciters, Satisfiers, and Dissatisfiers

Scenarios tend to focus on requirements of a solution that make users enjoy the solution and achieve their goals. You can think of these as *satisfiers*. When the goals are important and the scenario compelling enough to elicit a *"Wow!"* from the customer, we can call the scenario an *exciter*.

At the same time, there are potential attributes of a solution (or absence of attributes) that can really annoy users or disrupt their experience. These are *dissatisfiers*.[14] Both need to be considered in gathering a solution's requirements. Dissatisfiers frequently occur because qualities of service haven't been considered fully. "The system's too slow," "Spyware picked up my ID," "I can no longer run my favorite app," and "It doesn't scale" are all examples of dissatisfiers that result from the corresponding qualities of service not being addressed.

Customers and users rarely describe the dissatisfiers—they are assumed to be absent. Consider the Monty Python sketch, *The Pet Shoppe*, in which a man goes to a pet store to return a parrot he bought. He did not specify that the parrot must be alive, so the pet dealer sells him a dead one. The sketch is hilarious because it reveals such a frequent misunderstanding. Statements such as "You didn't tell me X," "The customer didn't specify X," and "X didn't show up in our research" are all symptoms of failing to consider the requirements necessary to eliminate dissatisfiers.

Python (Monty) Pictures LTD

Figure 3.7   The Pet Shoppe

Customer: I wish to complain about this parrot what I purchased not half an hour ago from this very boutique.

Owner: Oh yes, the, uh, the Norwegian Blue . . . What's, uh . . . What's wrong with it?

Customer: I'll tell you what's wrong with it, my lad. 'E's dead, that's what's wrong with it! [15]

Qualities of Service

Scenarios are extremely valuable, but they are not the only type of requirement. Scenarios need to be understood in the context of qualities of service (QoS). (Once upon a time, QoS were called "non-functional requirements," but because that term is non-descriptive, I won't use it here. Sometimes they're called *'ilities,* which is a useful shorthand.)

Most dissatisfiers can be eliminated by appropriately defining qualities of service. QoS might define global attributes of your system, or they might define specific constraints on particular scenarios. For example, the security requirement that "unauthorized users should not be able to access the system or any of its data" is a global security QoS. The performance requirement that "for 95% of orders placed, confirmation must appear within three seconds at 1,000-user load" is a specific performance QoS about a scenario of placing an order.

Not all qualities of service apply to all systems, but you should know which ones apply to yours. Often QoS imply large architectural requirements or risk, so they should be negotiated with stakeholders early in a project.

There is no definitive list of all the qualities of service that you need to consider. There have been several standards,[16] but they tend to become obsolete as technology evolves. For example, security and privacy issues are not covered in the major standards, even though they are the most important ones in many modern systems.

The following four sections list some of the most common QoS to consider on a project.

Security and Privacy

Unfortunately, the spread of the Internet has made security and privacy every computer user's concern. These two QoS are important for both application development and operations, and customers are now sophisticated enough to demand to know what measures you are taking to protect them. Increasingly, they are becoming the subject of government regulation.

- **Security:** The ability of the software to prevent access and disruption by unauthorized users, viruses, worms, spyware, and other agents.
- **Privacy:** The ability of the software to prevent unauthorized access or viewing of Personally Identifiable Information.

Performance

Performance is most often noticed when it is poor. In designing, developing, and testing for performance, it is important to differentiate the QoS that influence the end experience of overall performance.

- **Responsiveness:** The absence of delay when the software responds to an action, call, or event.
- **Concurrency:** The capability of the software to perform well when operated concurrently with other software.
- **Efficiency:** The capability of the software to provide appropriate performance relative to the resources used under stated conditions.[17]
- **Fault Tolerance:** The capability of the software to maintain a specified level of performance in cases of software faults or of infringement of its specified interface.[18]
- **Scalability:** The ability of the software to handle simultaneous operational loads.

User Experience

While "easy to use" has become a cliché, a significant body of knowledge has grown around design for user experience.

- **Accessibility:** The extent to which individuals with disabilities have access to and use of information and data that is comparable to the access to and use by individuals without disabilities.[19]
- **Attractiveness:** The capability of the software to be attractive to the user.[20]
- **Compatibility:** The conformance of the software to conventions and expectations.
- **Discoverability:** The ability of the user to find and learn features of the software.
- **Ease of Use:** The cognitive efficiency with which a target user can perform desired tasks with the software.
- **Localizability:** The extent to which the software can be adapted to conform to the linguistic, cultural, and conventional needs and expectations of a specific group of users.

Manageability

Most modern solutions are multitier, distributed, service-oriented or client-server applications. The cost of operating these applications often exceeds the cost of developing them by a large factor, yet few development teams know how to design for operations. Appropriate QoS to consider are as follows:

- **Availability:** The degree to which a system or component is operational and accessible when required for use. Often expressed as a probability.[21] This is frequently cited as "nines," as in "three nines," meaning 99.9% availability.

- **Reliability:** The capability . . . to maintain a specified level of performance when used under specified conditions.[22] Frequently stated as Mean Time Between Failures (MTBF).

- **Installability and Uninstallability:** The capability . . . to be installed in a specific environment[23] and uninstalled without altering the environment's initial state.

- **Maintainability:** The ease with which a software system or component can be modified to correct faults, improve performance or other attributes, or adapt to a changed environment.[24]

- **Monitorability:** The extent to which health and operational data can be automatically collected from the software in operation.

- **Operability:** The extent to which the software can be controlled automatically in operation.

- **Portability:** The capability of the software to be transferred from one environment to another.[25]

- **Recoverability:** The capability of the software to re-establish a specified level of performance and recover the data directly affected in the case of a failure.[26]

- **Testability:** The degree to which a system or component facilitates the establishment of test criteria and the performance of tests to determine whether those criteria have been met.[27]

- **Supportability:** The extent to which operational problems can be corrected in the software.

- **Conformance to Standards:** The extent to which the software adheres to applicable rules.

- **Interoperability:** The capability of the software to interact with one or more specified systems.[28]

What makes a good QoS requirement? As with scenarios, QoS requirements need to be explicitly understandable to their stakeholder audiences, defined early, and when planned for an iteration, they need to be testable. You may start with a general statement about performance, for example, but in an iteration set specific targets on specific transactions at specific load. If you cannot state how to test satisfaction of the requirement when it becomes time to assess it, then you can't measure the completion.

Kano Analysis

There is a useful technique, called "Kano Analysis" after its inventor, which plots exciters, satisfiers, and dissatisfiers on the same axes.[29] The X-axis identifies the extent to which a scenario or QoS is implemented, while the Y-axis plots the resulting customer satisfaction.

In the case of Monty Python's parrot, life is a satisfier, or in other words, a necessary QoS. (Like many other QoS, the customer assumes it without specifying it and walks out of the store without having tested it. Just as a dysfunctional project manager might, the shopkeeper exploits the lack of specification.)

Of course, removing dissatisfiers only gets you a neutral customer. The quality of service that the parrot is alive and healthy gets you a customer who is willing to look further. On the other hand, satisfying the customer requires adding the requirements that make a customer want to buy your solution or a user want to use it. For the parrot, this might be the scenario that the customer talks to the parrot and the parrot sings back cheerfully.

Health is a must-have requirement of the parrot—its absence leaves the customer disgusted; its presence makes the customer neutral. The singing scenario is a satisfier or "performance requirement"—customers will expect it, and will be increasingly satisfied to the extent it is present.

Exciters are a third group of scenarios that delight the customer disproportionately when present. Sometimes they are not described or imagined because they may require true innovation to achieve. On the other hand, sometimes they are simple conveniences that make a huge perceived difference. For a brief period, minivan manufacturers competed based on the number of cupholders in the back seats, then on the number of sliding doors, and then on backseat video equipment. All these pieces of product differentiation were small, evolutionary features, which initially came to the market as exciters and over time came to be recognized as must-haves.

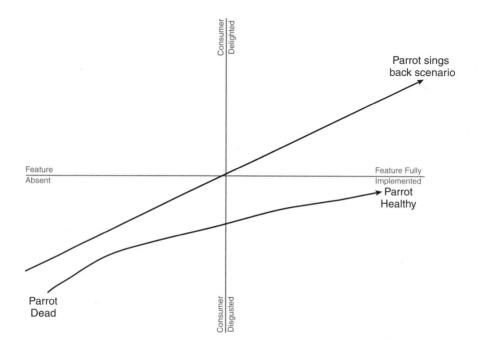

Figure 3.8   The X-axis shows the extent to which different solution requirements are implemented; the Y-axis shows the resulting customer response.

Returning to the parrot example, imagine a parrot that could clean its own cage.

You can generalize these three groups of requirements as *must-haves* (absence of dissatisfiers), *satisfiers*, and *exciters*, based on the extent to which their presence or absence satisfies or dissatisfies a customer. Must-haves constrain the intended solution, exciters optimize it, and satisfiers are expected but not differentiated. For completeness, there is a fourth set—*indifferent* features—that don't make a difference either way (such as the color of the parrot's cage).

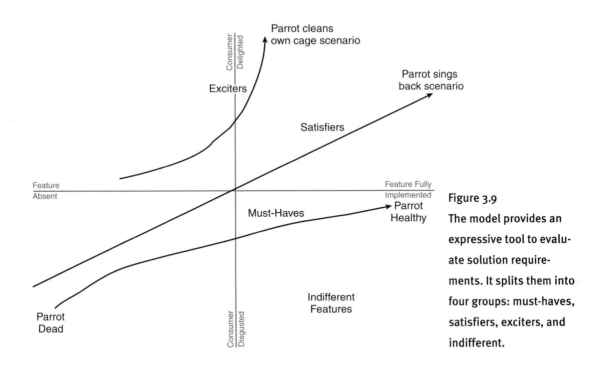

Figure 3.9

The model provides an expressive tool to evaluate solution requirements. It splits them into four groups: must-haves, satisfiers, exciters, and indifferent.

Technology Adoption Lifecycle

One last framework is useful in understanding the categorization of requirements and the differences among separate user segments. This framework is the technology adoption lifecycle, shown in Figure 3.10. It is a widely used model that describes the penetration of a product or technology into widespread use.[30]

The relative importance of dissatisfiers and exciters has a lot to do with where on the technology adoption lifecycle your users lie. If they are early adopters, who embrace a new solution out of enthusiasm for the technology, then they are likely to be highly tolerant of dissatisfiers and willing to accept involved workarounds to problems in order to realize the benefits of the exciters. On the other hand, the later in the adoption lifecycle your users lie, the less tolerant they will be of dissatisfiers, and the more they will expect exciters as commonplace. This is a natural market evolution in which users become progressively more sensitive to the entirety of the solution.

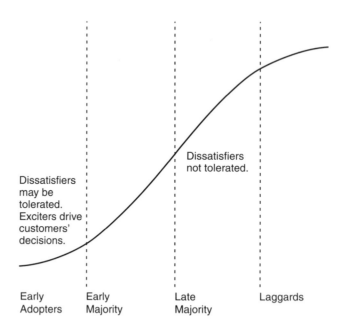

Figure 3.10   The S-curve is the standard representation of the Technology Adoption Lifecycle, broken into four segments for early adopters, early majority, late majority, and laggards.

Gathering the Data

Although the Monty Python parrot is a comic example, Kano Analysis is a very useful tool for thinking about your requirements. The easiest way to gather data for Kano Analysis is to ask questions in pairs, one about the appropriateness of a feature and the other about the importance, such as the following:[31]

- To what extent is the feature (scenario) that we just showed you (described to you) on target?
- How important is it that you can do what we just showed (or described)?

Whether you are doing broad statistical research or informal focus groups, you can gain insight into the solution by separating the scenarios and QoS, or the features as implemented, into the four groups.

Because it's easy to think of requirements, most projects end up having far too many of them (and not always the right ones). The Kano classification lets you see a total picture of requirements readily. This practice can shed light on different viewpoints and hidden assumptions about the relative importance of exciters, satisfiers, and dissatisfiers.

Kano Analysis provides a way of prioritizing scenarios and QoS. When planning an iteration, you can plot a set of requirements and evaluate the likely customer satisfaction. As you evolve a project across iterations, you will want to move up the Y-axis of customer satisfaction. This framework for differentiating the value of requirements gives you a powerful tool for assessing the impact of tradeoff decisions.

Summary

This chapter covered the description of a project's vision and requirements. As discussed in the previous chapter, MSF advocates iterative software development, in keeping with the value-up paradigm discussed in Chapter 1, "A Value-Up Paradigm." This implies that requirements be detailed an iteration at a time because they are perishable.

In MSF, the primary forms of requirements are scenarios and qualities of service (QoS). Scenarios are the functional requirements. A scenario addresses the goals of a persona or group of personas. Stated in the user's language, scenarios describe the sequence of steps and the interaction necessary for the persona to accomplish the intended goal. Scenarios can be elaborated in wireframes and storyboards.

QoS describe attributes of the intended solution in areas such as security, performance, user experience, and manageability. These are both global attributes and specific constraints on scenarios. QoS are often considered architectural requirements, both because they may have significant implications for architecture and because they often require specialist architectural knowledge to enumerate.

Not all requirements are created equal. It is important to understand the customer perception of these requirements as satisfiers, exciters, and must-haves (the removal of dissatisfiers). Scenarios alone rarely eliminate all dissatisfiers, which often lurk in poorly planned QoS. And scenarios by themselves do not design the architecture, the implementation details, or all the variant flows.

With requirements in hand, the next chapter looks at the process of managing a project.

Endnotes

1. Frederick P. Brooks, Jr., *The Mythical Man-Month: Essays on Software Engineering, Anniversary Edition* (Addison-Wesley, 1995), 199.

2. Adapted from Geoffrey A. Moore, *Crossing the Chasm: Marketing and Selling High-Tech Products to Mainstream Customers* (New York: HarperCollins, 2002), 154.

3. Beck 2000, op. cit., 60–61.

4. IEEE STD 830 is an example set of guidelines for such specifications.

5. Moore, *Crossing the Chasm*, 93–4.

6. Alan Cooper and Robert Reimann, *About Face 2.0: The Essentials of Interaction Design* (Indianapolis: Wiley, 2003), 59.

7. For a closer look at how Microsoft uses personas, see John Pruitt, *Persona Lifecycle: Keeping People in Mind Throughout Product Design* (Elsevier, 2005).

8. Cooper 2003, op. cit., 12.

9. Ibid., 35.

10. Hugh Beyer and Karen Holzblatt, *Contextual Design: Designing Customer-Centered Systems* (San Francisco: Morgan Kaufmann, 1998) and Cooper op cit., 44 ff.

11. Moore, *op. cit.*, 98.

12. Originally coined in Ivar Jacobson et al., *Object-Oriented Software Engineering: A Use Case Driven Approach* (Reading: Addison-Wesley / ACM Press, 1992), 159 ff., and elaborated by many including Alistair Cockburn, *Writing Effective Use Cases* (Pearson Education, 2000). The body of practice around use cases took a turn away from the intentions of these authors, and by using "scenarios," MSF connects to the separate tradition of the User Experience community.

13. For example, Mike Cohn, *User Stories Applied: For Agile Software Development* (Boston: Addison-Wesley, 2004).

14. J.M. Juran, *Juran on Planning for Quality* (Simon & Schuster, 1988).

15. Monty Python's Flying Circus, "The Dead Parrot Sketch," available on *The 16-Ton Monty Python DVD Megaset*, Disc 3 (A&E Home Video, 2005).

16. For example, ISO/IEC 9126 and IEEE Std 610.12-1990.

17. [ISO/IEC 9126-1/2001]

18. [ISO/IEC 9126-1/2001]

19. Section 504 of the Rehabilitation Act, 29 U.S.C. § 794d, available from http://www.usdoj.gov/crt/508/508law.html.

20. [ISO/IEC 9126-1/2001]

21. [IEEE STD 610.12-1990], 11

22. [ISO/IEC 9126-1/2001]

23. [ISO/IEC 9126-1/2001]

24. [IEEE STD 610.12-1990], 46

25. [ISO/IEC 9126-1/2001]

26. [ISO/IEC 9126-1/2001]

27. [IEEE STD 610.12-1990], 76

28. [ISO/IEC 9126-1/2001]

29. Kano, N., Seraku, N., Takahashi, F. and Tsuji, S. (1996), "Attractive quality and must-be quality," originally published in *Hinshitsu (Quality), The Journal of the Japanese Society for Quality Control*, XIV:2, 39–48, April 1984, translated in *The Best On Quality*, edited by John D. Hromi. Volume 7 of the Book Series of the International Academy for Quality (Milwaukee: ASQC Quality Press, 1996).

30. For example, Moore, op. cit.

31. For well documented questionnaires on gathering the data, see for example, *Center for Quality Management Journal*, II:4, Fall 1993.

4

Project Management

 Program Manager
Project Manager

"The deficiencies of the theory of the project and of the theory of management reinforce each other and their detrimental effects propagate through the life cycle of a project. Typically, customer requirements are poorly investigated at the outset, and the process of requirement clarification and change leads disruption in the progress of the project. The actual progress starts to drift from the plan, the updating of which is too cumbersome to be done regularly. Without an up-to-date plan, the work authorization system transforms to an approach of informal management. Increasingly, tasks are commenced without all inputs and prerequisites at hand, leading to low efficiency or task interruption and increased variability downstream. Correspondingly, controlling by means of a performance baseline that is not based on the actual status becomes ineffective or simply counterproductive. All in all, systematic project management is transformed to a facade, behind which the job actually gets done, even if with reduced efficiency and lessened value to the customer."[1]

—L. Koskela and G. Howell, "The Underlying Theory of Project Management Is Obsolete"

"A Friend in Need" by C.M. Coolidge, c. 1870

Figure 4.1   Without transparent data, project management can descend into a game of differing bets based on partial information and divergent perspectives of stakeholders. Poker is a good metaphor for this pattern.

The previous chapter addressed the gathering of requirements. This chapter focuses on managing a running project that implements those requirements. First, I'll cover three concepts that are core to the value-up paradigm:

- Variance to distinguish in- and out-of-control projects
- Descriptive rather than prescriptive metrics
- Multiple dimensions of project health

VSTS applies these concepts with its work item database and metrics warehouse to give you a practical basis for value-up project management. To illustrate this aspect of VSTS, I work through a large number of examples in this chapter using reports from the metrics warehouse. These are "happy day" examples, in contrast to troubleshooting the "unhappy" examples that I'll use in Chapter 9, "Troubleshooting the Project."

Finally, in this chapter I cover estimation and triage from a value-up perspective. These two essential project management practices rely closely on the metrics and queries that VSTS enables.

Understanding Variation

Fundamental to the Value-Up Paradigm is the concept of natural variation. Variation and its impact on quality were originally studied in manufacturing engineering and well taught by W. Edwards Deming:

> **Common causes and special causes.** [Dr. Walter A. Shewhart of Bell Labs] saw two kinds of variation—variation coming from common causes and variation from special causes . . . . Common causes of variation stay the same day to day, lot to lot. A special cause of variation is something special, not part of the system of common causes . . . . Dr. Shewhart also saw two kinds of mistakes . . . .
>
> **Mistake #1.** To react to an outcome as if it came from a special cause, when it actually came from common causes of variation.
>
> **Mistake #2.** To treat an outcome as if it came from common causes of variation, when actually it came from a special cause.[2]

The same distinction between common cause and special cause variation applies to software projects. Processes that exhibit common-cause variation are in control; those with special-cause variation are out of control. In software projects, some things take longer than anticipated, and some take shorter. Some software integrates perfectly; in other cases, bugs appear and need to be fixed. Some scenarios delight customers exactly as hoped; others need to be refined with usability testing and learnings from iteration to iteration. These are usually common-cause variations.

Mistake #1 is tampering with an in-control process showing this natural variation. This tampering only increases variance and quickly sends a process out of control. Perhaps more importantly, it leads to micromanagement that demoralizes the team.

Deming uses a beautifully simple experiment to illustrate the effect of tampering.[3] With a funnel, a marble, and a table, you point the funnel at a constant target and let the marble roll through many times (say 50), marking the spots where the marble falls. After each drop, you move the funnel to compensate for each error. Deming proposes three correction rules that, on their own, sound plausible. The first pass shows a constrained variance, while the others drift much more broadly.

At the same time, failing to identify and correct the special cause of a process going out of control can be disastrous (Mistake #2). This mistake leads to a vicious cycle of the process spinning further away from the desired target.

Special Causes as Issues in the Work Item Backlog

In VSTS, special causes are captured as issues.

- In MSF for CMMI Process Improvement, use the work item type called Issues and regularly work the issue log.

- In MSF for Agile Software Development, use the Issue field on other work item types.

In both processes, risks are a work item type for capturing potential issues that might create special causes.

Note also that the distinction between common and special causes is built into the staged "levels" of the CMMI, as it was in the Manufacturing Maturity Model from which it was derived. CMMI Levels 2–4 deal with reducing or eliminating special cause variation, and Level 5 aims to reduce common cause variation.

Determining variation has been too difficult for most software projects because the data have been too hard to collect. Even agile methods have suffered from this oversight. For example, the management pattern called "Yesterday's Weather," common to XP and SCRUM, specifies that "you can't sign up for more work in an iteration than you did in the previous iteration,"[4] which potentially leads to lower estimates with each iteration. This flies in the face of a primary value of iterations—that they allow for continuous learning, course correction, and improvement.

So how do you know what normal variation is? You observe and measure the running process without tampering. Fortunately, VSTS with its instrumentation of the process makes this observation easy, and an iterative approach with small batch sizes and short intervals provides frequent opportunities for observation and, when necessary, correction. You can never distinguish every common-cause variance from every special-cause one, but you can get very close by watching the reports described later in the chapter and managing the issues and risks in the project.

Using Descriptive Rather Than Prescriptive Metrics

Often there are tacit or even explicit assumptions about the "right" answers to questions of expectations. These expectations can determine how individuals are recognized or not recognized for their performance. Developers are praised for completing tasks on time. Testers are praised for running lots of tests or finding lots of bugs. Hotline specialists are praised for handling lots of calls and marking them resolved. Everyone is praised for keeping billable hours up. And so on. Using metrics to evaluate individual performance is horribly counterproductive, as Robert Austin describes:

> When a measurement system is put in place, performance measures begin to increase. At first, the true value of an organization's output may also increase. This happens in part because workers do not understand the measurement system very well early on, so their safest course is to strive to fulfill the spirit of the system architects' intentions. Real improvement may result as well, because early targets are modest and do not drive workers into taking severe shortcuts. Over time, however, as the organization demands ever greater performance measurements, by increasing explicit quotas or inducing competition between coworkers, ways of increasing measures that are not consistent with the spirit of intentions are used. Once one group of workers sees another group cutting corners, the" slower" group feels pressure to imitate. Gradually, measures fall (or, more accurately, are pushed) out of synchronization with true performance, as workers succumb to pressures to take shortcuts. Measured performance trends upward; true performance declines sharply. In this way, the measurement system becomes dysfunctional.[5]

These are *prescriptive* metrics. They can have unforeseen side effects. There is a well-identified pattern of organizational behavior adapting to fit the expectations of a prescriptive measurement program, as shown in Figure 4.2. Typically, a metrics program produces an initial boost in productivity, followed by a steep return to the status quo ante but with different numbers. For example, if bug find and fix rates are critically monitored, then bug curves start conforming to desirable expectations.

Consider some examples of prescriptive metric misuse:

- Imagine measuring programmer productivity based on lines of code written per day. An individual has a choice of calling a framework method (perhaps 5 lines with error handling) or of copying 200 lines of open-source example code. Which one gets rewarded? Which one is easier to maintain, to code-review, to security-review, to test, and to integrate? Or similarly, the individual has the chance to refactor three overlapping methods into one, reducing the size of the code base. (Now ask the same questions.)

- Imagine rewarding programmers based on number of bugs fixed. This was once the subject of a Dilbert cartoon, which ended with Wally saying, "I'm going to code me up a Winnebago."

- Imagine rewarding the team for creating tests and code to achieve 90% code coverage. Do they spend their time writing complex test setups for every error condition, or easily comment out the error handling code that tests aren't able to trigger? After all, if the tests can't invoke those conditions, how important can they be? (Not very, until a customer encounters them.)

- Imagine measuring testers based on the number of bugs found. Do they look for easy-to-find, overlapping, simple bugs or go after significant ones that require setting up complex customer data and configurations? Which approach gets rewarded? Which one yields more customer value?

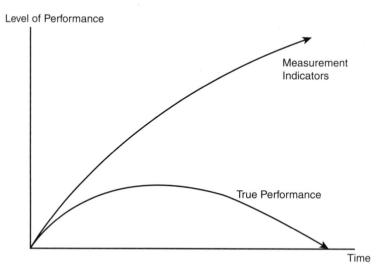

Robert D. Austin, *Measuring and Managing Performance in Organizations* (New York: Dorset House, 1996), 16

Figure 4.2   This graph summarizes the common experience with prescriptive, one-dimensional metrics programs. Performance shoots up early in accord with management aspirations, and the numbers get better and better, but the desired effect tapers off quickly.

Each example would lead to obvious dysfunction—discouraging reuse and maintainability, encouraging buggy check-ins, reducing error handling, and discouraging finding the important bugs. Other dysfunctions from metrics misuse will be less obvious but equally severe. People who don't get the best scores will be demoralized and will be faced with the choice of gaming the numbers or leaving the team.

Preventing Distortion

At the root of the distortion is the prescriptive, rather than descriptive, use of these metrics. This problem has several facets. First, the metrics are only *approximations* of the business objective, such as customer satisfaction or solution marketability. The team aims to deliver customer value, but that can't be counted easily on a daily basis. So the available metrics, such as task completion, test pass rate, or bug count, are imperfect but easily countable proxies.

A tenet of the value-up paradigm is to give credit only for completed, customer-deliverable units of work at known quality.[6] With iterations of two to four weeks and assessment at the end of the iteration, this practice allows for intervals of project monitoring at iteration boundaries. Treat all interim measurements as hypothetical until you can assess delivery of working scenarios at known qualities of service.

Second, the measurements are made *one dimension at a time*. The negative consequences of a one-dimensional view are dramatic. If you're only measuring one dimension at a time and are prescribing expected results, behavioral distortion is a natural consequence. Most experienced project managers know this. However, gathering data from multiple sources at the same time in a manner that lends itself to reasonable correlation is usually very difficult.

Third, when applied to individuals, metrics create all sorts of disincentives, as illustrated in the previous examples. Keep the observations, even descriptive ones, at the team level.

Fourth, expect common-cause variations and think in ranges. Don't reward the most prolific coder or highest-count bug finder. Expect the numbers to show variance and don't punish cases of in-control variance. Instead, reward a team based on completed customer-deliverable units of functionality and make the iteration cycle for that assessment frequent.

Many Dimensions of Project Health

Take a minute to think of the most common reports that you use in monitoring your projects. A typical list would include the following:

- Time spent on tasks (hopefully, planned and unplanned)
- Bug count (and hopefully, find and fix rates)
- Project task completion, as reported by the individual performers (hopefully measured by scenario, feature, QoS, or other customer-visible unit)
- Resource utilization, typically in accounting terms

Each is typically measured separately.

Software projects have many interacting dimensions, and any of them can be relevant. Looking at these dimensions provides an opportunity for early discovery of exceptions and bottlenecks that need course corrections. Yet having multiple dimensions helps you make sure that the measurements as a whole tell a consistent story.

In the first chapter, I describe how VSTS instruments the software process. A common project backlog is maintained in the single work item database. At the same time, version control, tests, and builds are instrumented so that many dimensions of project data can be gathered automatically and correlated in a metrics warehouse. This mechanism enables daily assessment of the project while it is running. This idea of a metrics warehouse is illustrated in Figure 4.3.

In estimation and monitoring, the backlog also helps considerably. You can do the same analyses on all work items regardless of type. Work item changes become metrics that automatically track progress for you to provide data for the next estimation, and you can assess the quality of your estimates to approve them next time. Quality can be measured against task progress using many simultaneous views.

Answering Everyday Questions

Any project manager should be able to answer the following questions, hopefully in the day-to-day course of business:

- How much work is left and when will it be done?
- How productive is the team?

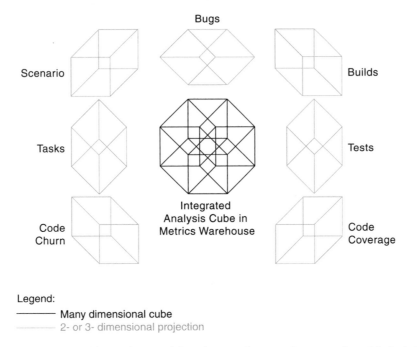

Figure 4.3 Unlike in many older project models, where project metrics are gathered in isolation, VSTS combines the measures in a metrics warehouse using a common set of analysis cubes and reports on the dimensions together.

- How much unplanned work do we have?
- What's the quality of the software we're producing?
- How effectively are we finding, fixing, and closing bugs?
- How many false task and bug resolutions do we have?
- Are we finding and triaging the right bugs?
- How fast can we go before quality suffers?

Each question is relevant at many scales—for the days within an iteration, for the iterations within a project, and for the projects within a program. The questions are also relevant for all kinds of work—scenarios and other requirements, tasks, bugs, and so on.

In the next few pages, I present graphs that help to answer these questions. Not unlike the way one develops scenarios, I show them first with "happy day" examples, and in Chapter 9, I show their use for troubleshooting unhealthy projects.

In VSTS, Reports Are Defined in the Process Template

Except where noted, all the following examples were produced with the standard reports available in MSF for Agile Software Development.

MSF for CMMI Software Improvement has the same models, usually with more detail in the data. Specifically, scenarios or other requirements start as Proposed and must be accepted by explicit decision before they become Active, so that you would see four states in the diagram rather than three.

Remaining Work

Of the several ways to track work, one of the most useful is a cumulative flow diagram (see Figure 4.4).[7] This is most useful when looking at days within an iteration or iterations within a project.

Every work item has state. In MSF for Agile Software Development, scenarios, which are a type of work item, have three states: Active (that is, in the hands of a developer and not yet coded), Resolved (that is, coded and ready for test), and Closed (that is, tested and verified).

Each data series is a colored band (reproduced here as shading), that represents the number of scenarios that have reached the corresponding state as of the given date. The total height is the total amount of work to be done in the iteration.

- If the top line increases, it means that total work is increasing. Typically, the reason is that unplanned work is adding to the total required. That may be expected if you've scheduled a buffer for unplanned work such as fixing newly discovered bugs. (See Figure 4.6.)

- If the top line decreases, it means that total work is decreasing, probably because work is being rescheduled out of the iteration.

Current status is measured by height on a particular date.

- The remaining backlog is measured by the current height of the leftmost area, *Active* in this case.

- The current completions are shown by the current height of the rightmost area, *Closed*.

- The height of the band in-between indicates the work in progress, in this case items *Resolved* but not *Closed*.

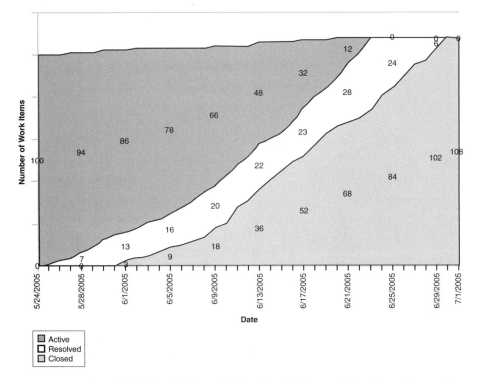

Figure 4.4 How much work is left and when will it be done? This cumulative flow diagram shows work remaining measured as the Scenario and QoS Work Items being resolved and closed in the iteration.

Watch for variation in the middle bands. An expansion can reveal a bottleneck, for example, if too many items are waiting to be tested and testing resources are inadequate. Alternatively, a significant narrowing of the band could indicate spare capacity.

Visually, it's easy to extrapolate an end completion inventory or end date for the backlog from a cumulative flow diagram like Figure 4.4. A small caution applies, however. Many projects observe an S-curve pattern, where progress is steepest in the middle.[8] The common-sense explanation for the slower starting and ending rates is that startup is always a little difficult, and unforeseen tough problems need to be handled before the end of a cycle.

Project Velocity

The rate at which the team is processing and closing work items is captured in the Project Velocity graph (see Figure 4.5). Similar to Remaining Work, this is most useful when looking at days within an iteration or iterations within a project.

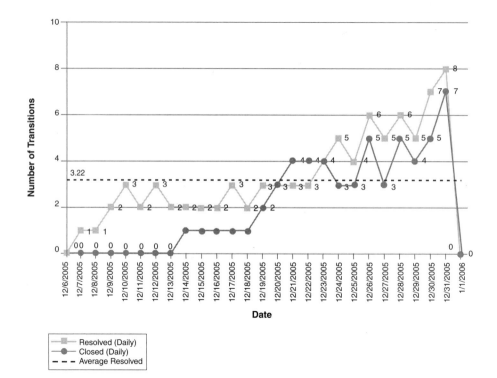

Figure 4.5   How productive is the team? Unlike the cumulative flow diagram, velocity shows the count of work items resolved and closed on each day. In this example, the range is 4 ± 2 scenarios/day after a seven-day lag.

This chart is one of the key elements for estimation. It shows how quickly the team is actually completing planned work and how much the rate varies from day to day or iteration to iteration. In examining variance, be sure to distinguish between common-cause and special-cause events. Special-cause variances include team illness, power outage, an office move, and so on. If you eliminate them, you can look at the actual normal variance to get a feel for the upper and lower bounds of your team's normal productivity. Use this data to plan a target range for the next iteration in conjunction with the quality measures discussed in the following.

Unplanned Work

Very few project teams know all the itemizable work to be done ahead of time, even within the iteration. This condition can be perfectly acceptable if you schedule a sufficient buffer for handling the load of unplanned work (for example, maintenance tasks and bugs). On the other hand, it can be a real problem if you have not scheduled the capacity and can force you to cut back on the planned work.

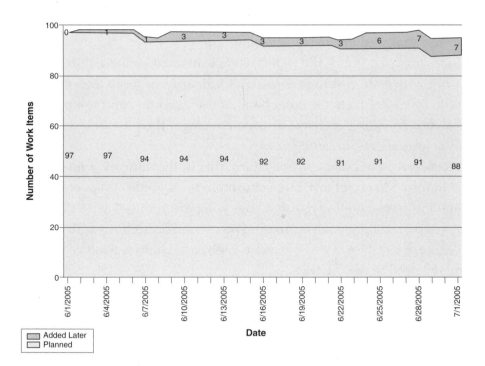

Figure 4.6   How much unplanned work do we have? This graph breaks down the total work from the Remaining Work chart into the planned and unplanned. In this example, planned work is declining slightly. This might be due to the unplanned work added later, forcing planned work items to be triaged out of the iteration or due to overestimation, or it might be occurring simply because certain items were discovered to be no longer necessary.

The top line of Figure 4.6 matches the top line of the Remaining Work graph in Figure 4.4. The total height is the total amount of work to be done in the iteration.

The areas then divide that work into the planned and unplanned segments, where "unplanned" means unscheduled as of the beginning of the iteration.

For monitoring, use this graph to determine the extent to which unplanned work is forcing you to cut into planned work. For estimation, use this to determine the amount of schedule buffer to allow for unplanned work in future iterations.

Quality Indicators

Quality needs to be seen from many dimensions. Figure 4.7 combines the test results, code coverage from testing, code churn, and bugs to help you see many perspectives at once.

The bars show you how many tests have been run and of those, how many have returned Pass, Fail, and Inconclusive results.

The first series of points is the code coverage attained by those tests (specifically, the ones run with code coverage enabled). Ordinarily, as more tests are run, more code should be covered. On the other hand, if test execution and test pass rates rise without a corresponding increase in code coverage, then it can indicate that the incremental tests are redundant.

The second series of points is code churn, that is, the number of lines added and modified in the code under test. High churn obviously indicates a large amount of change and the corresponding risk that bugs will be introduced as a side effect of the changes. In a perfectly refactored project, you can see code churn with no change in code coverage or test pass rates. Otherwise, high code churn can indicate falling coverage and the need to rewrite tests.

The third series is the active bug count. Clearly, there should be a correlation between the number of active bugs and the number of test failures. If the active bug count is rising and your tests are not showing corresponding failures, then your tests are probably not testing the same functionality in the same context that the bugs are reporting. Similarly, if active bug count is falling and test pass rates are not increasing, then you may be at risk for a rising reactivation rate.

The different series are scaled by different powers of ten to make the graph legible with one Y-axis. This is comparable to a Performance Monitor graph, which has different counters at different orders of magnitude.

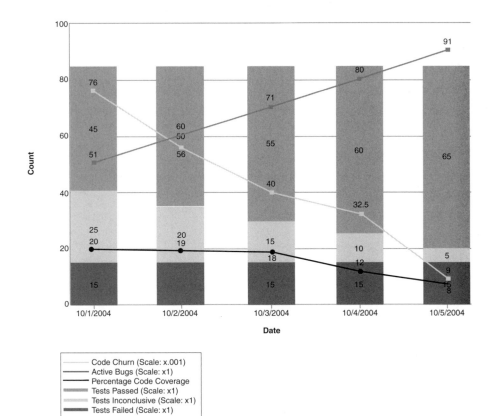

Figure 4.7   What's the quality of the software? Ideally, test rates, bugs, and code churn would all produce the same picture, as they do in this example. Test passes and code coverage rise, while bugs and code churn fall. On the other hand, when you find a discrepancy in these relationships, you need to drill down into the appropriate build and data series.

Bug Rates

Bugs are, of course, a key part of the team workload and a key risk area. To assess bugs, you need to look at three trends (see Figure 4.8):

- What is the total active bug count (sometimes called "bug debt")?
- How quickly are we finding new bugs?
- How quickly are we fixing bugs already found?

Bug rates are best interpreted with your knowledge of all the current project activities and the other metrics on the Quality Indicators graph (see Figure 4.7). For example, a high find rate can be a sign of sloppy code (a bad thing), newly integrated code (an expected thing), effective testing (a good thing), or exceptional events, such as a bug bash (an infrequent event, where large numbers of people try ad hoc testing for a day). On the other hand, a low find rate can indicate a high-quality solution or ineffective testing. Use code coverage, code churn, and test rates to help you assess the meaning.

Similarly, a high resolve rate is usually a good thing, but check Work Progress to make sure that the resolved bugs are getting promptly closed and check Reactivations to make sure that the resolutions are not premature.

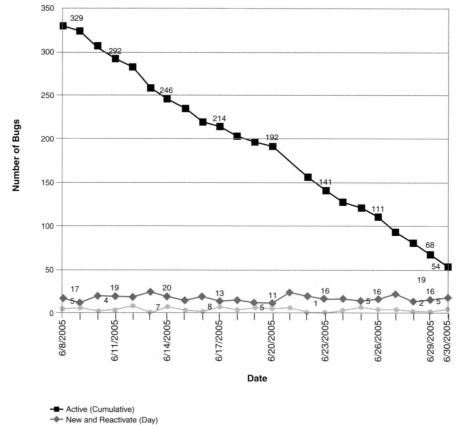

Figure 4.8   How effectively are we finding, fixing, and closing bugs? When the fix rate exceeds the find rate, the active bug count falls.

Reactivations

Reactivations occur when work items have been resolved or closed prematurely. They are a huge warning sign of project dysfunction.

People sometimes record bugs as resolved when the underlying problem has not been fixed. (Similarly, they can record scenarios resolved before they are working or development tasks closed when the work hasn't been finished.) Every time this happens, it introduces significant waste into the process. Someone has to test and reopen the work item, the developer needs to scrap and rework the original code, and then the code needs to be retested. At a minimum, the reactivation *doubles* the number of handoffs and usually more than doubles the total effort required to complete the corresponding work.

Watching the reactivation rate (also sometimes called the Fault Feedback Ratio) is important.[9] A small amount of noise (for example, less than 5% of the work items resolved at any time) might be acceptable, but a high or rising rate of reactivation should warn the project manger to diagnose the root cause and fix it.

The top line of Figure 4.9 shows the number of total work items of the selected types (for example, bugs) resolved in the build.

The height of the top area is the number of reactivations, that is, work items previously resolved or closed that are now active again.

The height of the lower area is the difference, that is, the number of work items resolved less the reactivations.

Bugs by Priority

Bugs happen, and finding them is a good thing. Often, however, the easy-to-find bugs aren't the ones that will annoy customers the most. If the high-priority bugs are not being found and a disproportionate number of low-priority bugs are, then you need to redirect the testing efforts to look for the bugs that matter.

In triage, it is easy to over-prioritize bugs beyond your capacity to resolve them or under-prioritize them to the point where customers will be highly dissatisfied.

Figure 4.10 assesses the effectiveness of two things: bug hunting and triage, that is, the process of prioritizing the bugs to fix, which is described later in this chapter.

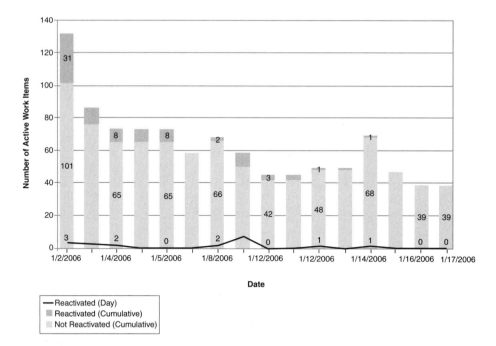

Figure 4.9   How many false task and bug resolutions do we have? These false resolutions show up as reactivations—bugs or tasks that were made active again because the original work wasn't completed. The line shows the count of reactivated items each day. The bars show the cumulative active bugs as of that day, broken into the reactivations (top segment) and non-reactivations (bottom segment).

In Figure 4.10, the three series of bars represent similar data to the Bug Rates graph (Figure 4.8). The series are as follows:

- Total active bugs at the time of the build
- Number found in build
- Number resolved in build

Each series is further broken into priority so that each bar stacks from highest to lowest priority, with lowest on top.

If you have too many high-priority bugs active, you need to be sure that you have capacity to address them. On the other hand, a significant lack of low-priority bugs can also lead to customer dissatisfaction. (See the discussion of the Broken Windows theory in the "Defining 'Good Enough'" section of Chapter 7.)

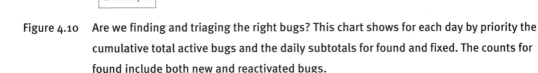

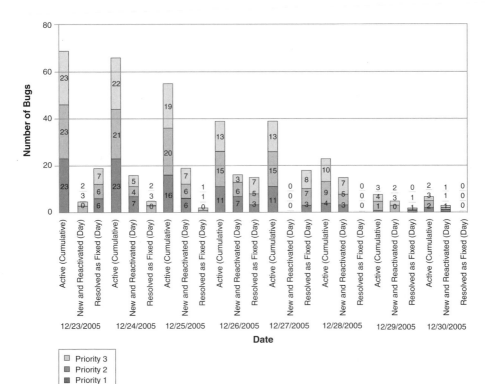

Figure 4.10   Are we finding and triaging the right bugs? This chart shows for each day by priority the cumulative total active bugs and the daily subtotals for found and fixed. The counts for found include both new and reactivated bugs.

Actual Quality Versus Planned Velocity

As much as teams believe the saying, "Haste makes waste," there is usually a business incentive to go faster. A project manager's goal should be to find the maximum rate of progress that does not make quality suffer. Figure 4.11 presents the relationship for each iteration of estimated size to overall quality.

The X-axis is the number of scenarios actually closed (completed) in the iteration.

The Y-axis is the total number of bugs found divided by the scenarios closed (in other words, the average number of bugs per scenario).

Each bubble is labeled according to its iteration.

On screen, stoplight colors go from green for the lowest bugs per iteration to red for the highest. Here you see them reproduced as lightest to darkest for green-amber-red.

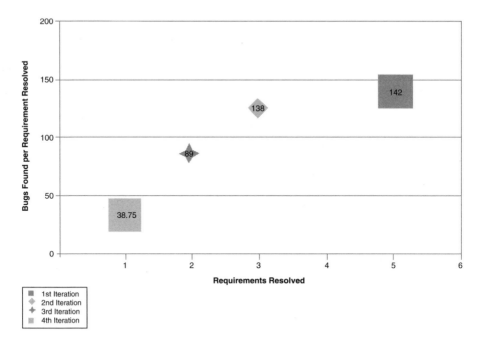

Figure 4.11 How fast can we go before quality suffers?

If haste is in fact making waste, position of the iterations to the right (larger iterations) will be higher, indicating more bugs per requirement, and smaller (left) ones will be lower, indicating fewer bugs. If you are working at a comfortable pace and have not seen quality drop with planned iteration size, then all iterations will be at roughly the same height on the Y-axis.

Estimating an Iteration

This section describes a simple process for estimating projects at the level of person days using the data from the project health reports shown previously. With Visual Studio Team System, all of the backlog is one database, and all the historical metrics are in one data warehouse, so it's easy to get the numbers that you need here.

Estimating the work for an iteration is best done in multiple passes.

Top-Down

Before the Renaissance and the advent of celestial navigation, explorers (such as Christopher Columbus) relied on a technique called *dead reckoning*. While imperfect, dead reckoning did enable the discovery of the New World and the drawing of early maps, which in turn made further exploration and settlement possible. Here's a standard definition of dead reckoning:

> Dead Reckoning is the process of estimating your position by advancing a known position using course, speed, time and distance to be traveled. In other words figuring out where you will be at a certain time if you hold the speed, time and course you plan to travel.[10]

Top-down estimation is like dead reckoning:

1. Calculate the number of team-days available in the iteration. This is your gross capacity.

2. Looking at the actual data in the Unplanned Work chart, make a rough estimate of the buffer you will need for unplanned work. Subtract this from the gross capacity to determine your net capacity for planned work.

3. Looking at the Project Velocity chart, determine the number of scenarios and QoS per day that your team can resolve and close. This is your gross velocity. Consult the Quality Indicators and Actual Quality versus Planned Velocity charts to look for possible negative side effects of your current pace. If you see them, adjust gross velocity downward to a sustainable net velocity.

4. Multiply net capacity for planned work with sustainable net velocity to determine the number of scenarios and QoS that you can implement in the iteration. On your ranked list of scenarios and QoS, count down from the top until you have reached that number. Draw a cut line there. Everything above the cut line is your candidate list.

Dead reckoning might just be good enough, especially if you have low variance among your scenarios and QoS on the Project Velocity chart (see Figure 4.5). If you have high variance, then you can attack the problem both by breaking down scenarios and QoS into more consistently sized work items and by estimating bottom-up.

Bottom-Up

After you have a candidate list of scenarios and QoS, you can perform bottom-up estimation as well. (You could do it earlier, but this is not recommended. You'd spend a lot of time estimating work that won't be done yet, and you might never be done according to the current understanding of the requirements.)

1. If necessary, the business analyst and architect should refine the scenarios, QoS, storyboards (refer to Chapter 3, "Requirements"), and solution architecture (see Chapter 5, "Architectural Design"). These need to be articulated to the point where they communicate sufficiently to all team members the details needed to estimate work for the next iteration.

2. Next, individual team members decompose these into tasks, typically to a granularity of one to three days.

3. The team triages bugs to identify work needed to fix bug backlogs for the iteration.

4. Working with the teams, the project manager rolls up the total volume of these task estimates to see whether they fit the iteration capacity for planned work.

To the extent that the estimates and capacity don't match, you should lather, rinse, and repeat. If you do bottom-up estimation, don't forget the feedback loop of the retrospective to assess how actuals compare to estimates.

Refinements

Obviously, there are some refinements to this method you want to make.

Variance in Size

The way I described the technique previously, I assumed that all scenarios and QoS are roughly the same size, with little variance. Depending on your project and your styles of solution definition and architecture, this might be true. If the variance in the Project Velocity graph is small, then it is a good assumption.

Alternatively, it might be more useful to categorize your scenarios and QoS into "T-shirt size" groupings, that is, Large, Medium, and Small. You can plan, track, and graph these separately.

Another alternative is to use Rough Order of Magnitude (ROM) estimates as part of top-down costing. Both alternatives let you draw the cut line for the iteration based on more careful initial estimation. Again, depending on your project, it may or may not be worth the extra effort because you will calibrate the top-down estimates based on bottom-up costing.

Changes in Team

I also simplified the previous technique to assume static team size and composition. Clearly, that's often false. When your team grows or shrinks, capacity changes. As skills and domain expertise improve with experience, your capacity grows, too.

Differences in Iterations

Not all QoS are alike. For example, at Microsoft, it is typical to single out blocks of time, usually a month or more, for a "Security Push." This is a period when all architecture, designs, and code are reviewed for security considerations. This enables experts to assist the team in an intensive focus on a particular QoS that requires specialized analysis and addresses specialized risks. Usability, Manageability, and Performance are other QoS that might, again depending on your project, lend themselves to specific emphasis in particular iterations when specialists are available.

Similarly, some scenarios may be more important than others for solution success, or they may require integration of several components and therefore be possible only after a number of prerequisites have been finished.

It is also common to see an S-curve pattern in the Remaining Work chart, in which startup and finish iterations (or tasks within an iteration) take longer than the middle ones. If you anticipate this pattern, you can plan capacity around it.

Working on Multiple Projects

Note that in the techniques described previously, estimation and monitoring do not require explicit time or effort tracking. Because work items track changes automatically, and the changes are all time-stamped for auditability, the data for actual elapsed time is available for free. This makes it very easy to do the estimates based on days planned and track on days actually spent.

The limitation is that calendar time estimation assumes that the team members are *working on only one project at a time.* If that's not true, or in other words, if some of you are working on multiple projects, then you do need to introduce effort tracking. Just as importantly, you also need to significantly alter your capacity estimates to accommodate the overhead cost of switching contexts.

Estimation Quality

Twenty years ago, Tom DeMarco introduced the idea of an Estimating Quality Factor (EQF) as a way of tracking and tuning the accuracy of estimation.[11] The idea is simple and powerful. Keep track of your estimates, compare them to your actual completion time, compute the difference, and analyze the reasons for the difference. Use this information to tune your next estimation. Over multiple project cycles, you can assess whether you're getting better and how much variance there is in your estimation accuracy.

Originally proposed for a project as a whole, EQF is

$$1 \ / \ \Sigma t \ | \ (\text{estimated completion} - \text{actual completion}) \ |$$

You can also apply this idea to iterations. On a time-boxed iteration or project, you can use this technique against the backlog size. On a feature-boxed one, you can use it against time.

Tracking Historical Estimates

In VSTS, you can track historical estimates. Work item data, as covered before, is round-tripped between the Team Foundation Server and Microsoft Project or Microsoft Excel. When you use Project to edit work items, Estimated Work, Remaining Work, and Baseline Work fields are stored in the work items and pushed into the metrics warehouse for reporting.

Accordingly, if you use Project to create a project baseline for your work items, that data is available to you for reporting from the metrics warehouse.

EQF can also be a way of surfacing project concerns among the team members. Survey the team members during the retrospectives to ask when they think the project will be "done" or when a certain milestone, such as live deployment, will be reached. Then ask follow-up questions to drill into the perceptions. If there are changes, ask, "What did you see or hear that made you change your estimate?" This approach can yield great information about risks, unplanned work, skills gaps, or other factors that need to be addressed.[12]

Alternatively, if the team is not worried about dates and functionality, that is great information. Frequently, teams get optimistic in the middle of a project as they become more proficient at closing a level of tasks and have not yet encountered hard integration issues. This optimism will produce an S-curve in the Remaining Work chart and a hump in the EQF tracking.

Of course, your mileage may vary. Unless you are running a project very much like one you've run before, with a very stable team, it is reasonable to expect variation in the estimation quality. Excluding special causes (half the team was diverted to an emergency project, the company was reorganized, and so on) and examining the residual variance will give you good guidelines for the factors to apply in the next round of estimates.

Retrospectives

One of the great benefits of iterative development is that you can learn and correct course frequently. *Retrospectives* are meetings in which you distill the learning from the iteration. The most important prerequisite for a retrospective is a blame-free environment. A great mindset to bring is summarized by Norman L. Kerth in his book and web site:

> Regardless of what we discover, we understand and truly believe that everyone did the best job they could, given what they knew at the time, their skills and abilities, the resources available, and the situation at hand.[13]

During the retrospective, you should strive to identify the common- and special-cause variances. Look at the charts and identify unusual dips in Velocity, bloats in Remaining Work, or inconsistencies in the Quality Indicators. Look for root causes of problems, reusable lessons learned, and corrective actions. In other words, find where the real bottlenecks are. For example, testing may appear slow, but on further investigation you find frequent unusable builds. Looking into builds, you discover that services on which you depend or incoming components that you integrate were not performing adequately. So the appropriate corrective action might be to provide better component acceptance tests that must pass before those external services or external components are accepted into your lab and to have the providing teams run these as build verification tests (BVTs).

The output of the retrospective should inform the next iteration plan. The scenarios, QoS, tasks, and their prioritization may all change based on the discoveries you make in the retrospective.

Triage

In addition to planning, monitoring, and estimating, a good project manager needs to prioritize and schedule the work to fit available resources and time. This process is called *triage*. The term was introduced from medical practice into the software world. Originally, triage only described the handling of bugs, but now it is equally applicable for all work items.

Triage is successful only if the workload is cut to the point where it fits the available hours, skills, and schedule of the team. In ordinary, daily triage sessions, the resources and time dimensions are fixed, so it is the prioritization of the work that changes the functionality and quality levels of the planned solution.

A Triage Exercise

To illustrate the point of triage, here is a simple exercise: I'll use bugs only, not all work item types, and I'll assume that there is no other work on the team.

Suppose you are approaching the end of an iteration. Along the way, you have an iteration goal to reduce your bug backlog to zero. There are currently 10 P1 ("must fix") bugs outstanding, as shown in Figure 4.12. Your team of five developers can average two verified bug fixes per person per day. Your team of three testers is averaging four bugs found per tester per day. Every four days, their find rate decreases by one bug per tester.

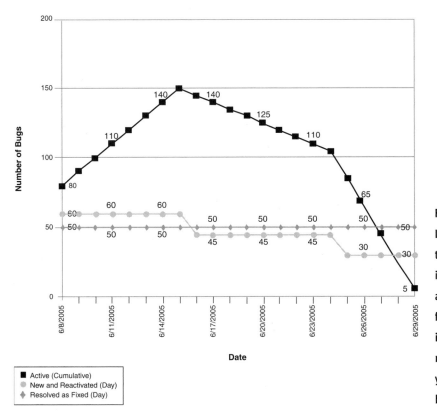

Active Bugs [Results]   ▾ ✕

Query Results: 10 results found (1 currently selected). The query has been modified. You must re-run the query to see the changes.

✐	ID	Work Item Type	Assigned To	Priority △	Title	State
	10535	Bug	Juan Perez	1	Credit Card payment form doesn't use HTTPS/SSL	Active
	10537	Bug	Kim Tapia St Amant	1	Application hangs during splash screen	Active
	10538	Bug	Kim Tapia St Amant	1	Not all application users required to register upon downloading application	Active
	10539	Bug	Juan Perez	1	Possible security vulnerability with payment backend	Active
	10533	Bug	Kim Tapia St Amant	2	Password text box doesn't hide text	Active
	10542	Bug	Sam Guckenheimer	2	Registration Web Service causing incorrect Log	Active
	10534	Bug	Juan Perez	3	Delay while submitting exception report via web service	Active
	10536	Bug	Kim Tapia St Amant	3	FAQ #4 is incorrect	Active
	10540	Bug	Sam Guckenheimer	3	Sample UI should be isolated into a different assembly	Active
	10541	Bug	Juan Perez	3	Documentation states incorrect system requirements	Active

Figure 4.12   In VSTS, you can query work items from the backlog, here the Active Bugs, for daily triage meetings.

When will you hit zero backlog at those rates? (Don't look ahead—try to solve this by yourself first. Even with such simple numbers, it's not easy.) After you have solved this, check your answer against Figure 4.13.

Figure 4.13

In this idealized chart, the capacity of the team is static at 50 per day, and the find rate drops from 60 to 30 in even increments, but it is still not obvious at first when you'll eliminate the backlog.

Legend:
- ■ Active (Cumulative)
- ● New and Reactivated (Day)
- ◆ Resolved as Fixed (Day)

In practice, of course, the rates are not constant and may not be reliable. There are several points to note here:

- As long as the find rate is above the fix rate, backlog will increase.
- When the find rate is slightly below the fix rate, convergence will be slow.
- It's easy to cheat—artificially lowering the find rate, for example, by deprioritizing bugs, can make the numbers look much better than they should look.
- These are only averages. (Refer to the earlier Bug Rates chart, Figure 4.8, for a more realistic example of variance.)

The point remains: Every day you should assess workload, progress, impediments, and probability of success.

A History of Triage

Triage was a medical term long before it was adapted to software engineering:

triage – 1727, from Fr. *triage* "a picking out, sorting," from O.Fr. *trier* "to pick, cull" (see *try*), hence "action of assorting according to quality." There seems to be some influence from or convergence with L. *tria* "three" (e.g., *triage* for "coffee beans of the third or lowest quality"). In World War I, adopted for the sorting of wounded soldiers into three groups according to the severity of their injuries.[14]

Casualties in World War I far exceeded the capacity of the available medical staff at the front, so the wounded were sorted into three groups: those who would die regardless of intervention, those who would heal without intervention, and those who would recover only if they received prompt care. The term is still used in medicine—when you walk into a hospital emergency room, the first person you see is the triage nurse.

Similarly, the first person to handle a bug is the project manager or committee performing triage. Analogous to the medical practice, triage selects work items and bugs that require prompt attention. Chapter 8, "Reporting Bugs," describes how triage heuristics from the medical world can help classify bugs.

What Makes Triage Effective: The Red Line

Averages, like in the previous exercise, can be deceiving. Averages don't tell you who has the heavy backlog, where the bugs are being found, and who's fixing them and how quickly they are doing it.

It is typical to see big differences in all these areas. (See the Quality Indicators chart, Figure 4.7, to relate the different measures.) Take the exercise a little further. Imagine that there are five components, with one developer each, and that 50% of the backlog and found bugs are in Component A. You'd see a breakdown on day four like Figure 4.14.

The Red Line: (Fix Rate – Find Rate) × Days Available < Backlog

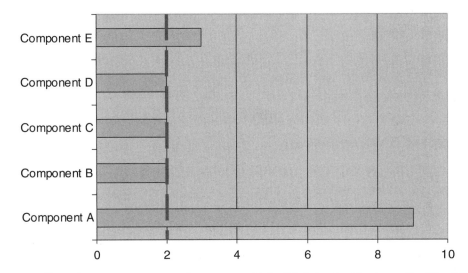

Work Item Distribution Among Components

Figure 4.14   Bug rates among components can vary widely. It is important to draw a "red line" that tracks capacity and to load balance or reprioritize the excess beyond available capacity.

The red line on your car's tachometer shows you the speed at which your engine is likely to fail. Similarly, the red line on your work item distribution chart is the level at which your project or one of its components will overheat. It is the level beyond which you are at risk of not hitting the planned iteration exit with current find and fix rates.

Bear in mind that sometimes you will let your queues climb past the red line, just as a racecar driver lets the tachometer needle cross the red line for short periods. For example, to focus on increasing bug find rates, you might hold a "bug bash" where everyone on the team tests for a period and triage is deferred. Part of your plan just needs to be bringing the queues and red line back in balance. It's important to manage your red line regularly and consciously.

What Happens During Triage

Triage is your opportunity to manage the red line in real time. During triage, you can use the Bugs by Priority report in VSTS to understand the current red line distribution and the query All Active Work Items to manage priorities and ownership.

Depending on your process, your triage group may be a committee, with a representative of each discipline, or it may be a select group. It is important that the owner be clearly designated (usually the project manager or test manager) and have ultimate responsibility for the resulting priority list.

The mechanics are very easy. VSTS lets you use a standard query (like the previous one) or a bound Excel worksheet to walk through the queues and edit priority, owner, and other appropriate fields.

Escalating and Resolving Issues

It is important not only to plan to capacity but also to remove any blocking issues that prevent team members from completing their tasks. In MSF for Agile Software Development, any work item can be escalated using the Issue field, and you can see these with a simple query called Issues. If it is not done elsewhere, the triage process should pick up all these issues and address them to unblock the corresponding work.

Iterations and Triage

One of the primary benefits of iterative development (described in Chapter 2, "Value-Up Processes") is that you can plan for now and later, rather than now and never. Use the iterations to manage the quantity of bugs in the current queues and keep them off the red line.

Many project managers, especially in agile projects, believe that you should not allow any bugs to be carried forward. According to this view, any backlog of bugs greater than zero is bad, and those bugs should be fixed before any new feature work proceeds. This is certainly true of bugs caused by simple coding errors. These bugs are cheapest to catch in the development process with unit tests (see Chapter 6,

"Development"). Unless you have specific reasons otherwise, the unit tests should pass before you check in code.

Unfortunately, however, not all bugs are caused by coding errors, and not all bugs are caught before check-in. Many bugs appear for subtler reasons of scenarios, QoS, architecture, configurations, data, and so on, and will not be caught by unit tests. In these cases, there may be good reasons to postpone bug fixes to the next iteration, and there will be nothing wrong with revisiting the priorities when you plan that iteration.

Triage Goals Early, Middle, and Late in the Iteration

As you enter an iteration, you need to be clear about how much time will be spent on the bug backlog and how much on other work items, and you need to re-triage bug priorities accordingly. As scenarios become available for testing, you may focus on finding bugs for a period, intentionally letting queues lengthen. Watch the find rates. As they stabilize and fall, even after you vary testing techniques (see Chapter 7), you need to be very clear about your fix capacity and triage the queues accordingly.

Triage Daily, Unless You Have a Good Reason Otherwise

Long lists are hard to manage. The easiest way to keep the incoming lists for triage short is to triage daily, especially during the middle and end of an iteration.

Satisfying the Auditor

It is now common for software teams to face regulatory requirements. For example, all financial systems of U.S. public companies are subject to audit under the Sarbanes-Oxley Act of 2002. Fortunately, VSTS automatically keeps an audit trail of all changes to work items and automatically links work items to all changes in source code and tests.

If you are subject to audit, you should enforce the association of work items to check-ins in order to make sure that the changes to source code are associated with work item changes. For the developer, this means nothing more than ticking a box at check-in. (See Figure 6.17.) With the policy on, the developer can't forget without being warned and generating email notification to an appropriate team member.

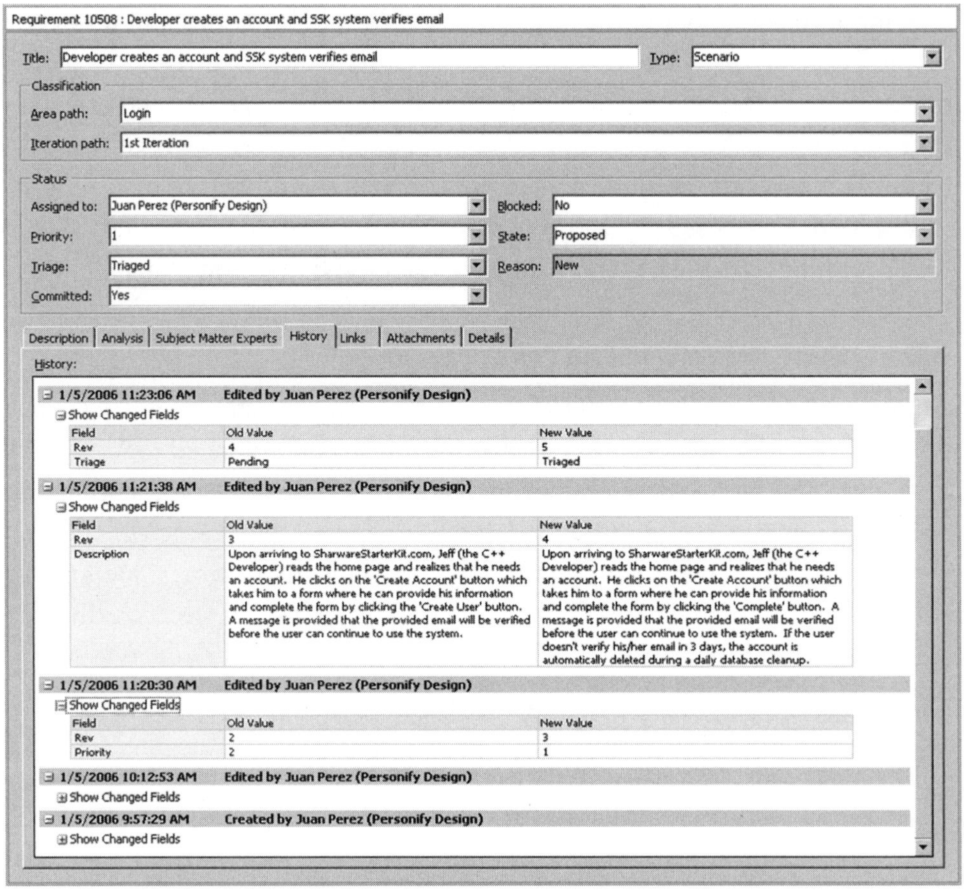

Figure 4.15   Every work item, in this case a scenario, accumulates its full change history every time it is edited and saved. This gives you a complete audit trail.

Setting Check-In Policy to Require Associating Work Items to Check-Ins

In VSTS, MSF for CMMI Process Improvement defines Auditor as one of the Product Management roles. The guidance for the Auditor focuses on collecting evidence for conformance to CMMI Level 3 process. This is the same evidence needed for regulatory audits, and it is largely automated by VSTS.

Be sure that you have configured check-in policies to include the requirement of associating work items on check-in. See the MSDN topic:

Development Tools and Technologies

   Visual Studio Team System

      Team Foundation

         Team Foundation Walkthroughs

            Team Foundation Server Administration Walkthroughs

               Walkthrough: Customizing Check-in Policies and Notes

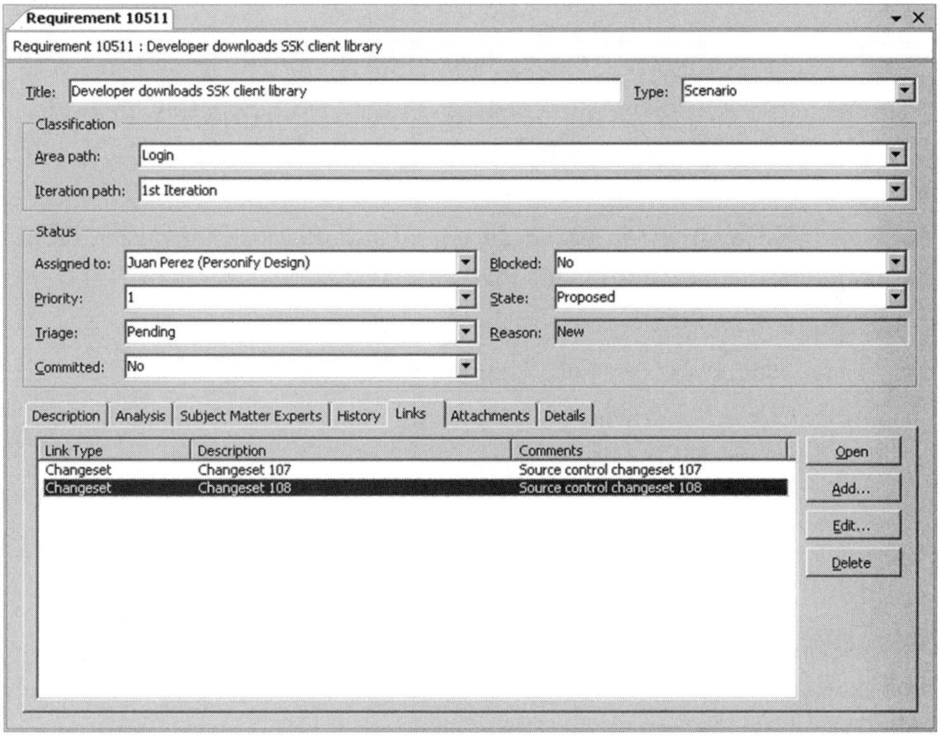

Figure 4.16   Change sets, containing the code changes for each check-in, are automatically linked to the scenario or other work item so that you can see both what changed and why. These changes and associations flow through to the build reports, discussed in Chapter 6.

Summary

In this chapter, I covered the basics of project management with VSTS. First, I covered three value-up concepts that inform the activities: understanding variance, using descriptive rather than prescriptive metrics, and keeping multiple dimensions of project health in mind. Then I reviewed examples of several of the reports in VSTS and how to use them. Finally, we looked at applying these reports and work item queries to estimation and triage. I did not yet explore troubleshooting with these reports, as that will be covered in Chapter 9.

In the next chapter, I will look at the architecture and design of a solution.

Endnotes

1. L. Koskela and G. Howell, (2002), "The Underlying Theory of Project Management is Obsolete." Proceedings of the PMI Research Conference, 2002, 293–302, available at http://www.leanconstruction.org/pdf/ObsoleteTheory.pdf.

2. W. Edwards Deming, *The New Economics: For Industry, Government, Education, Second Edition* (Cambridge: MIT Press, 1994), 174.

3. Ibid., 190 ff.

4. http://www.c2.com/cgi/wiki?YesterdaysWeather

5. Robert D. Austin, *Measuring and Managing Performance in Organizations* (New York: Dorset House, 1996), 15.

6. For example, Beck (2000), op. cit., 72–3.

7. Cumulative flow diagrams were introduced to software in Anderson 2004, op.cit., 61.

8. Ibid., 90 ff.

9. For example: Johanna Rothman, "What's Your Fault Feedback Ratio?," *ComputerWorld* (November 04, 2002), available from http://www.computerworld.com/developmenttopics/development/story/0,10801,75654,00.html.

10. http://www.auxetrain.org/Nav1.html

11. Tom DeMarco, 12. http://www.jrothman.com/pragmaticmanager.html

12. http://www.jrothman.com/pragmaticmanager.html

13. http://www.retrospectives.com/pages/retroPrimeDirective.html

14. http://www.etymonline.com/

5

Architectural Design

 **Architect**

"Every system has an architecture, encompassing the key abstractions and mechanisms that define that system's structure and behavior as seen from the perspective of different stakeholders, each with a different set of concerns. In every case—from idioms to mechanisms to architectures—these patterns are either intentional or accidental, but insofar as they are visible, such patterns reflect the style and inner beauty of each system."[1]

—Grady Booch, *Handbook of Software Architecture*

Figure 5.1

Every system has an architecture. The honeycomb of a beehive is a great example of an architecture whose conceptual integrity allows and applies patterns, continual evolution, flexibility, scaling, and reuse.

Architectural design transforms the requirements, as captured in scenarios and qualities of service into designs that can be built to satisfy and delight users. The analogy between the work of software architects and civil architects has been made countless times to illustrate the point. Civil architecture, however, consists not only of the work of professional architects but also of thousands of years of craftsmanship in the application of patterns that work.[2]

A good architecture reflects a conceptual integrity that makes the architecture easy to understand, use, maintain, and evolve. This conceptual integrity is typically achieved through the choice, application, and specialization of the right patterns to the broad qualities of service and scenarios defined for a system.

Although there is broad agreement on the characteristics of a good architecture, there is controversy about the process of architectural design. The extremes range from the concept that architectural design should be practiced independently of implementation[3] to the idea that architecture should emerge from implementation.[4] Accordingly, architecture is sometimes an explicit process, whereas at other times it is a set of activities combined closely with development.

A Value-Up View of Architecture

A value-up approach asserts that architecture needs to be explicit but can emerge from the implementation, and it absolutely needs to be current with the implementation. VSTS follows this view. In VSTS, architectural designs are views on source code at whatever state of implementation the code happens to be. Architecturally significant updates to diagrams, source code, or configuration simultaneously update the architecture and the implementation.

VSTS supports the architectural design process by enabling an architect to design the architecture of software to be built, and it exposes to the architect aspects of the architecture of software that already exists. VSTS focuses on the deployment structure, which is expressed in terms of configurations of applications, which are defined as discrete packages of resource that are deployed together.

Service-Oriented Architecture

Conceptual integrity is a key part of good architecture. Service-oriented architecture (SOA), the predominant modern conceptual framework for software and systems architecture, provides that integrity. The rise of SOA has been driven by two over-riding business concerns—the need for business agility and the desire for maximum reuse of existing assets. Together, these two collapse into the twenty-first century edict: "Do more with less."

Business agility is all about "doing more" faster. IT systems have historically suf-fered from much less flexibility than the business demanded. As the pace of business change has increased in the last couple decades (ironically, often spurred by IT), the gap between the evolving business needs and IT's ability to adapt to them has widened. The promise of SOA is that IT capabilities can be exposed as services that are closely aligned with business services, flexibly recombined, and changed as needed in small increments.

A business process can be seen as a thread of control flowing through the capa-bilities of the organization. Exposing the organization's capabilities as discrete gran-ular services allows flexibility in the way they can be combined into business processes and increases the ease with which the processes can be changed and the capabilities or their implementation can be altered.

This style contrasts with the historic approach of monolithic systems that attempted to circumscribe large problems, anticipate all requirements in advance, and address them in very large projects. In many ways, SOA is an architectural par-adigm aligned with continuous improvement.

Maximum reuse is about doing it "with less." First, almost every enterprise has large sunk costs in legacy systems. These systems were not often built for main-tainability or flexibility, and the costs and business risks of replacement are often high. SOA enables these legacy systems to be wrapped with facades that expose them as web services so that they can be recomposed flexibly into larger systems. Additionally, SOA enables interoperability among diverse operating systems and technical platforms. The WS-* standards make it possible to orchestrate distributed applications across Windows, Linux, and mainframes, spanning .NET and J2EE implementations.[5]

Another business trend favoring SOA is the need for geographic and organiza-tional flexibility in locating and composing systems. Increasingly, what appears to the users as one system may be developed and managed as many separate services, and over time, those services may be migrated or replaced as business needs war-rant. Consider the typical web experience of looking up directions and a map. There are only a handful of GIS mapping services, whose interfaces are exposed through web services to hundreds of thousands of web sites that provide the appearance of customized maps. The visitors to those sites couldn't care less whose engine is drawing the map and directions—the web site owner makes a simple business choice and can change the choice as business conditions evolve.

The same flexibility applies to proprietary services. By using SOA and making services self-contained and granular, organizations can retain significant choices in how to locate, outsource, or contract for the development and management of the business capabilities on which they rely. Similarly, choices about maintenance, upgrade, and tuning can be made at the level of the services, affording a flexibility not found with more monolithic systems.

Web Services and SOA

In theory, SOA does not require web services, but in practice, the technology for implementing web services as been almost completely aligned with the WS-* standards, if only for the reason that this enables technical interoperability. When developing with Visual Studio, the Microsoft .NET Framework makes it easy to implement the web services. Of course, there is more to interoperability than just the standards.

Contract-First Design

The key to interoperability is that services describe themselves in terms of interface contracts. For web services, these interfaces are expressed in the Web Services Description Language (WSDL).[6]

A valuable SOA practice is *contract-first* design, or in other words, specifying the message formats and the WSDL among participating services before being concerned with implementation details. Contract-first design can ensure loose coupling and prevent decisions about how to implement services from creeping into the overall distributed system design.

Practices for contract-first design are still evolving. WSDL and XSD do not yet describe message sequence or pre- and post-conditions as examples. Fuller contracts need to specify the messages that the services publish and consume, the sequence of handling, and the constraints in order to isolate the public contracts from the private details of the implementation. One approach to improving contracts can be found in the Windows Communication Foundation Services (WCF), previously known as project "Indigo," part of Windows Vista.[7]

Constraints with Degrees of Freedom

A value-up approach requires an explicit architecture, but it may emerge from the implementation. This creates an apparent contradiction. On one hand, you must consider all the QoS and deployment constraints in the context of the scenarios. On the other hand, value-up considers running tested code to be the best measure of system progress, and the act of developing *is* the act of designing, albeit at a very detailed level. It is exactly the act of development, in small fixed-scope iterations, that enables design to emerge from the implementation.

The answer lies in the creation of a baseline architecture early in the project lifecycle.

Baseline Architecture

A baseline architecture is a executable skeletal application designed expressly to mitigate technical risk and provide a solid, stable basis for project iterations. Some agile developers refer to this as "iteration zero" when platform infrastructure components are installed and a "thin vertical slice" of the system is built, exercising a very simple scenario from end to end (for example, from the user interface to the database). The goal here is to flush out and validate the project's architecturally significant mechanisms unambiguously. Removing ambiguity mandates that the baseline architecture be executable.

As an example, consider a popular application style—a web application using a relational database. A number of fundamental questions need to be answered early to determine the best fit based on good citizenship and all the perspectives of the advocacy groups described in Chapter 2, "Value-Up Processes." Should this application be bought or built? Should the application be a smart client or a web application? If it is a web application, what processing should be done on the client using technologies such as Asynchronous Java Script and XML (AJAX), and what processing should be done on the server? As for persistence (assuming a relational database), what are the organizational standards for the choice of a relational database? Should a new database instance be created, or should tables be added to an existing database instance? What is the source of reference data for this application? How does this application integrate with other applications in the enterprise? How many business transactions per day must this system be able to execute to support the project's economic justification? Will this application be deployed, operated, and maintained in a corporate datacenter? If so, what are the technical constraints of the datacenter? As these fundamental kinds of decisions are made early in the project lifecycle, they result in constraints that guide and stabilize the project under development.

There is a delicate balance to strike. As you work through these technical issues, try to defer decisions to the "last responsible moment." The last responsible moment, however, will vary depending on project complexity. Pull together all the advocacy groups from Chapter 2 early in the project lifecycle to agree on the high-level decision policy. Often, you will let detailed design issues, such as interfaces and method factoring, evolve from implementation. In more complex projects with many dependencies, you may need to pin down interfaces and mitigate architecturally significant risks early to avoid later rework. Then, within the agreed policy, build an executable baseline that implements these high-level design decisions so that they can become architectural constraints on the project.

Defining this baseline early benefits developers by providing stable platform infrastructure components and protocols for application development. Defining these constraints early also enables predictability and planning for other stakeholders. For example, Release/Operations can plan for the deployment and management of the application in production and can ensure datacenter readiness. Product management in the line-of-business can create marketing plans designed to attract levels of usage at transaction rates the system can support. Business analysts can design business process monitoring reports to analyze the application's return on investment, which will feed planning for the next version. Enterprise architects can design and implement reusable services across the enterprise, migrating toward an enterprise-level SOA. Defining these constraints early enables a stable, predictable basis for multiple stakeholders.

Validate Architectural Decisions

This process is not just top-down. You need to validate these constraints bottom-up by building an executable skeletal architecture. VSTS enables you to model your "as-is" datacenter using the Logical Datacenter Designer (shown in Figure 5.5) and your "to-be" application using the System and Application Designers (shown in Figures 5.3 and 5.4) and then to run a validation report to identify conflicts between the two. Then your System and Application models can be used to generate skeletal code that can become part of your executable baseline.

Doing so provides many benefits. The running code is unambiguous—should areas of design seem unclear, the source code can be consulted. The running code can be performance tested to validate initial transaction rates of the system. System settings can be verified against datacenter policies to identify potential conflicts. Also, building an executable system forces lower-level design decisions to become explicit, further refining the baseline.

Refining the Baseline

As you build out the skeletal architecture to run end-to-end, you are forced to consider lower-level design decisions. How will you structure your application logic? What is your data access approach? Will you deploy the business logic on the same server as the web server, or will you deploy them on separate application servers? What authentication and authorization mechanisms will you use? What protocols will you use between servers?

Don't try to address all the concerns yet. Choose the areas of highest technical risk to validate and let the other decisions emerge through implementation. Think about building the simplest skeletal application that will meet your constraints, mitigate technical risks, and still provide a sound, stable basis for development iterations.

> **Detailed Example of Refining the Baseline**
>
> For a detailed example of this technique, see the MSDN Tech Note:
>
> TN_1111: Top-Down System Design
>
> http://msdn.microsoft.com/vstudio/teamsystem/reference/technotes/system_designer/topdown_sys.aspx

You should also leverage the design knowledge and experience of others who may have also solved similar problems before and captured the learning in patterns.[8] Patterns also give you a language with which you can concisely describe solutions, mitigate risk by reusing known good designs, and enable future maintenance and reuse of your work.

.NET Framework-Specific Patterns

For patterns specific to the .NET framework, see msdn.microsoft.com/ practices.

Reference Architectures

In many cases, you can use a reference architecture as a baseline. For example, Microsoft has created a reference application called Applied Integration Baseline (AIB), which uses a pattern-based approach to build an executable baseline (see Figure 5.2). This application ships with more than twelve Visual Studio projects and is based on ASP.NET, BizTalk Server, SQL Server, Host Integration Server, and VSTS.

Windows Server System Reference Architecture

For planning infrastructure and datacenters, you can download the Windows Server System Reference Architecture from http://www.microsoft.com/ technet/itsolutions/wssra/raguide/default.mspx.

In a similar way, the Windows Server System Reference Architecture (WSSRA) offers the infrastructure architect a baseline for the configuration of a datacenter. Obviously, actual circumstances will vary, but the WSSRA baseline provides a preferred model to set up the server environments.

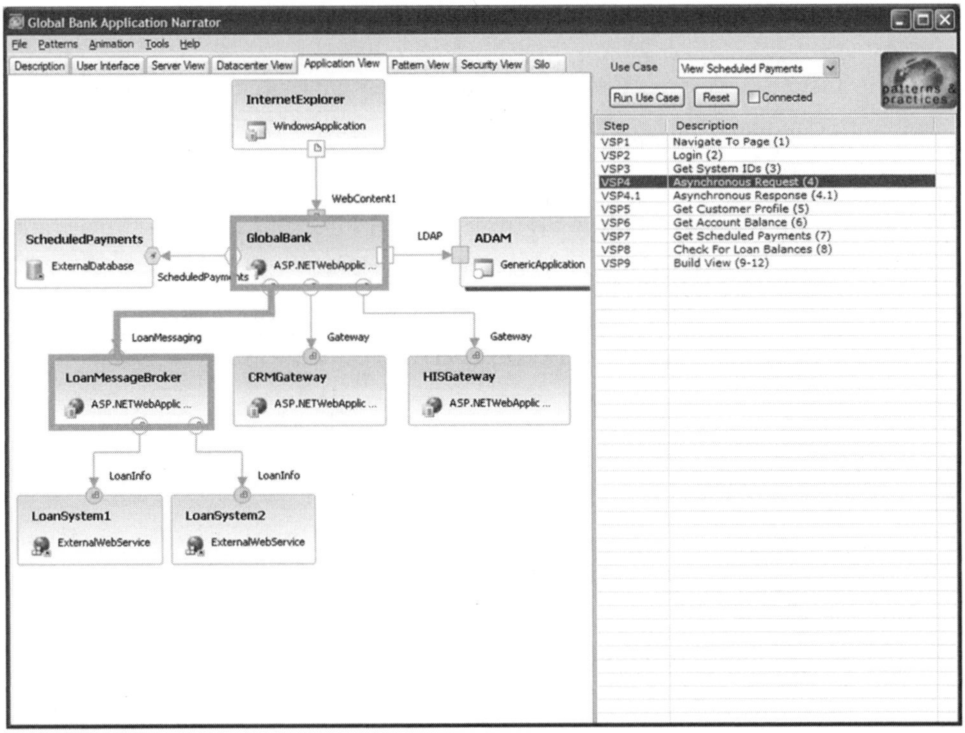

Figure 5.2   The Application Integration Baseline provides an interactive "Narrator" to visualize the baseline architecture. The visual models include VSTS Application Designer and Logical Datacenter Designer models as well as a pattern-based description of the system. Here the narrator is illuminating a scenario one step at a time by rendering each step on the Application Designer diagram.

Download the Application Integration Baseline

You can download the Application Integration Baseline from

MSDN Library

    Servers and Enterprise Development

        Enterprise Architecture, Patterns, and Practices

            Microsoft Patterns & Practices

                Reference Implementations

VSTS and Service-Oriented Architecture

For all the following reasons, VSTS focuses on the practical aspects of implementing a distributed system using a SOA. VSTS provides four designers that handle the major activities involved:

1. The Application Designer (see Figure 5.3) enables you to design the application components that expose and consume web services.

2. The System Designer (see Figure 5.4) enables you to compose and configure the applications into systems and potentially reusable subsystems.

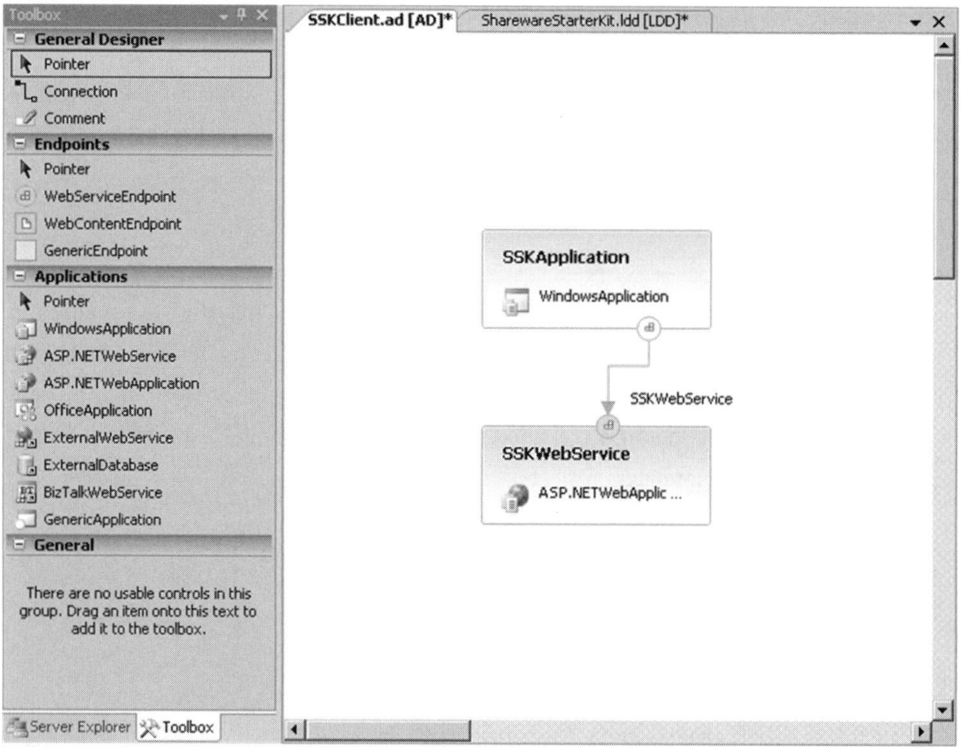

Figure 5.3   Use the Application Designer to describe the components that will communicate with web services. Note that you can add your own custom types to the toolbox.

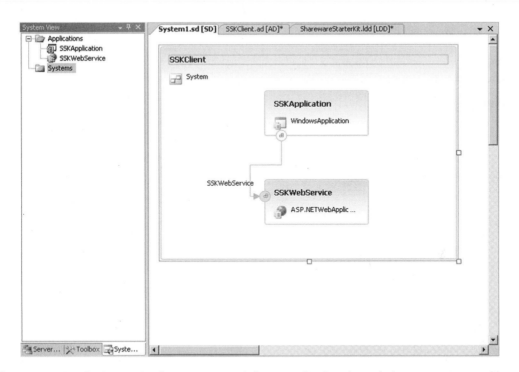

Figure 5.4   Use the System Designer to compose these applications into whole systems or reusable subsystems.

3. The Logical Datacenter Designer (see Figure 5.5) captures servers (such as IIS), their configurations, and network trust zones as you use them in a datacenter into which one or more systems will be deployed.

4. The Deployment Designer (see Figure 5.6) enables you to map each component in a system to the servers in a logical datacenter to specify how the distributed parts of the system need to be deployed.

In VSTS, the designs generate source code and XML files and therefore become live views into the source code and configuration files. As architecturally significant changes are made in source code and configuration files, these diagrams update automatically.

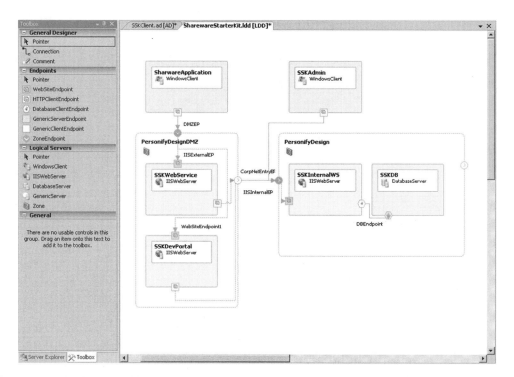

Figure 5.5   Use the Logical Datacenter Designer to capture the configuration of the servers and the network trust zones that are in operation or planned for the datacenter.

Quality of Service Mindset

MSF describes a QoS mindset as follows:

> The idea is that qualities of service such as performance and security should not be considered late in the project but throughout it. When ignored, these qualities of service are ultimately consumer dissatisfiers.[9]

Architectural design needs to reflect this QoS mindset. Often the architect is the team member most able to consider the implications of QoS requirements, implicit or explicit. In turn, the decisions with the greatest impact on QoS are typically made during design.

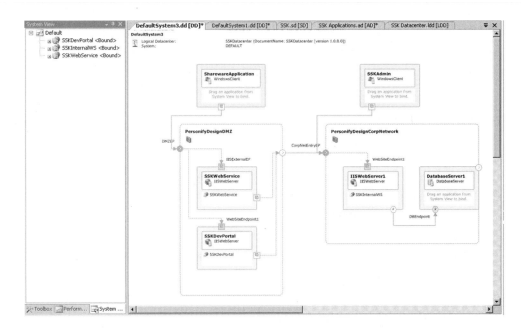

Figure 5.6   Use the Deployment Designer to map each application component to the corresponding server and thereby specify how the distributed application needs to be deployed.

Security

Security is a primary architectural concern. The primary architectural analysis technique for security is threat modeling, which looks for potential vulnerabilities of the planned system.[10]

Fortunately for web services, the security profiles are implemented in the Web Services Enhancements (WSE) Microsoft .NET Framework.[11] WSE enables you to sign and encrypt web services and set trust domains.

Performance

Performance is another leading architectural concern. A typical trap in architecture is that performance problems usually are not detected until late in product development, leading to costly redesign or rework. VSTS mitigates this risk in two ways. Because the SOA designers generate code, you can create application skeletons early that can be submitted to trial deployment and performance testing, well before the system is complete. And because the systems are made of autonomous services, reconfiguration is straightforward, and tuning can be optimized to the problem areas.

Citizenship Mindset

The shift from self-contained applications to services requires a change in mindset, which MSF calls *Citizenship*. As applications move from being self-contained projects to consumers and publishers of services, the project team needs to think differently about its approach. Consumers need to look for services to consume and not bypass the infrastructure that is available to them. Publishers need to realize that many of their consumers are unknown. Published services need to act reliably for any consumer adhering to the service contract and protect against malicious hackers who are looking to exploit the service with ill-formed messages or other attacks.

This mindset presumes a transparency and trust that are typical of high-performing organizations. Here's a description from Philip Evans' and Bob Wolf's "Collaboration Rules" that plays equally to the services of an SOA as to the appropriate culture for developing one:

> Where trust is the currency, reputation is a source of power. In a dense network . . . . there is more power to being an information source than an information sink. Consequently, individuals are motivated to maximize both the visibility of their work and their connections to those who are themselves broadly connected.[12]

Design for Operations

A typical problem that most organizations face is the complexity of moving a system as designed into a datacenter as configured. The development and operations teams typically have different vocabulary, different staffs, and different physical locations (sometimes on different continents or in different companies). The information flow between development and operations can be very dissatisfying, often inaccurate and incomplete.

Particularly with distributed systems, there are many parts to deploy on many servers, each with its own configuration requirements. For example, applications that run in test environments don't run in production environments because the applications violate policies that developers were not aware of. In this situation, architectural design changes are sometimes required to bring applications into conformance, or conversely, applications need to make requirements of the datacenter, such as specific versions or service packs. These operational requirements may conflict with the existing deployments of other applications. The consequence of these communication mismatches may be a delay of weeks or months between the time that architects, developers, and testers announce that an application is ready to deploy and the readiness of operations to actually deploy it.

In the value-up approach of embracing change and enabling business agility, these delays are a huge barrier. VSTS starts to remove these disconnects by enabling Design for Operations. The principle is simple. Rather than waiting until an application is implemented to attempt deployment, VSTS tests the deployability of the application during its design. The solution architect and infrastructure architect can then resolve any incompatibility between the application requirements and the datacenter constraints well ahead of actual deployment and significantly reduce the bake time needed for successful deployment.

Design for Operations is made possible by the System Definition Model (SDM):

> At the heart of SDM is the notion of a system. In its most basic form, a system is an independently deployable configuration of resources. For software systems, resources are ultimately directories and files, such as binaries, XML files, configuration files, SQL script files, and so on. For hardware systems, such as graphics systems, motherboards, network interface cards and power supplies, resources might include the boards, processor chips, memory chips, fans, and other lower-level components.

> If a system enables access to its resources, or if its resources access services offered by resources in other systems, it exposes those resources via endpoints. For example, a motherboard might provide an IDE endpoint for peripherals; web service endpoints provide a means for an application to expose or consume web services; HTTP endpoints provide a means for a server to enable access using the HTTP protocol.[13]

The SDM is visualized on the Deployment Designer (as shown in Figure 5.6). It marries the application design (typically from the solution architect) with the logical datacenter design (from the infrastructure architect). Directly on this diagram, you can validate the architecture—that is, you can determine whether the application as designed will deploy in the datacenter as configured. Any exceptions appear directly as warnings with glyphs on the diagram as needed (see Figure 5.7).

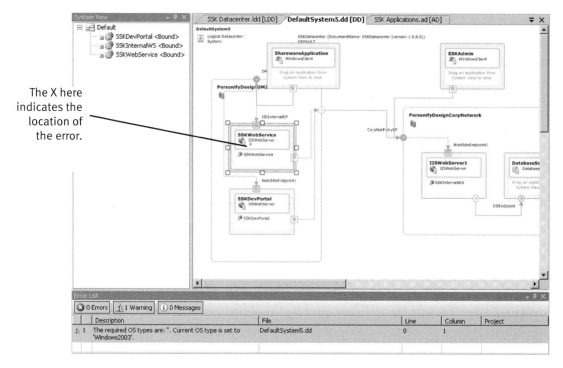

The X here indicates the location of the error.

Figure 5.7   Validation of the Deployment Designer can identify conflicts between the application as designed and the datacenter as configured. In this example, the application requires Windows Server 2003, but it is intended for deployment on a server with an earlier OS.

The SDM defines a model of the system and a model of the datacenter and enables a deployment to be defined and validated. Models allow validation of a design, even before coding has begun. After the application has been implemented, changes to the application's configuration to resolve errors are directly synchronized with code and configuration files. The fact that models reflect real code is very important for deployment validation. Models also describe how configuration can be overridden.

In addition to enabling the validation at design time, VSTS facilitates the verification at test time by enabling test labs to run in virtual machines (which is discussed in Chapter 7, "Testing").

Summary

In this chapter, I briefly discussed a value-up approach to architectural design, the process of creating a solution architecture. It is highly iterative, working both top-down and bottom-up, emerging from choices about implementation and driven by the scenarios and qualities of service that define user value and contract boundaries.

SOA is the dominant super-pattern that governs overall design of modern distributed systems because it enables business alignment, agility, interoperability, and reuse. The MSF mindsets for Qualities of Service and Citizenship bring essential points of view to SOA—the consideration of all aspects of experience and creation or application of reuse wherever possible. Contract-first design is an important practice for successful SOA.

The web services standards are the main enabler of SOA. VSTS supports architectural design of web services and composition of systems directly based on these services. VSTS introduces Design for Operations to reduce the complexity of preparing distributed systems for deployment. VSTS provides a Deployment Designer that marries the logical datacenter design to the system design, enabling you to see whether the application as designed will deploy in the datacenter as it is configured.

The next chapter looks at the value-up practices of development.

Endnotes

1. Grady Booch, *Handbook of Software Architecture*, work in progress, available at http://www.booch.com/architecture/index.jsp.

2. Christopher Alexander first introduced the notion of patterns of building in civil architecture, and this spawned the patterns community in software architecture. [Alexander 1964] Christopher W. Alexander, *Notes on the Synthesis of Form* (Harvard University Press, 1964).

3. For example, Brooks, op. cit., 45.

4. For example, http://xp.c2.com/TheSourceCodeIsTheDesign.html.

5. www.ws-i.org

6. http://www.w3.org/TR/wsdl

7. http://msdn.microsoft.com/library/default.asp?url=/library/en-us/dnlong/html/introtowcf.asp

8. Three important works here are Eric Evans, *Domain-Driven Design: Tacking Complexity In the Heart of Software* (Boston: Addison-Wesley, 2003); Martin Fowler et al., *Patterns of Enterprise Application Architecture* (Boston: Addison-Wesley, 2002); and Joshua Kerievsky, *Refactoring to Patterns* (Boston: Addison-Wesley, 2004).

9. MSF, both instances

10. http://msdn.microsoft.com/security/

11. http://msdn.microsoft.com/webservices/webservices/building/wse/default.aspx

12. Philip Evans and Bob Wolf, "Collaboration Rules," Harvard Business Review, July–August 2005.

13. http://msdn.microsoft.com/vstudio/teamsystem/reference/technotes/apps_designer/sdm.aspx

6. Development

Developer
Development Manager

"Working software over comprehensive documentation"
—The Agile Manifesto[1]

Figure 6.1 Newton's Cradle is a common desktop toy. When you apply force from one end, the balls swing in a predictable regular motion. When you add a force from the opposite end, the balls start bouncing chaotically against each other. It's a metaphor for development practice. Simple, directional force encourages predictability, while contradictory forces can create chaos.

This chapter is not about programming languages or coding techniques. These important topics are well covered in many other books. Rather, this chapter is about the activities that VSTS enables a developer to perform as a complement to writing production code that help to make that code successful.

There's no religion here. I completely recognize that many readers will think that the practices I describe don't go far enough. Again, many books cover methodologies or individual practices in considerable depth, whereas I only have space to touch the surface.

Rather, my goal here is to give you enough of the reasoning behind and tooling in VSTS to do a better job right away. I hope it makes you want to dig deeper faster through the other sources, too.

> **More Detail on Development Techniques**
>
> For a how-to description of the development techniques discussed here, see Will Stott and James Newkirk, *Visual Studio Team System—Better Software Development for Agile Teams* (Addison-Wesley, 2006).

A Value-Up View of Development

The value-up approach measures only deliverables that the customer values. More than anything else, this means working code of quality suitable for customer delivery. For twenty-five years, we've known that ensuring quality early is much cheaper than removing bugs late.[2] Only in the last ten years, however, have practices shifted from notions like "Code Complete," which treats bug removal as a deferrable activity, to "Test-Driven Development," which focuses on bug prevention with 100% of tests passing at the time of check-in.

For purposes of this chapter, I'm going to assume that you are a skilled developer. Also, I'm going to assume that you, like virtually every developer I've ever met, want to do quality work and remove the impediments to delivering quality.

Quality from a Developer's Point of View

In the vast majority of cases, there are five broad process problems that lead (directly or indirectly) to quality problems in a developer's work:

1. **Poorly communicated, misunderstood, or out-of-date requirements**. Chapter 3, "Requirements," discusses how to define and manage scenarios and QoS requirements to contain problems related to requirement misunderstandings. However, as a developer, you can take responsibility for forcing good requirements, as discussed later.

2. **Programming errors**. People write code, and people make mistakes. In particular, it is often very hard to write code that takes all the necessary qualities of service into account, such as security, performance, localization, and maintainability. This is true for both managed and unmanaged code, although unmanaged C and C++ incur the additional security hazards of buffer overruns, unallocated memory reads, and similar memory violations.

3. **Lack of testing feedback**. Even developers who know that they should be writing unit tests often find themselves facing too many disincentives. Unit testing takes time; it's often hard to tell how much code has been tested and under which conditions, and the tests often do not get reused or noticed. Without thorough unit testing and its immediate feedback to a developer, though, it is very easy to change code and not discover undesirable side effects until much too late.

4. **Version skews**. Even developers who would never consider working without source control often find that their source control does not deal adequately with the many non-source files on which the project depends, such as the build system, tests, and configurations. Differences in these files often lead to those hard-to-diagnose bugs that provoke from the observation, "But it worked on my machine!"

5. **Lack of transparency**. The development infrastructure, project management system, and bug/change request tracking and metrics (if any) are treated as disconnected black boxes. In this situation, the team has little visibility into the workings of the actual coding activity other than the commonly hated and not always reliable status reports.

Fortunately, VSTS addresses these five broad categories. The first is only partially a development responsibility. The remaining four, however, can't be solved by improving the requirements gathering process and instead need to be solved by focusing on development and downstream activities. These five are the focus of this chapter.

Using Test-Driven Development to Ensure Requirements Clarity

Test-Driven Development (TDD) is a practice in which you do not write a single line of code until you have written a test that fails in the absence of that code. Next, you write just enough code to pass the test, then write a new test that fails, and keep repeating the tight loop. Advocates of TDD document that the practice forces clear requirements, catches mistakes, enables refactoring, and removes stress.[3]

Figure 6.2 VSTS supports unit testing directly in the IDE. This is a view of test run results from the last run with the source code under test in the upper window. The dark shading (red on a color screen) indicates an uncovered exception handler.

The strongest argument in favor of TDD is that it uses tests as technical product requirements. Because you must write a test before writing the code under test, you are forced to understand the requirements and wring out any ambiguity in order to define the test. This process, in turn, makes you think in small increments and in terms of reuse so that you do not write any unnecessary code. In other words, TDD imposes a clear and atomic design, which is easier to grow and maintain. To facilitate TDD, VSTS supports direct test creation and execution, with code coverage, inside the IDE (see Figure 6.2).

The next argument is that TDD enables continual refactoring to keep the code lean (see Figure 6.3). If you have tests that cover 100% of the code and immediately report failing results when there are any side effects from refactoring, you have the safety net to refactor with confidence. Indeed, the experience of TDD is that you do much less debugging of your code because your unit tests pinpoint errors that you would otherwise isolate only by laboriously stepping through the execution with the debugger.

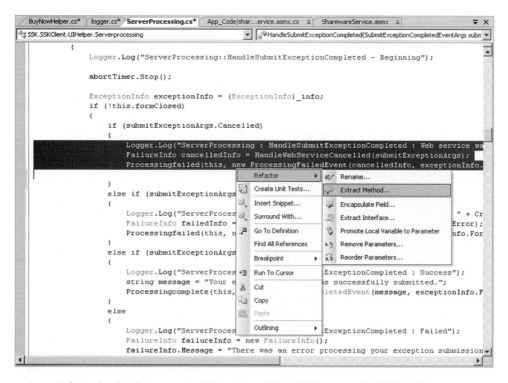

Figure 6.3   Refactoring is also supported directly, making VSTS a powerful IDE for TDD.

Addressing Programming Errors with Code Reviews, Automated and Manual

The most frequent prescription for catching programming errors is the code review. Code review approaches include informal walkthroughs, formal inspections, and pair programming, which is a continuous review as the code is being written. Success with manual code reviews varies according to the experience of the reviewer and the degree of safety created in the review environment.

Automated code analysis, often called static analysis, is a technique that has received less attention because it depends on sophisticated tools that can scan code for subtle errors, such as security risks. Microsoft developed code analysis tools for its own product teams (FXCop for managed code and PreFAST for unmanaged code) that are now included as part of VSTS. They cover coding practices in the areas of design, globalization, interoperability, maintainability, mobility, naming conventions, performance, portability, reliability, and security.

To encourage consistent practices across the team, VSTS enables you to set a check-in policy that ensures that code analysis has been run before every check-in (see Figure 6.4; more on check-in policies later).

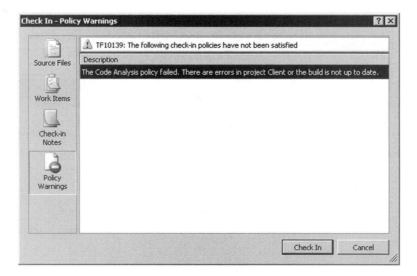

Figure 6.4   Check-in policies warn you when you have skipped steps before checking in your source code. In this example, static code analysis hasn't been run before the attempted check-in.

Automated Code Analysis

VSTS enables automated code analysis as a set of options on the local build (F5) and presents the code analysis warnings and errors in the same window as the rest of the build output (see Figure 6.5).

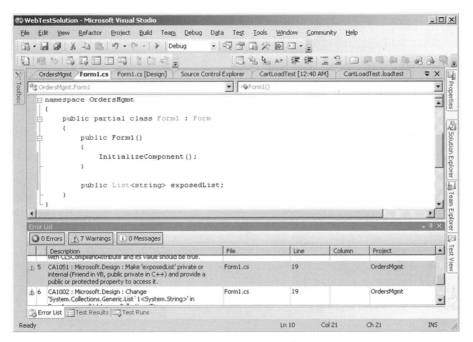

Figure 6.5   The warnings from code analysis appear in the IDE in the same way as build warnings. You can click on each warning and jump to the source for viewing and editing.

Managed and Unmanaged Code Analysis

In VSTS, there are two different code analysis mechanisms—one for C/C++ that works from the source and one for managed code that works from the managed assemblies. The steps that you need to follow vary depending on which you use.

See these MSDN topics:

Development Tools and Technologies

   Visual Studio Team System

      Team Edition for Developers

         Writing Quality Code

            Detecting and Correcting C/C++ Code Defects

            Detecting and Correcting Managed Code Defects

Manual Code Reviews

To facilitate manual code reviews, VSTS lets you *shelve* your code changes and share them privately with your reviewers prior to check-in (see Figure 6.6; more on shelving later.) In return, reviewers can give you suggestions and comments on the code in a shelveset, and only when you're ready do you check it in for the build.

Working With Shelvesets for Code Reviews and Other Uncommitted Changes

To understand how to create and use shelvesets in VSTS, see the MSDN topic:

Development Tools and Technologies

   Visual Studio Team System

      Team Foundation

         Team Foundation Project Members

            Working with Team Foundation Source Control

               Working with Source Control Files and Folders

               Working with Source Control Shelvesets

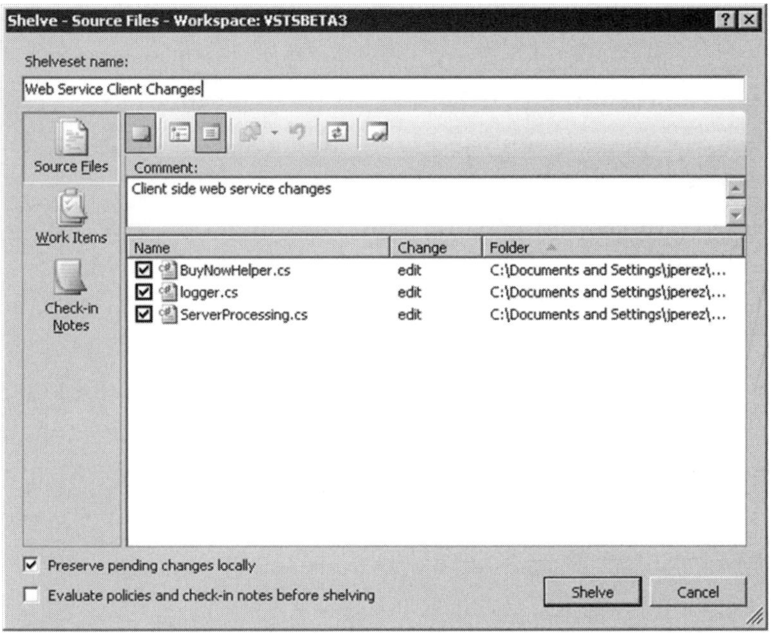

Figure 6.6   In the version control database, a shelveset is a temporary set of changes that may or may not be checked in later. One use of shelving is to make new source code available for a code review before check-in.

Providing Immediate Feedback with Unit Tests and Code Coverage

Unit testing is probably the single most important quality practice for a developer. As a practice, unit testing has been advocated for at least thirty years.[4] However, in the last ten years, simple tools, such as NUnit and JUnit, have made the practice much more widespread, often as part of TDD as previously described.

Unit tests support programming, as shown in Figure 6.2. Their purpose is to check that your code does what you intend it to and does not do what you don't want it to. Except in rare cases, they are not tests from a customer viewpoint, they do not validate scenarios, and they might not have a lot of meaning to users other than the owners of the code under test.

The concept of a unit test is straightforward: It is a test of the unit of functionality in which you write the program, such as a method in C# or a routine in VB. You can have multiple unit tests for each method, such as a positive test, checking that the method behaves as expected with valid input, and a negative test, validating that it does not behave as unexpected with invalid input.

As a developer, you should usually write your own unit tests. You know what you intend your code to do. You know how to validate it. Writing the unit tests ensures that you have thought this subject through, and it provides a necessary safety net for the future when you have to maintain the code.

Generally, whether you practice TDD or not, you should not check in code without having written and run unit tests that exercise all delivered functionality, including any parts of the software that are dependent on any of this functionality. Normally in VSTS, a check-in policy ensures that the newly delivered code passes unit testing prior to check-in.

Test First or Code First?

Everyone I have met who practices TDD finds it a liberating practice. (That's not surprising; otherwise, they wouldn't do it.) At the same time, there are accomplished developers who do quality work and achieve similar results by coding first and then writing unit tests. In either case, two principles hold:

1. Unit tests should be written in the same session as the code and checked in to source control at the same time in the same changeset as the code.
2. Unit tests should strive for maximum code coverage.

The result of these two principles is that you do not check in code that does not have unit tests that run and pass with it, and if someone else (or the build system) gets your code and runs your tests, they should pass. In that way, your unit tests become a safety net not just for yourself but also for the whole team.

VSTS makes both approaches easy (test first and code first) while supporting these principles. If you write tests first, you can right-click and refactor to generate the code under test, as shown in Figure 6.3. If you write the code first, you can right-click and generate tests for that code, as shown in Figure 6.7.

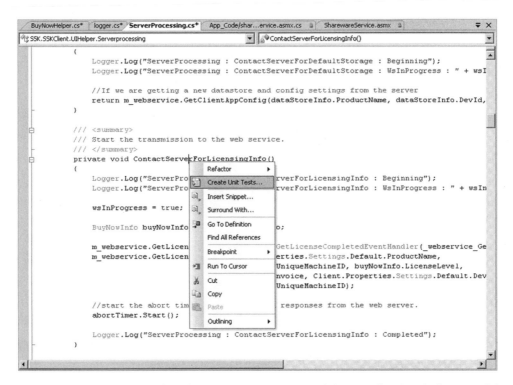

Figure 6.7 If you are writing code before tests or want to extend the tests for a particular area of the code (by method, class, or namespace), you can right-click and generate tests from the source.

Code Coverage

Regardless of whether you write the tests or the code first, when you run the tests, VSTS provides code coverage reporting with the test run results (see Figure 6.8). Code coverage choices are stored in the *Test Run Configuration* settings (more on the rest of these later). You need to choose which assemblies to instrument for coverage because not all might be relevant to the testing at hand.

At the completion of a test run, you can use the toolbar of the Test Results Viewer to show the coverage in the source that you just exercised. This lets you pinpoint any code that your tests failed to exercise—skipped code is painted red (see Figure 6.9). You can then right-click on this code to generate a new test for it, or you can extend an existing test to cover it.

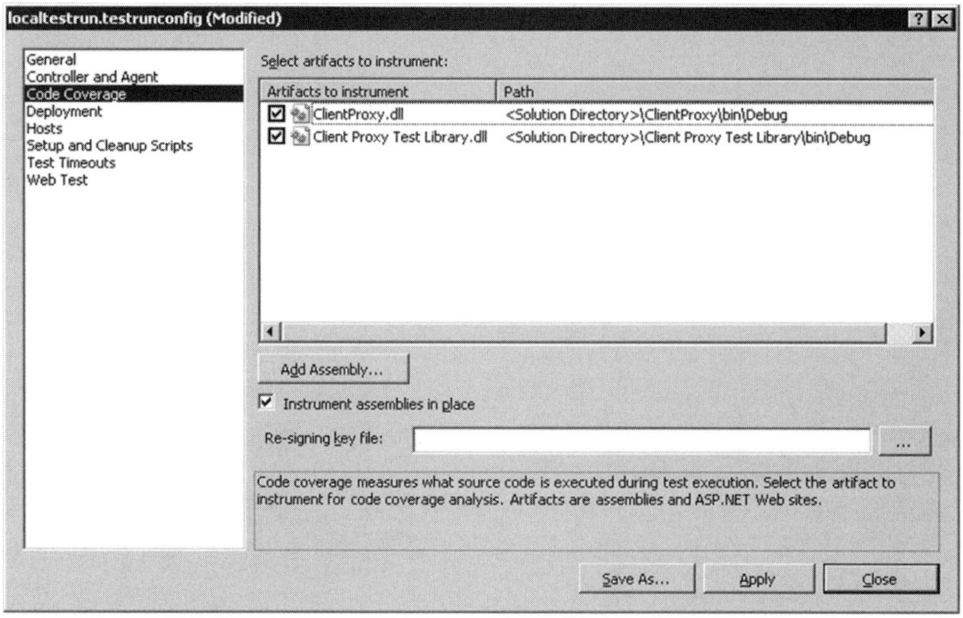

Figure 6.8   When you create or edit a test run configuration, you choose the assemblies for which you want to collect code coverage. Only select those from the code under test.

Code coverage is an exquisite tool for showing you which blocks of code have not been exercised by your tests. Use code coverage to identify gaps where you need more unit tests. Do not let good code coverage make you too confident, however. Code coverage tells you neither that your tests are good nor that the customer-visible scenarios and QoS have been met.

How much code coverage is enough? The ideal is obviously 100%, but this is rarely obtainable. Frequently, there is some error-handling or integration code for which it is impractically expensive to write unit tests. In these cases, you need to perform careful code reviews and exercise the code in the debugger. In every case, when you check in code that does not have matching unit tests passing, you should make the choice consciously and document it in the check-in notes.

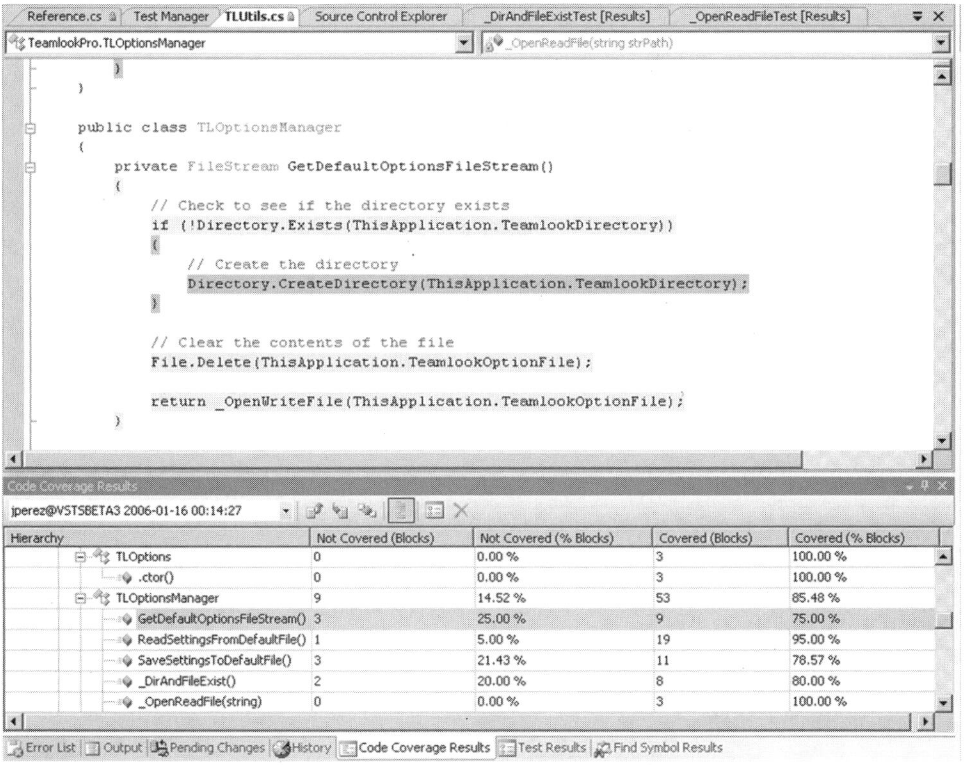

Figure 6.9   At the completion of a test run, you can see the source code under test painted to show code coverage. This lets you identify at a glance blocks of code that are not being tested. In this monochrome rendering, they are darker; in color, they appear red. You can then right-click in the uncovered code to create a new test to exercise this area.

Making Unit Tests Better

When you're thinking about unit tests, it's key that you start with a good test list.[5] Consider simultaneously the four variables: output, methods invoked, code path, and error conditions. Make sure that you have inputs that maximize the diversity of those variables. Include negative tests that broadly check for error conditions. You may want a buddy or a tester to help brainstorm possible error conditions that you haven't thought of handling yet.[6]

Varying the Data and Configurations Used By Your Tests

Think of using your unit tests more broadly by varying the data and by running them with multiple configurations. VSTS makes this straightforward.

See these MSDN topics:

Development Tools and Technologies

   Visual Studio Team System

     Team Edition for Developers

       Working with Unit Tests

         Creating Unit Tests

           Coding a Data-Driven Unit Test

Development Tools and Technologies

   Visual Studio Team System

     Team Edition for Testers

       Testing Tools Tasks

         Configuring Test Execution

           How to: Specify a Test Run Configuration

Using Data

Usually when you write a unit test, you start it with a single set of values. One of the best ways to extend a test is to drive the test with broader data, which exercises more paths through the code, including more error conditions. Think about values that force different behavior and throw exceptions. VSTS lets you do this easily, as shown in Figure 6.10.

Configurations

If your program needs to run in different configurations, you need to test against those configurations, too. There are usually at least two: one for development and one for production. If you distribute your software commercially, to support diverse datacenters or desktops you will need many more configurations. VSTS lets you manage these as test run configurations, which encapsulate the data needed to run the tests in the right environment (see Figure 6.11).

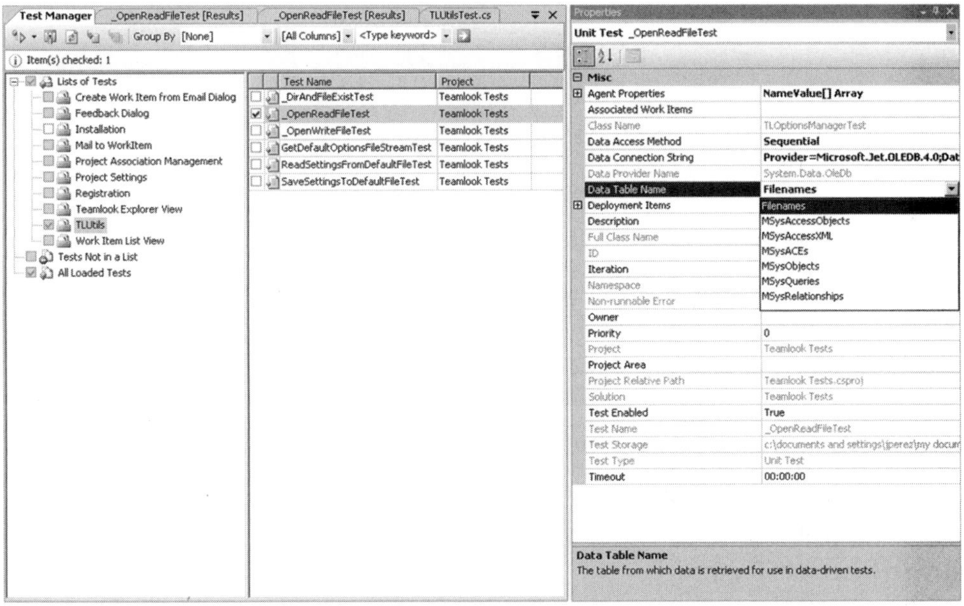

Figure 6.10   You can drive your unit tests with variable sets of data. Data sets can be maintained in OLEDB providers and specified as properties on the test.

Component Integration Tests

Depending on the software project, it might be appropriate to supplement unit tests with component integration tests. The purpose of these tests is to protect against unforeseen impacts on other parts of a system. In service-oriented architectures, for example, each service has many consumers. These consumers can provide component integration tests that act as compliance tests, ensuring that the published service continues to meet the consumers' requirements and contracts. When available, these component integration tests should be run before check-in as well.

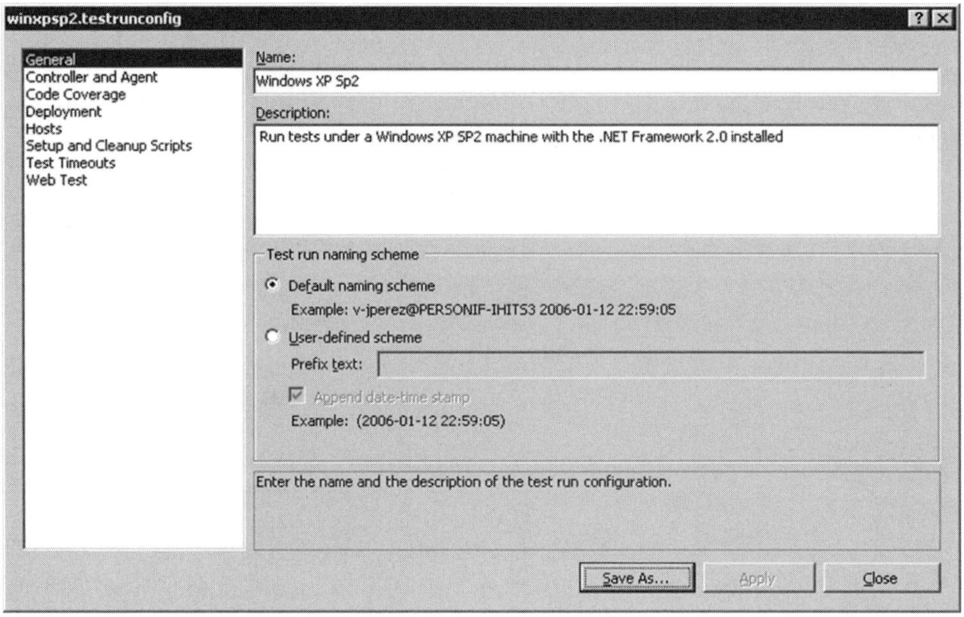

Figure 6.11 Test run configurations let you test multiple deployment configurations and track each test result against the intended deployment target.

Build Verification Tests

Build verification tests (BVTs) are tests that run as part of the automated build. The purpose of BVTs is to look for unforeseen side effects and errors due to changes in the new code.

Any automated tests that do not require manual setup make good BVTs. This should include the vast majority of unit tests and component integration tests and the majority of scenario tests (see Chapter 7, "Testing"). To achieve this purpose, BVTs need to achieve very high code coverage. If they don't, you have no idea how many unforeseen issues slipped by the net. To set up BVTs in VSTS, you must create a test list that identities which tests to use (see Figure 6.12) and then refer to the list on the Build Type Creation Wizard, as shown in Figure 6.13.

Specifying Tests for BVTs

In VSTS, BVTs are ordinary tests that have been included on the appropriate *test list*. You need to create a test list for your BVTs.

See the MSDN topics:

Development Tools and Technologies

    Visual Studio Team System

        Team Edition for Testers

           Testing Tools Tasks

               Managing Tests

                    Managing Large Numbers of Tests

                       How to: Create a Test List

Development Tools and Technologies

    Visual Studio Team System

        Team Edition for Testers

           Testing Tools Tasks

               Managing Tests

                    Managing Large Numbers of Tests

                       How to: Configure and Run Build Verification Tests (BVTs)

Tuning Performance

Unit testing and code analysis are techniques that you should apply before every check-in to make sure that your code does the right thing in the right way. Performance profiling is different. When you have performance problems, it is usually a small portion of your code that is culpable, so you should focus your tuning efforts there. Frequently, the problems appear under load tests (discussed in Chapter 7); sometimes, though, you can discover them through routine functional testing or exploratory walkthroughs.

To diagnose performance errors, you launch a profiling session and select from the current solution the code projects on which you want to collect data (see Figure 6.14).

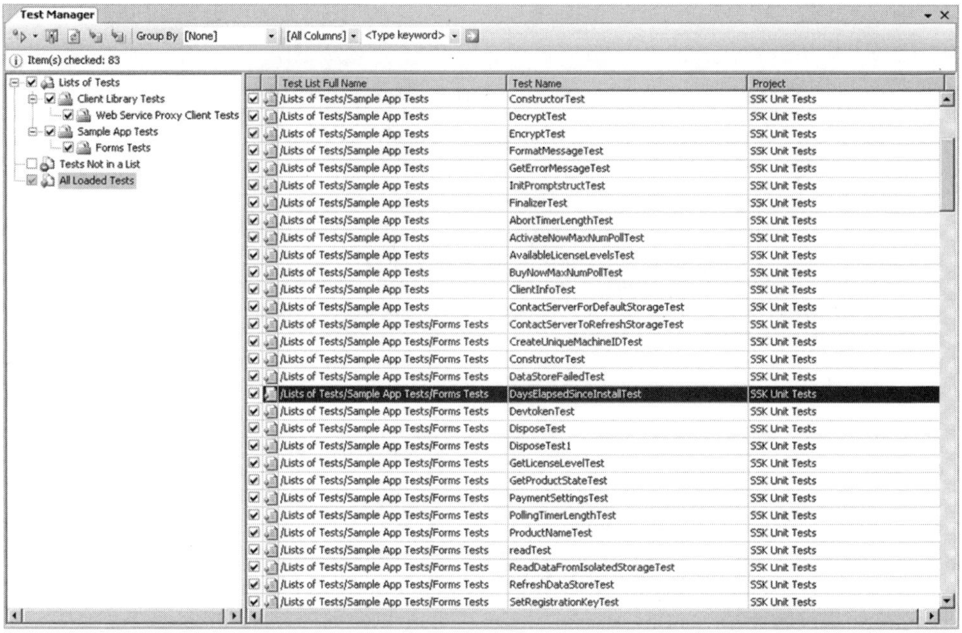

Figure 6.12   VSTS lets you organize your tests into test lists so that you can group them for execution. Typically, you add new tests to these lists as they become available.

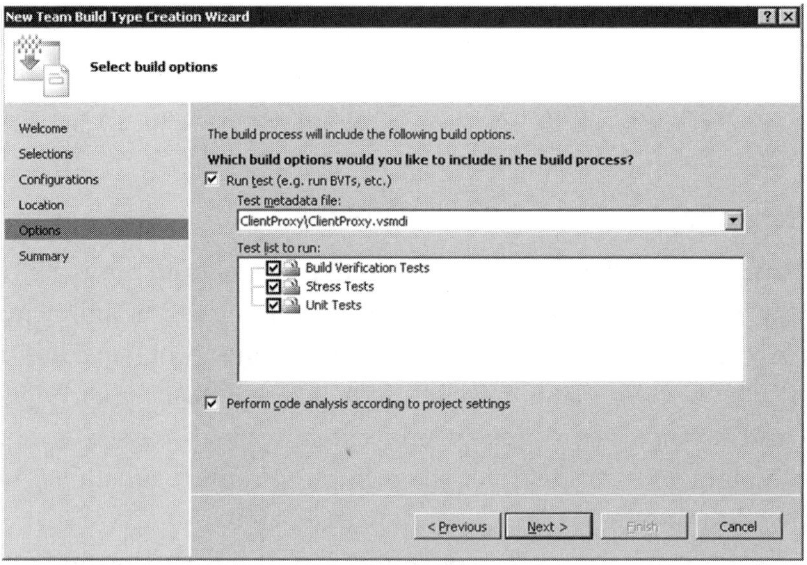

Figure 6.13   VSTS Team Build includes the designation of the test lists that you want to run as the build verification tests.

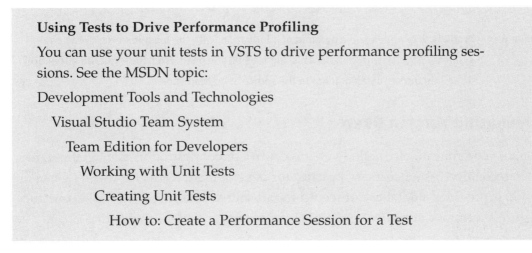

Figure 6.14   VSTS provides a wizard that instruments the code under test for profiling. When you choose the source project to profile, VSTS automatically chooses the instrumentation mechanism for you.

Using Tests to Drive Performance Profiling

You can use your unit tests in VSTS to drive performance profiling sessions. See the MSDN topic:

Development Tools and Technologies

   Visual Studio Team System

     Team Edition for Developers

       Working with Unit Tests

         Creating Unit Tests

           How to: Create a Performance Session for a Test

You need to choose between two profiling techniques. Sampling enables you to collect data without perceivable overhead indicating how often a method appears in the call stack, as shown in Figure 6.15. Typically, you start with sampling. Instrumented profiling, on the other hand, lets you walk traced call sequences with much more data, at the cost of some overhead and expanded binary size. Use instrumented profiling to drill into the hot spots that sampling reveals.

After you have selected your target and the technique, you can either drive the application manually or run a test that exercises it. When you stop the profiling session, you'll see a report that lets you drill down from a high-level summary into the details of the calls.

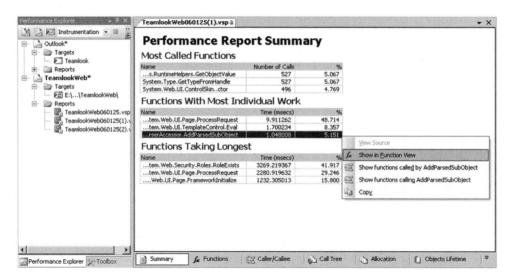

Figure 6.15 Profiling data appears in a pyramid of information, with the most important data on the summary page, as shown here. This might be all you need. From here you can either drill down into further detail or jump to the source of method shown.

Preventing Version Skew

Source code control, also called version control or configuration management, has been recognized as a necessary practice for development teams for twenty years or more. It provides a database of record for all source code, an ability to reconstruct historical versions of source, and a place of record for the build system.

Checking In

VSTS has built-in version control that keeps the full history of changes to the team's source base, all the related files open in your Visual Studio solution, and any others that you include. When you start to edit a file, it is automatically checked out for you, unless someone else has it locked. (By default, only one person can edit a file at a time, but you can enable multiple checkout from the Team menu.)

The primary explicit way that you interact with version control is by checking in files. When you check in, you are in effect saying that your files are ready to be used in the team build (see Figures 6.16, 6.17, and 6.18).

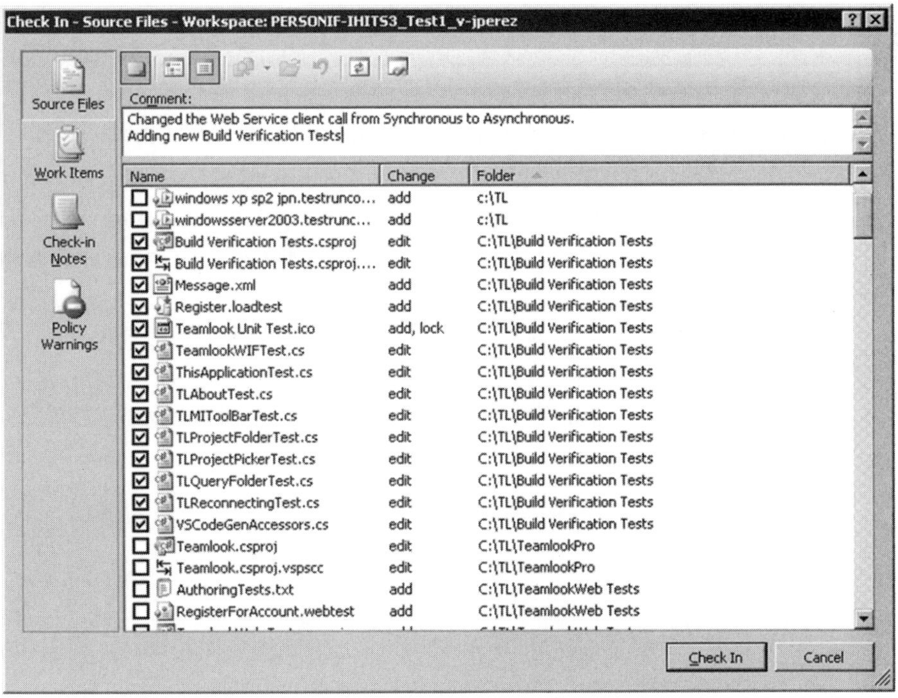

Figure 6.16   The Check In dialog shows you files that have been changed on the first pane so that you can select the ones to check in. Note the four tab icons on the left that let you flip among source files, work items, check-in notes, and policy warnings.

When you check in, VSTS prompts for three things: the list of files, the work items that you are resolving with this check-in, and the check-in notes that you are using to describe the changes. Together, these three items form a *changeset*, which ties

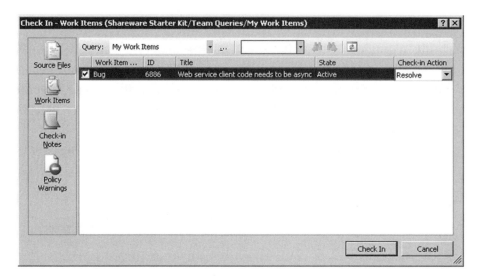

Figure 6.17   The second tab shows the work items that you want to associate with the check-in. If your check-in completes the delivery of the code for a task or other work item, you set the Check-In Action to Resolve. The resolution happens on the next successful team build. If you are making a partial delivery and keeping the work item active, then change the Check-in Action to Associate.

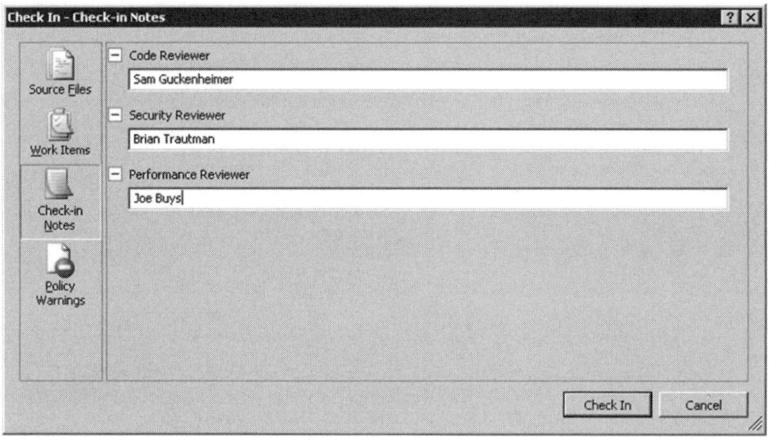

Figure 6.18   On the third pane, enter notes for this check-in. The fields used for the notes are determined by your setting for the team project on the Team Foundation server.

together the data of a check-in. The changeset includes the newly added, modified, or deleted lines of code, the work item state changes associated with that code, and the check-in notes.

A major benefit of changesets in VSTS is that they allow the build system and the metrics warehouse to track fine-grained relationships of work items changes with source code and test changes. The build system can identify all the changesets that have been delivered to the build and thereby identify all the work item transitions and calculate the code churn. Reports—such as the Build Report in Figure 6.21 and the Quality Indicators shown in Figures 4.7, 9.12, 9.15, 9.18, and 9.20 through 9.22—rely on the changeset structure.

Check-In Policies

When you check in, VSTS also verifies that you have complied with the team's check-in policies, as shown previously in Figure 6.4. Three standard check-in policies make sure that you have associated work items with your changes, have run unit tests, and have performed static code analysis. Your team may choose to write other policies and have these evaluated at check-in, too.

Shelving

Often you want to back up, store, or share your code without submitting it for the next build. Because changesets delivered by check-in automatically feed the build system, you need a different mechanism. In VSTS, you *shelve* your code in these cases, as shown previously in Figure 6.6. When you shelve your code, it is stored centrally, and others can view your changes (assuming you give them permission), but nothing is submitted for the next build. When you subsequently unshelve your code, there is no record of the shelveset and correspondingly no history to clean up in the source database.

Shelving is very useful for a number of cases. If you need to leave the office when your code isn't ready for the build, you can back it up. If you need to share your code with someone else prior to check-in, for example for a code review or buddy test, you can shelve your code and let someone review it from the shelveset. When you want to experiment with two solutions to a problem, you can try one, shelve it, try the second, and switch between the shelvesets for local testing.

Branching

If you've used other source control systems, you're probably familiar with the concept of branching. Having branches lets you keep parallel versions of files that evolve separately. Probably the most frequent use of branches is to track multiple released versions of a solution. When releasing version 1, you can branch to start work on version 2. If you subsequently need to fix bugs or issue a service release (perhaps for new environments) for version 1, you can do so in its branch without having to pull in any version 2 code.

Use branches sparingly. Whenever you branch, you may be creating a future need to merge. The bugs you fix for version 1 probably need to be fixed in version 2 as well. If you have multiple branches, then you will have multiple merges to consider.

What to Version

Versioning is not just for source code. You should version all files associated with compiling, configuring, deploying, testing, and running your system (see Figure 6.19). By default, the tests and most of the configuration files are part of your Visual Studio solution and appear as files to check in when you look at the Check In dialog.

If you expect to maintain your solution for a long time, it is worth creating a "tools" team project in which you keep the versions of the compiler and support programs (for example, *msbuild* and *mstest*) that you use to recreate and retest the solution. For example, commercial software companies may have contracts to support products for ten years, and in many government situations, contracts are longer. It won't take ten years for newer projects to retool, so having a record copy of the build and test environment is valuable.

Automating the Build

Version control is incomplete without an automated build system. The build system needs to automate not only compilation but also the tracking and testing of the binaries against the source versions. The build needs to provide as many quality checks as possible so that any errors can be corrected before investment of further testing. This approach ensures that testing time (especially human time) is used appropriately.

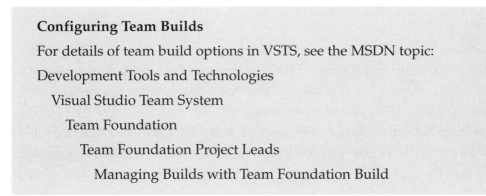

Figure 6.19   "Source control" actually tracks all the files in your workspace, including tests, XML files, icons, and so on. Check in your tests with your source.

In VSTS, you can configure an automated build from the Team Explorer (see Figure 6.20). You can have different named build types, such as a daily build, a continuous integration build, and a branch build, each running separate scripts and tests.

Configuring Team Builds

For details of team build options in VSTS, see the MSDN topic:

Development Tools and Technologies

   Visual Studio Team System

      Team Foundation

         Team Foundation Project Leads

            Managing Builds with Team Foundation Build

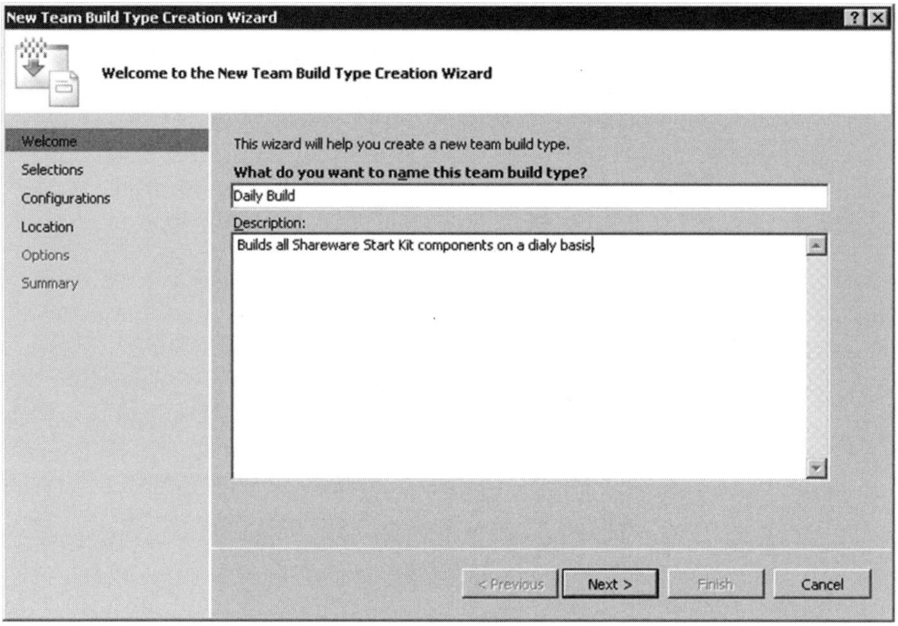

Figure 6.20   VSTS gives you a wizard to create a "team builds," that is, the daily build and other regular builds that you automate for the full solution.

Daily Build

The heartbeat of your project is the daily build. At a minimum, you should have a build configuration for daily builds that not only creates the binaries that you install but also runs all the code analysis and BVTs and generates the metrics that track the health of your project.

Build Report

On completion of the daily build, you get a build report (see Figure 6.21). This shows you the results of build completion, code analysis, and BVT runs. In the case of a failed build, it gives you a link to the work item that was created to notify the appropriate team member to fix and restart the build.

Use the Build Report, as shown in Figure 6.21, to monitor the execution of a build and view the details of a completed build and the work item changes documenting what went into the build. Opening the test result details shows you the BVT results and the code coverage from BVTs. Build warnings include the static code analysis results. In the case of a build failure, a work item will have been automatically created to track the failure, and it is shown here, too. From this report you can publish the build quality status.

Build Nightly_20060119.2

Summary	Successfully Completed
Build name:	Nightly_20060119.2
Team project:	Teamlook
Type:	Nightly
Build machine:	PERSONIF-IHITS3
Started on:	1/19/2006 5:46:35 PM
Completed on:	1/19/2006 5:47:38 PM
Quality:	Unexamined
Work items opened:	Not available
Log:	\\personif-ihits3\tfrobotdrops\Nightly_20060119.2\BuildLog.txt

Build steps Successfully Completed

Build Step	Completed On
Initializing build	1/19/2006 5:46:41 PM
Getting sources	1/19/2006 5:46:43 PM
Compiling sources	1/19/2006 5:46:55 PM
Compiling TeamlookPro.sln for Any CPU/Release	1/19/2006 5:46:55 PM
Compiling Teamlook.csproj	1/19/2006 5:46:49 PM
Compiling SetupHelper.csproj	1/19/2006 5:46:52 PM
Compiling Build Verification Tests.csproj	1/19/2006 5:46:54 PM
Generating list of changesets and updating work items	1/19/2006 5:47:01 PM
Running tests	1/19/2006 5:47:37 PM
Running tests for Any CPU/Release	1/19/2006 5:47:36 PM
Copying binaries to drop location	1/19/2006 5:47:37 PM
Copying log files to drop location	1/19/2006 5:47:37 PM
Successfully Completed	1/19/2006 5:47:37 PM

Result details for Any CPU/Release 0 Errors, 12 warnings, 425/434 tests passed, 31 (Release.txt)

Associated changesets

ID	Checked In By	Comments
31	jperez	Created team project folder $/Teamlook via the Team Project Creation Wizard
32	jperez	Initial Checkin
33	jperez	Added tests
34	jperez	Created via Build Type creation wizard
35	jperez	Created via Build Type creation wizard
36	jperez	Adding PD Trace. Removing Setup Project
37	jperez	Adding Microsoft.TeamFoundation.WorkItemTracking.Controls to the project so that it can build
38	jperez	Checking in a bunch of new unit tests
39	jperez	Fixing bugs and closing out tasks

Associated work items

ID	Title	State
2353	Create Personas	Closed
2473	Create more tests for the Query Managment area	Closed
2474	Work Item type not showing correctly when converting email to Work Item	Resolved
2475	Teamlook seems to hang Outlook on Startup	Resolved
2476	Need new images for Teamlook reports form	Closed
2477	Adding multiple servers to Teamlook causes exception	Resolved

Note: All dates and times are shown in Pacific Standard Time (GMT -08:00:00).
Provided by: Microsoft Visual Studio® 2005 Team System.

Figure 6.21 The Build Report both monitors the real-time execution of a build and aggregates the details of a build on completion.

Note that you can navigate to the changesets that are included, the code analysis warnings, and the test results directly from the build report. The data shown on the build report is fed directly to the metrics warehouse to create historical data for the project.

Build Verification Tests (BVTs)

Every build should go through a consistent series of BVTs, and on many projects, these are the primary regression tests performed. The objectives of the BVTs are to

1. Isolate any errors introduced by check-ins or the build process, including unanticipated integration errors.

2. Determine whether the software is ready for further testing.

BVTs should include all unit tests and component integration tests that are run prior to check-in, plus any other tests that are needed to ensure that it is worth spending time testing the software further. BVTs are automated.

Typically, a tester or designated developer "scouts" a build for the team—that is, he or she installs the software and runs a further series of tests beyond the BVTs, often manually. For example, scenario tests may require using a new GUI that is still rapidly evolving, and automation may not be cost effective yet. For this reason, there is a *Build Quality* field on the report that can be manually set. Its initial value on build completion is *Unexamined*. You can set it after that to *Rejected, Under Investigation, Ready for Initial Test, Lab Test Passed, Initial Test Passed, UAT Passed, Ready for Deployment, Released,* or other values that you have customized.

Continuous Integration

Continuous integration refers to the practice of triggering a build after every check-in.[7] It has been proven very successful in eXtreme Programming and other agile practices in that it delivers immediate feedback on integration errors to a developer who has just checked in. With VSTS, you can set up a build type for continuous integration and trigger the build from check-in events (see Figure 6.22). When you do this, use a separate build type from the daily build so that you still have daily metrics from the daily build.

Making Work Transparent

VSTS applies the same transparency to the developer activities that it does to the work item backlog and the rest of the team activities. It treats all team members as part of one integrated workflow. Because all work items of all types are stored in the common database, when you check in you can (and should) identify the tasks *and the requirements* (for example, scenarios or QoS) that the delivered code and tests implement. This creates a link from those work items that traces their resolution to the corresponding changesets.

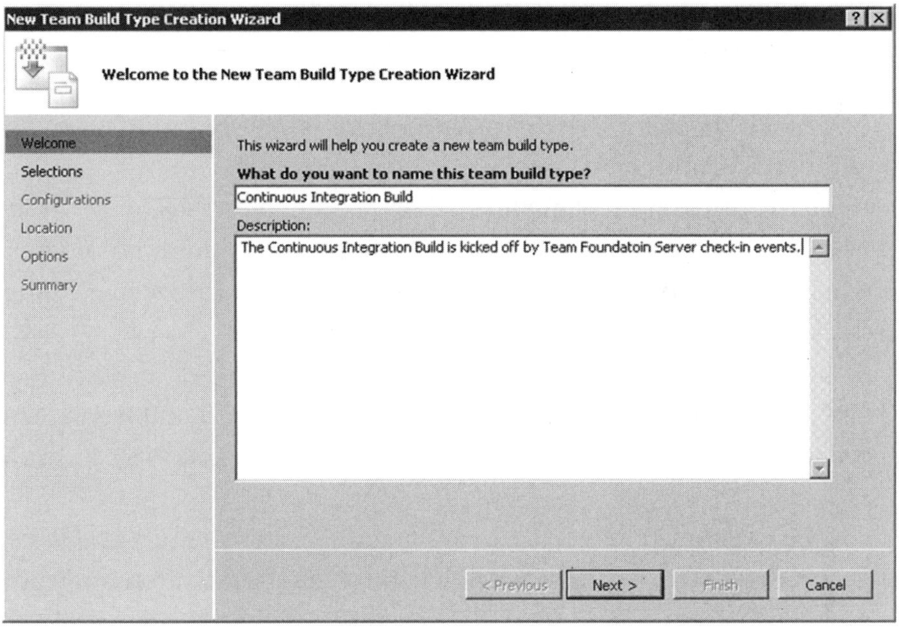

Figure 6.22   Create a separate build type to perform continuous integration. Keeping the daily build as a separate build type will keep metrics tracked to the daily build.

This traceability in turn drives reports such as Remaining Work and Velocity, discussed in Chapter 4. When it is time to estimate the next iteration, you have a daily record available of the current and prior iterations' history. These metrics are collected for you, and they take the guesswork (and grunt work) out of determining the actual baseline trends.

Similarly, this traceability drives the build report so that the whole team (notably testers) can automatically see what work is available in which build with what quality. There's no mystery of "Did feature X make it in?" or "Did it pass BVTs?" The build report provides a reliable, friction-free view to trigger the testing cycle based on accepted builds.

Summary

A value-up approach development is all about delivering working code of customer-ready quality. In this chapter, I described the major impediments to that delivery and how VSTS addresses them.

The first issue is dealing with requirements that may be inadequate or hard to understand. VSTS supports Test-Driven Development as a practice to force clarification of requirements before you begin implementation. The testing support directly inside VSTS makes it easy to create and run unit tests and to promote these for reuse with every build.

Second is the consideration of qualities of service and the check for programming errors that might not be caught in unit testing. VSTS supports automated code reviews with its static code analysis. Workflow for manual reviews is supported through shelving, a feature of VSTS version control.

Third is the issue of direct feedback from tests and the need to see code execution and performance as a part of testing. VSTS lets you extend unit testing with test data and configurations and supports direct performance profiling from the test runs.

Fourth is the complexity of version control and the tracking of as-built software to the source code. VSTS integrates version control and build automation and provides an audit trail of source and work item changes going into every build. Check-in policies work as reminders to support hygienic practices for the team.

The last issue is the difficulty of keeping track of all the information sources. VSTS supports transparency of the process with its common work item database and metrics warehouse and with the integration of code and test changes with work items and the build system. In this way, VSTS lets you as a developer focus on the substance of the work, not the ceremony.

The next chapter looks at the extended testing process and its contribution to value-up development.

Endnotes

1. http://www.agilemanifesto.org/

2. Barry W. Boehm, *Software Engineering Economics* (Englewood Cliffs, NJ: Prentice Hall, 1981).

3. For example, K. Beck and E. Gamma, "Test infected: Programmers love writing tests," *Java Report*, 3(7):51–56, 1998.

4. Glenford J. Myers, *The Art of Software Testing* (New York: John Wiley & Sons, 1979).

5. For example, http://www.testing.com/writings/short-catalog.pdf.

6. Brian Marick, "Faults of Omission," first published in *Software Testing and Quality Engineering Magazine*, January 2000, available from http://www.testing.com/writings/omissions.html.

7. For example, http://www.martinfowler.com/articles/continuousIntegration.html.

7

Testing

Tester
Test Manager

"Lesson 1: You are the headlights of the project.
A project is like a road trip. Some projects are simple and routine, like driving
to the store in broad daylight. But most projects worth doing are more like
driving a truck off-road, in the mountains, at night. Those projects need head-
lights. As the tester, you light the way. You illuminate the road ahead so that
the programmers and managers, however they bicker over the map, can at least
see where they are, what they're about to run over, and how close they are to
the cliff. The detailed mission of the testing group varies from company to
company. Behind those details, though, is a common factor. Testing is done to
find information. Critical decisions about the project or the product are made
on the basis of that information."[1]

—Cem Kaner, James Bach, and Bret Pettichord,
Lessons Learned in Software Testing

Figure 7.1   Thinking of testing as the headlights of a project can keep your activities focused on providing useful information.

For any professional software application, there are an infinite number of possible
tests. Accordingly, most software development and IT organizations devote a significant amount of their budget to testing, whether done in-house or outsourced. Yet
surprisingly, most test managers and project managers express much frustration at
their inability to answer fairly basic questions about the effectiveness of their testing.

Similarly to earlier chapters, I start with a couple pages on the value-up tenets of
the discipline, in this case, testing. The rest of the chapter drills into those frustrating basic questions and illustrates how VSTS helps you answer them.

A Value-Up View of Testing

Probably no discipline acts as more of a lightning rod for confused discussions of
software process paradigms than testing. A great many books discuss testing in isolation and assume a work-down paradigm.[2] The negative effect of these works has
been so great that in early days of the Agile movement, it was unclear whether there

was a role for testing at all because developers were responsible for their own unit testing.[3] Lots of confusion remains.

The first source of confusion is that testing activities have two purposes:

- **To support development activities.** In MSF, these tests belong to the development role, and I described them in the previous chapter. I'm not going to repeat them here.

- **To assess customer value.** In MSF, this is the responsibility of testers, and it is the subject of this chapter.

The next source of confusion concerns the appropriate output of testing activity. Before continuing to describe value-up testing, indulge me in a small exercise that brings some of this confusion to light.

What Makes a Good Tester?

Consider this exercise.[4] Caliban and Ariel are testers on a project. They work independently. It is close to the release date. Their project has five subsystems, all equally important, and all bugs that they might find are of equal priority. (Of course, this oversimplification never happens, but for the exercise, please suspend disbelief.)

Prospero, their project manager, is reviewing the state of the project. He sees that Caliban reported 100 bugs, and Ariel reported 74. Then, Prospero decides to look at the breakdown of their bug reports (see Table 7.1).

Table 7.1   Caliban's and Ariel's Found Bug Counts

	Caliban	Ariel
Subsystem 1	100	50
Subsystem 2	0	6
Subsystem 3	0	6
Subsystem 4	0	6
Subsystem 5	0	6
Total	**100**	**74**

Here's what he sees: Caliban has found 100 bugs in one component and none in the others. Ariel has found some in all components. Prospero asks the two testers to explain their work.

> **Caliban:** I have tested Subsystem 1 very thoroughly, and we believe we've found almost all of the priority 1 bugs. Unfortunately, I didn't have time to spend on the remaining five subsystems.

> **Ariel:** I've tested all subsystems in moderate depth. Subsystem 1 is still very buggy. The other subsystems are about 1/10th as buggy, though I'm sure bugs remain.

Now consider whose information is more useful. Many professional testers believe that the only role of testing is to find bugs, and that the more bugs found, regardless of context, the better the testing. Where organizations ferociously track bug rate curves, this assumption can be reinforced. Caliban behaves perfectly for such a situation. He focused on the buggiest component and reported the highest number of bugs. On the other hand, he only reported 20 percent of the information that Ariel reported.

Prospero, on the other hand, must decide whether it would be better to hold on to the solution for more work or to ship it now. If more work is needed, where should the investment be made? Prospero can make much more informed decisions from Ariel's work than from Caliban's, even though she found far fewer bugs. Indeed, Prospero might decide based on Ariel's investigation to scrap Subsystem 1 and replace it. In that case, 20 percent of her work will need to redone, whereas all of Caliban's work will be thrown away.

Ariel also follows some useful tenets that are captured in three great value-up heuristics:[5]

1. **Important problems fast.** Testing should be optimized to find important problems fast rather than attempting to find all problems with equal urgency.

2. **Focus on risk.** Test strategy should focus most effort on areas of potential technical risk while still putting some effort into low-risk areas just in case the risk analysis is wrong.

3. **Maximize diversity.** Test strategy should be diversified in terms of test techniques and perspectives. Methods of evaluating test coverage should take into account multiple dimensions of coverage,

including structural, functional, data, platform, operations, and requirements.

In a value-up view of testing, Ariel's work is far more useful. Ariel and Caliban work to optimize different values—information versus bug counts—because they were working toward different missions. (Of course, in a work-down paradigm, Caliban might be considered more productive.) Like the opening quote of this chapter, Ariel's informational approach acts as "the headlights of the project."

Basic Questions

What is the information you need to assess customer value? It comes down to some pretty basic questions:

- Are we delivering the customer value?
- Are the qualities of service, such as performance and security, fit for use?
- Have we tested the changes?
- What haven't we tested?
- Does it work in production as well as in the lab?
- Are we testing enough?
- When should we be running the tests?
- Which tests should be automated?
- How efficient is our team, or our outsourced team?

These are fundamental questions that members of a well-run project should be able to answer, and they are a good way to think of the testing that you do. In the rest of this chapter, I'll show how VSTS helps with the answers.

Are We Delivering the Customer Value?

As discussed in Chapter 3, "Requirements," scenarios are a primary statement of customer value. Good scenario testing requires putting yourself in the role of customer advocate. This means testing well beyond the stated scenario requirements. Cem Kaner has a good checklist to put you in the right mindset:[6]

Designing scenario tests is much like doing a requirements analysis, but is not requirements analysis. They rely on similar information but use it differently.

- The requirements analyst tries to foster agreement about the system to be built. The tester exploits disagreements to predict problems with the system.
- The tester doesn't have to reach conclusions or make recommendations about how the solution should work. Her task is to expose credible concerns to the stakeholders.
- The tester doesn't have to make the solution design tradeoffs. She exposes the consequences of those tradeoffs, especially unanticipated or more serious consequences than expected.
- The tester doesn't have to respect prior agreements. (Caution: testers who belabor the wrong issues lose credibility.)
- The scenario tester's work need not be exhaustive, just useful.

Scenario tests need to represent the primary business flows you expect to cover 80% of the software's usage. Typically, they use broad data sets, representing a realistic mix of business cases that you expect your solution to handle.

As much as testing should cover identified requirements, such as known scenarios, good testing also discovers new ones. A value-up tenet is that your knowledge grows throughout the project, often emerging from use and discovery. Do not hesitate to recognize and capture the new scenarios that you find in planning and executing tests.

Scenario tests can be manual or automated. If you have experienced testers who can play customer advocates, you may want to document the manual tests only to the extent of customer goals and appropriate data. In this case, you do not need to enumerate manual tests step by step, but can provide a more general test ideas list. On the other hand, if you delegate manual test execution to people who do not understand the customer well, you may need to document the steps in detail (see Figure 7.2).

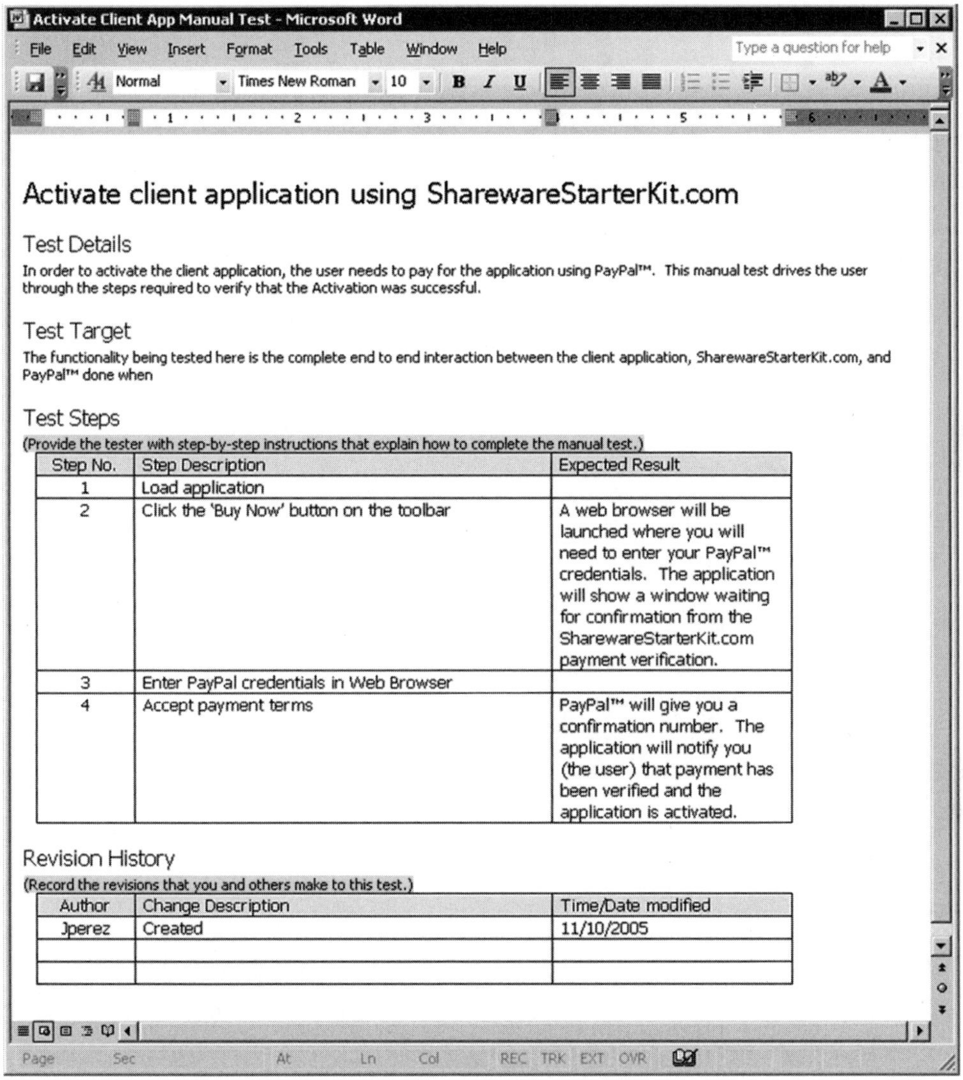

Activate Client App Manual Test - Microsoft Word

File   Edit   View   Insert   Format   Tools   Table   Window   Help   Type a question for help   ▾ ×

Normal   ▾   Times New Roman   ▾   10   ▾   **B**   *I*   U   ▐▀ ▀ ▀ ▀ ▐ ▐ ▐ ▐ ▐ ▐ ▐ ▐ · **A** ·

Activate client application using SharewareStarterKit.com

Test Details

In order to activate the client application, the user needs to pay for the application using PayPal™. This manual test drives the user through the steps required to verify that the Activation was successful.

Test Target

The functionality being tested here is the complete end to end interaction between the client application, SharewareStarterKit.com, and PayPal™ done when

Test Steps

(Provide the tester with step-by-step instructions that explain how to complete the manual test.)

Step No.	Step Description	Expected Result
1	Load application	
2	Click the 'Buy Now' button on the toolbar	A web browser will be launched where you will need to enter your PayPal™ credentials. The application will show a window waiting for confirmation from the SharewareStarterKit.com payment verification.
3	Enter PayPal credentials in Web Browser	
4	Accept payment terms	PayPal™ will give you a confirmation number. The application will notify you (the user) that payment has been verified and the application is activated.

Revision History

(Record the revisions that you and others make to this test.)

Author	Change Description	Time/Date modified
Jperez	Created	11/10/2005

Page   Sec   At   Ln   Col   REC   TRK   EXT   OVR

Figure 7.2   In VSTS, you can describe manual tests in documents like this. The test results are captured, tracked, and fed to the warehouse in the same manner as automated tests.

Create a Test Project to Get Started

To get started with testing in VSTS, you will need to create a test project. See the MSDN topic:

Development Tools and Technologies

    Visual Studio Team System

        Team Edition for Testers

            Getting Started with Team System Testing Tools

            How to: Create a Test Project

Create a Manual Test

To create a manual test in VSTS, see the MSDN topic:

Development Tools and Technologies

    Visual Studio Team System

        Team Edition for Testers

            Testing Tools Tasks

            Creating and Editing Tests

                How to: Create a Manual Test

Automated Scenario Tests

The primary way to automate scenario tests in VSTS is as *web tests* (see Figure 7.3). These test any application that presents itself through a web browser. Whether you create web tests by recording or programming, you can enhance and maintain them in Visual Basic or C#.

Although web tests are created by recording, they are not dependent on the browser UI for running because they exercise the software under test where it counts—at the server level. During playback, you can see both the browser interaction and the HTTP or HTTPS traffic (see Figure 7.4).

Figure 7.3   When you add a web test in VSTS, you drive the scenario as a user would—through an instrumented web browser. This captures the interaction not just at the GUI level but also at the HTTP protocol level and produces a parameterized test.

Create a Web Test

To create a web test in VSTS, see the MSDN topic:

Development Tools and Technologies

   Visual Studio Team System

      Team Edition for Testers

         Testing Tools Tasks

            Creating and Editing Tests

               How to: Record a Web Test

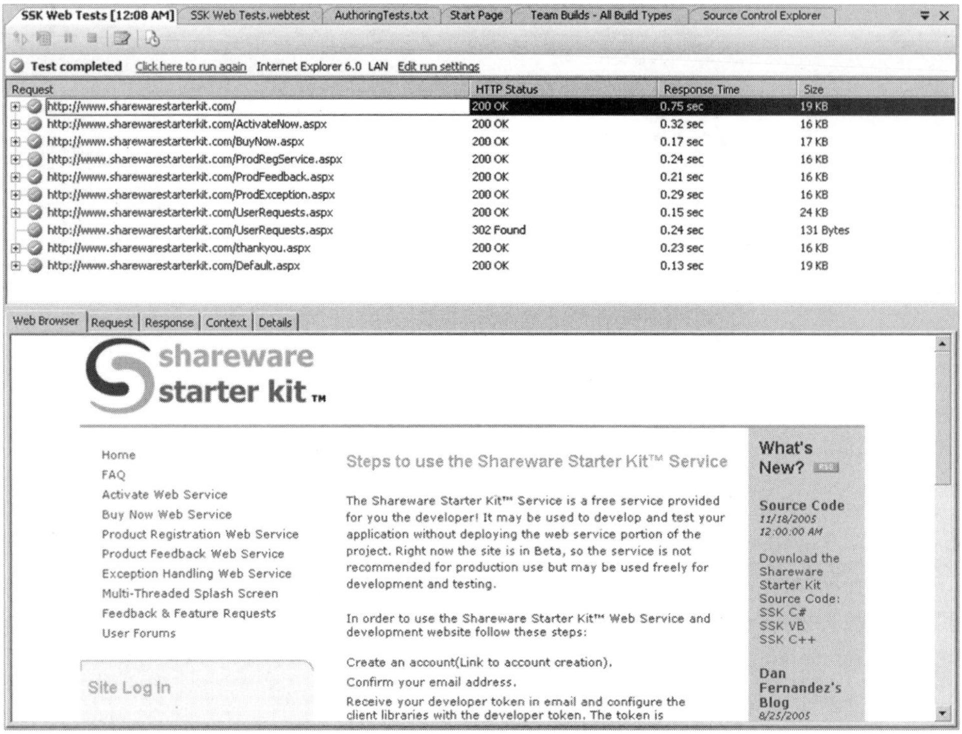

Figure 7.4   The playback of the test shows you both what was rendered in the browser and what happened in the HTTP stream so that you can watch the full server interaction, including the invisible parts of the traffic.

Using Test Data

Varying test data to represent a mix of realistic inputs is an important part of scenario testing (see Figure 7.5). Seeing a test pass for one data set does not mean it will pass for all, especially when you've paid careful attention in designing your equivalence classes. Accordingly, you can have your web tests access external test data from any OLEDB data source, including .csv files, Excel, Access, and SQL Server databases.

Because web tests are easy to create, they are also easy to *re*create when a scenario changes.

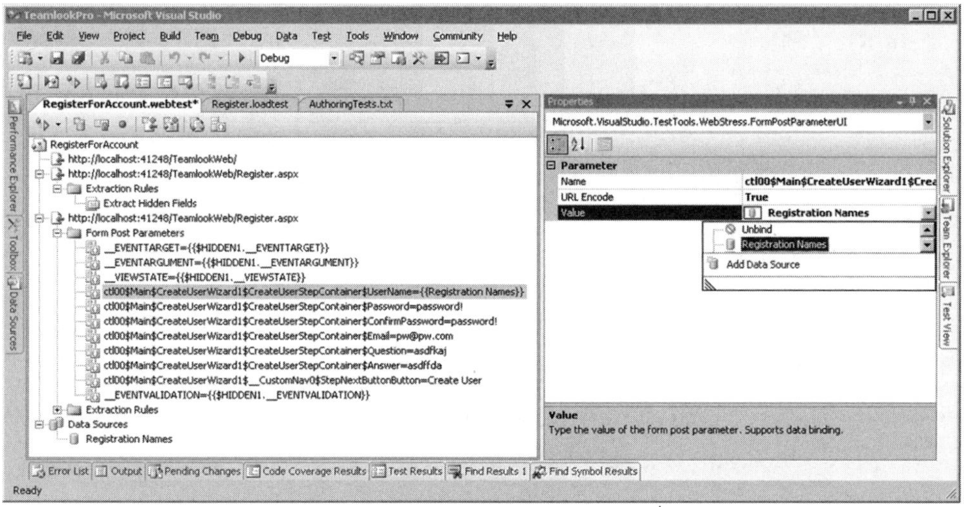

Figure 7.5   In almost all cases, you should vary the data used for testing either to cover different combinations based on different equivalence classes or to apply unique values for each transaction present in a multiuser workload.

Data Substitution for Web Tests

To set up data substitution for web tests, see the MSDN topic:

Development Tools and Technologies

   Visual Studio Team System

    Team Edition for Testers

     Testing Tools Tasks

      Test Types

       Working with Web Tests

        Data Binding in Web Tests

Testing Rich Clients

You can record tests in VSTS from the UI of web applications but not rich client applications. Several partners companies, such as Compuware, provide products that plug into VSTS for rich-client test automation. See http://msdn.microsoft.com/vstudio/teamsystem/downloads/partners/default.aspx for a current list.

Insulating Your Tests from UI Changes

There's an old joke about Mr. Smith kneeling on a deserted sidewalk at night under a street lamp. A policeman comes by and asks if there's a problem.

Mr. Smith: I lost my car keys.

Policeman: Where did you lose them?

Mr. Smith: Around the corner in the parking lot, near my car.

Policeman: Then why are you looking here?

Mr. Smith: Because it's dark there and the light's so much better over here!

Most software is tested through the user interface, and the "light" is indeed brightest there. However, in modern distributed architectures, most of the program's logic is actually implemented on a server, and the user interface is a thin veneer on top of that logic. Accordingly, most of the potential failures are on the server side. The UI is also likely to change considerably based on usability testing and other customer feedback. You don't want those changes to break the tests, or worse, you don't want to use the test maintenance cost as a reason not to improve the UI.

If you limit your tests to user interface tests, you almost certainly must rewrite over the course of the project as the UI changes. Fortunately, VSTS web tests exercise server-side APIs (see Figure 7.6). They can be turned into C# or Visual Basic programs that enable you to maintain the tests independent of the UI changes. Of course, the test data that they use is already separately bound and maintained.

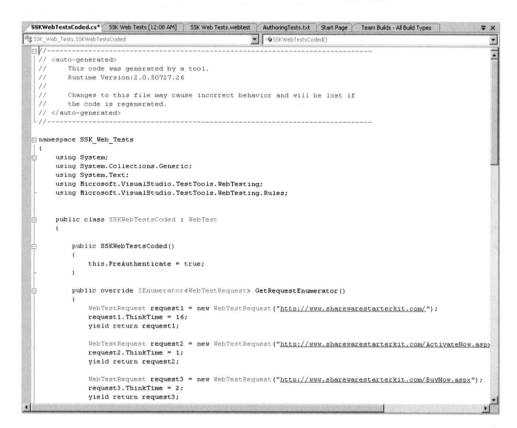

Figure 7.6   An alternate view of the test shown in Figure 7.3 as generated code. Note that the test code is really driving a set of server interactions, not clicking in the user interface.

Are the Qualities of Service Fit for Use?

As discussed in Chapter 3, qualities of service (QoS) are captured in the work item database. Tests specialize according to the different qualities of service. For example, load tests, configuration tests, security tests, and usability tests are all radically different.

Load Testing

Load testing aims to answer two primary questions:

1. **Does the software respond appropriately under expected load conditions?** To answer this, you compose performance tests that combine reasonable scenario tests, data, and workloads.

2. **Under what stress conditions does the software stop responding well?** For this, you take the same scenarios and data and crank up the workload progressively, watching the corresponding effect on performance and system indicators.

All the automated tests managed by VSTS—web tests, unit tests, and any additional test types you create—can be used for load testing (see Figures 7.7 through 7.10). With VSTS, you can model the workload to represent a realistic mix of users, each running different tests. Finally, VSTS automatically collects diagnostic data from the servers under test to highlight problems for you.

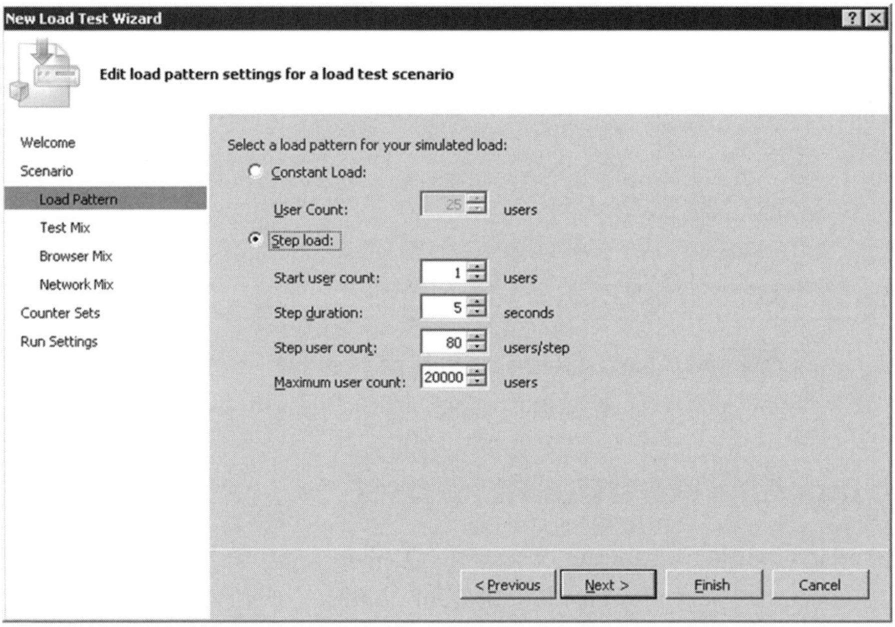

Figure 7.7   In VSTS, a load test is a container for any arbitrary set of tests with workload settings. First, you choose how to ramp the load. Often you want to observe the system with gradually increasing user load so that you can spot any "hockey stick" effect in the response time as the user load increases.

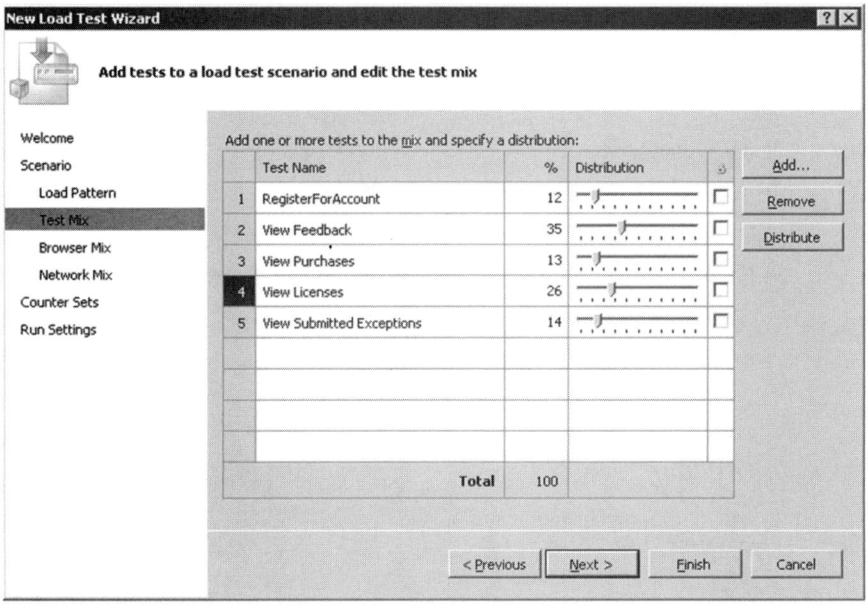

Figure 7.8
Next, you choose
the tests (unit,
web, or other)
and the percentage
of load to create
from each of the
atomic tests.

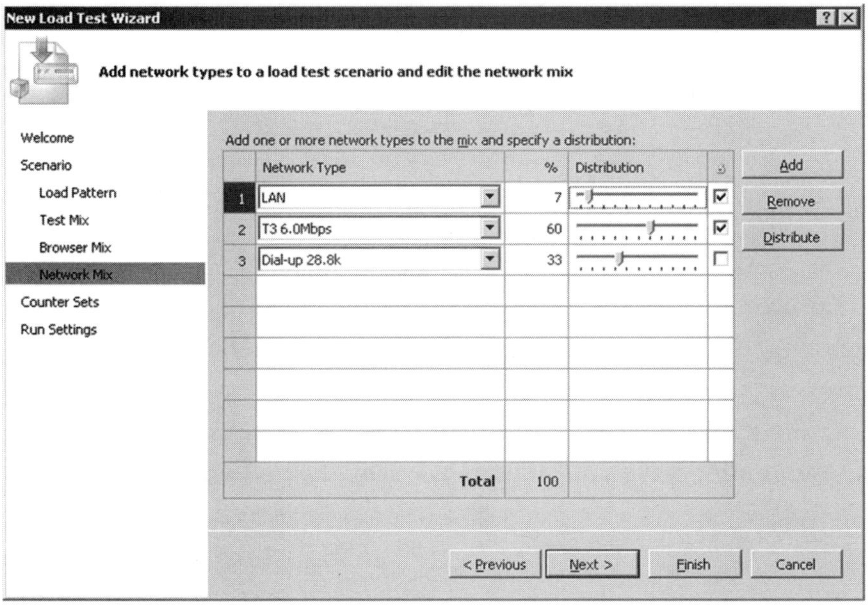

Figure 7.9
The next steps
are to choose the
browser and
network mixes
that best reflect
your end-user
population.

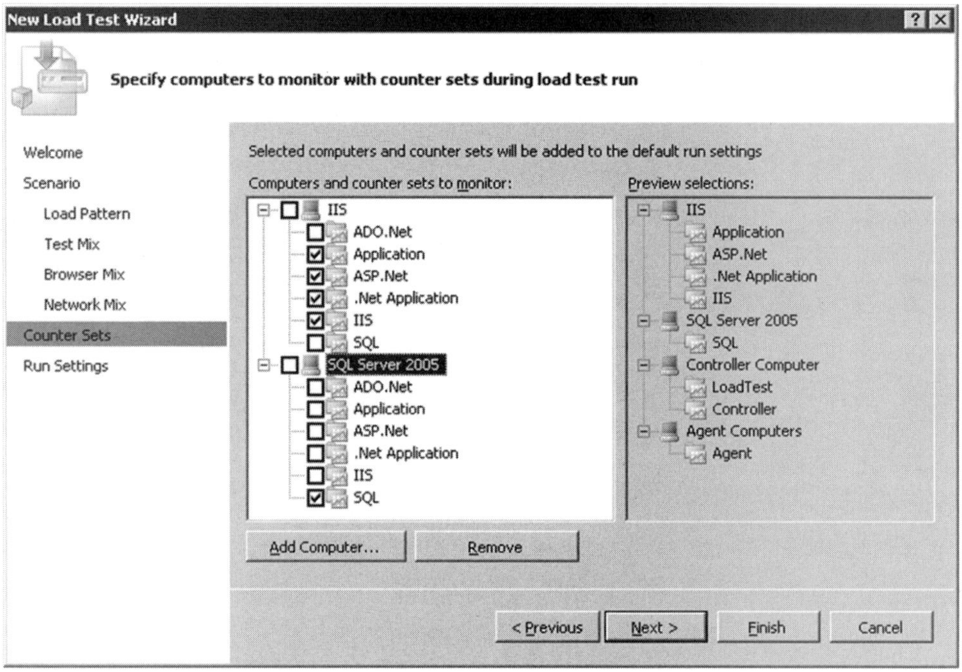

Figure 7.10   Load tests can generate huge amounts of data from the servers under test, and it's often hard to know what's relevant. VSTS simplifies this by asking you to choose only which services to watch on which machines and automating the rest of the decisions.

Understanding the Output

While a load test runs, and after it completes, you need to look at two levels of data (see Figure 7.11). *Average response time* shows you the end-to-end response time for a page to finish loading, exactly as a user would experience it. That's straightforward, and you can assess whether the range is within acceptable limits. At the same time, while the test runs, all the relevant performance data is collected from the chosen servers, and these counters give you clues as to where the bottlenecks are in the running system.

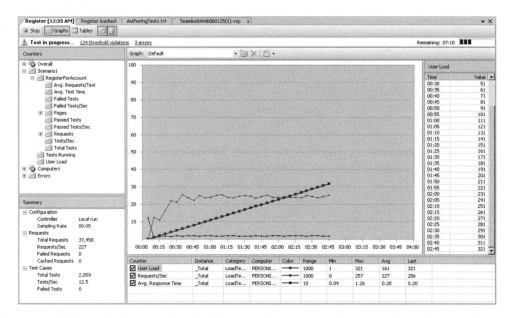

Counter	Instance	Category	Computer	Color	Range	Min	Max	Avg	Last
☑ User Load	_Total	LoadTe...	PERSONI...	—■—	1000	1	321	161	321
☑ Requests/Sec	_Total	LoadTe...	PERSONI...	—●—	1000	0	257	227	256
☑ Avg. Response Time	_Total	LoadTe...	PERSONI...	—■—	10	0.09	1.26	0.20	0.20

Figure 7.11 This graph shows two kinds of data together. *Average Response Time* is the page load time as a user would experience it. *Requests/Sec* is a measurement of the server under test, indicating a cause of the slowdown. Note additionally the warning and error icons that flag problems among the tree of counters in the upper left. Some of these may lead you to configuration problems that can be tuned in the server settings; others may point to application errors that need to be fixed in code.

Diagnosing

When a load test points to a likely application performance problem, the developer of the suspect code is usually the best person to diagnose the problem. As a tester, you can attach the test result to a bug directly to forward it to an appropriate teammate, and when your teammate opens the bug, the same graphs will be available for viewing. He or she can then use the Performance Wizard to instrument the application and rerun the test that you ran, as shown in Figure 7.12.

The profiling report can rank the actual suspect functions and lead you straight to the code that may need optimizing. This sequence of load testing to profiling is a very efficient way to determine how to tune an application. You can use it in any iteration as soon as enough of the system is available to drive under load.

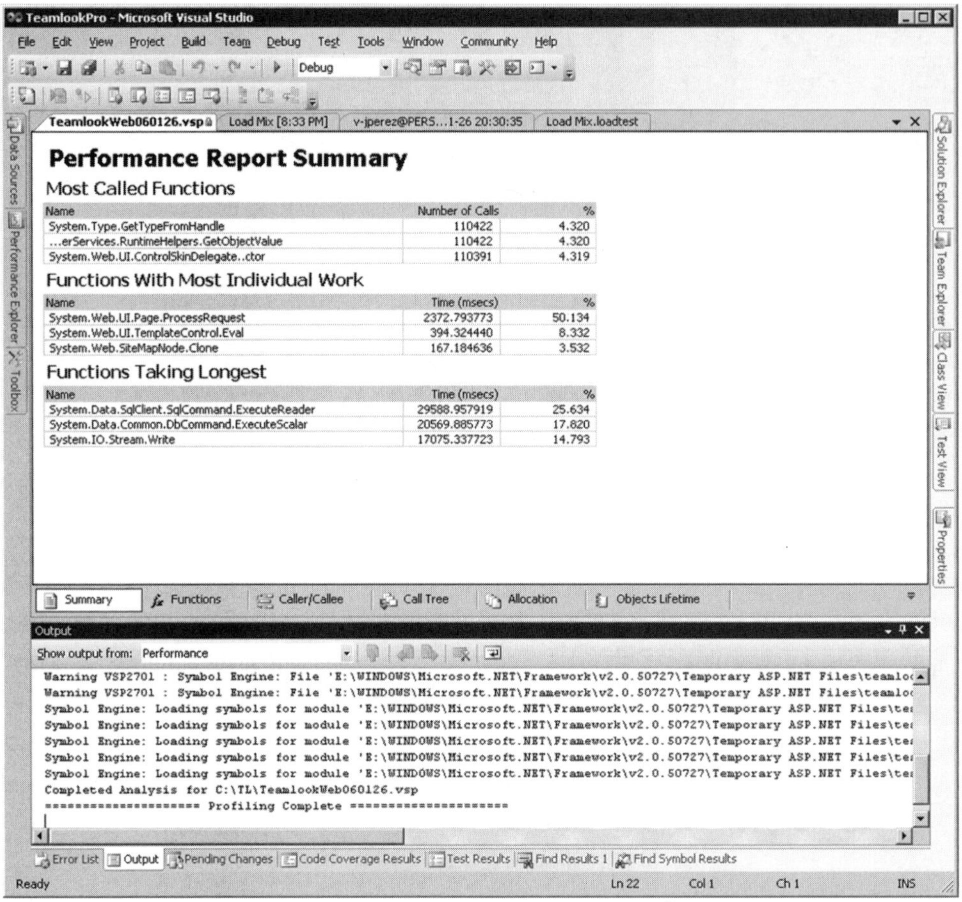

Figure 7.12   In addition to the information offered by the perfmon counters, you can rerun the test
with profiling (or attach the test result to a bug and have a colleague open it and rerun
with profiling). This takes you from the system view to the code view of the application
and lets you drill into the specific methods and call sequences that may be involved during the slowdown.

Security Testing

Security testing is a specialized type of negative testing. In security testing, you are trying to prove that the software under test is vulnerable to attack in ways that it should
not be. The essence of security testing is to use a fault model, based on vulnerabilities
observed on other systems, and a series of attacks to exploit the vulnerabilities.

There are many published attack patterns that can identify the vast majority of vulnerabilities.[7] Many companies provide penetration testing services, and many community tools are available to facilitate security testing. You can drive the tools from VSTS test suites, but they are not delivered as part of the VSTS product itself.

> **Testing for Security Violations**
>
> The only checks for security in VSTS are in the code analysis described in the previous chapter, but partners such as SPIDynamics offer solutions that plug into the test framework. See http://msdn.microsoft.com/vstudio/ teamsystem/downloads/partners/default.aspx for a current list.

Usability Testing

In Chapter 3, I discussed usability testing as part of the requirements process, so I won't repeat it here. It is equally relevant, of course, throughout the lifecycle.

Have We Tested the Changes?

Throughout the lifecycle, the application changes. *Regressions* are bugs in the software under test that did not appear in previous versions. *Regression testing* is the term for testing a new version of the software to find those bugs. Almost all types of tests can be used as regression tests, but in keeping with the tenet of "Important problems fast," your regression testing strategy must be very efficient.

Ideally, you should test the most recent changes first. Not only does this mitigate the risk of unforeseen side effects of the changes, but also if you do find bugs and report them, the more recent changes are more current in everyone's memory.

One of the challenges in most test teams is identifying what exactly the changes are. Fortunately, the daily build report shows you exactly what changesets have made it into the build and what work items (scenarios, QoS, tasks, and bugs) have been resolved, thereby identifying the functionality that should be tested first (see Figure 7.13). Moreover, if you have reasonable build verification tests (BVTs), then you can check their results and code coverage.

Nightly_20060119.2				▾ ✕
(i) Last refreshed on 1/24/2006 10:52:27 PM.				

⊞ Summary — ◔ Successfully Completed
⊞ Build steps — ◔ Successfully Completed
⊞ Result details for Any CPU/Release — ⚠ 0 error(s), 12 warning(s), 1289 test(s) total, 10 passed, 676 failed
⊟ Associated changesets — 9 associated changesets

ID	Checked In By	Comments
31	REDMOND\v-jperez	Created team project folder $/Teamlook via the Team Project Creation Wizard
32	REDMOND\v-jperez	Initial Checkin
33	REDMOND\v-jperez	Added tests
34	REDMOND\v-jperez	Created via Build Type creation wizard
35	REDMOND\v-jperez	Created via Build Type creation wizard
36	REDMOND\v-jperez	Adding PD Trace. Removing Setup Project
37	REDMOND\v-jperez	Adding Microsoft.TeamFoundation.WorkItemTracking.Controls to the project so that it can build
38	REDMOND\v-jperez	Checking in a bunch of new unit tests
39	REDMOND\v-jperez	Fixing bugs and closing out tasks

⊟ Associated work items — 6 associated work items

ID	Title	State	Assigned To
2353	Create Personas	Closed	Juan Perez (Personify …
2473	Create more tests for the Query Managment area	Closed	Ted Hardy (ALT)
2474	Work Item type not showing correctly when converting email to Work Item	Resolved	Juan Perez (Personify …
2475	Teamlook seems to hang Outlook on Startup	Resolved	Juan Perez (Personify …
2476	Need new images for Teamlook reports form	Closed	Ted Hardy (ALT)
2477	Adding multiple servers to Teamlook causes exception	Resolved	Juan Perez (Personify …

Figure 7.13   One of the many purposes of the daily build report is to focus testing activity on the newly built functionality. This list of work items resolved in the build is like an automatic release note, showing what new functionality needs to be tested.

What Haven't We Tested?

Identifying gaps in testing involves looking at the test results from multiple dimensions:

- **Requirements.** Have the tests demonstrated that the intended functionality was implemented?
- **Code.** What code has been exercised during testing?
- **Risks.** What blind spots might we need to guard against? What events do we need to be prepared for?

Requirements

One view of coverage in VSTS is the results of tests against requirements such as scenarios or QoS (see Figure 7.14). Tests and their results can be tracked to these specific work items.

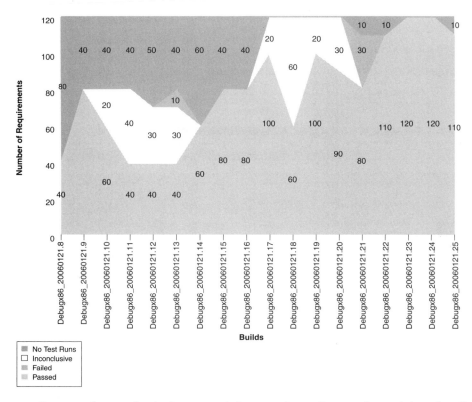

Figure 7.14 One way of measuring test coverage is by scenario or other requirement, based on the useful discipline of clearly identifying the scenario that a test tests. The aggregation is, by requirement, showing how many requirements are in which state of testing.

Tracking Tests Against Requirements

The Requirements Test History report shown in Figure 7.14 is standard in the MSF for CMMI Process Improvement but not in MSF for Agile Software Development. The requirement associated with a test case is captured in the Test Case Properties window.

Code

A second view of coverage is against source code (see Figure 7.15). This is just a second, orthogonal measure that can be taken from the same test runs that demonstrate the testing against requirements shown in Figure 7.14.

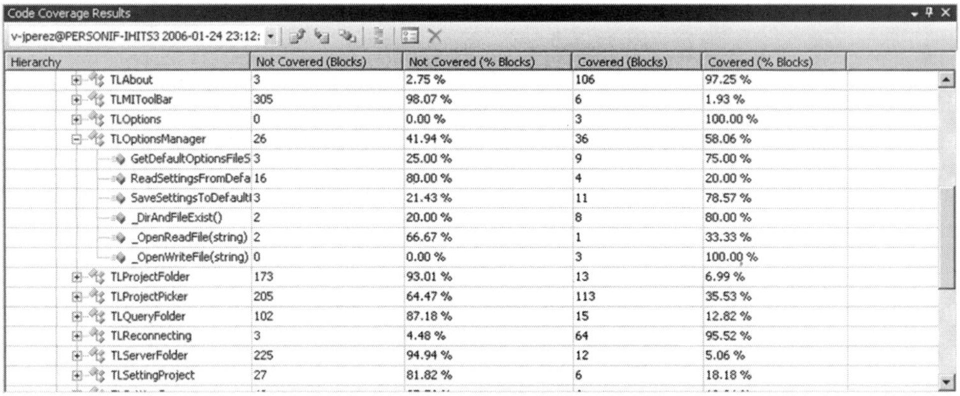

Hierarchy	Not Covered (Blocks)	Not Covered (% Blocks)	Covered (Blocks)	Covered (% Blocks)
TLAbout	3	2.75 %	106	97.25 %
TLMIToolBar	305	98.07 %	6	1.93 %
TLOptions	0	0.00 %	3	100.00 %
TLOptionsManager	26	41.94 %	36	58.06 %
GetDefaultOptionsFileS	3	25.00 %	9	75.00 %
ReadSettingsFromDefa	16	80.00 %	4	20.00 %
SaveSettingsToDefaultI	3	21.43 %	11	78.57 %
_DirAndFileExist()	2	20.00 %	8	80.00 %
_OpenReadFile(string)	2	66.67 %	1	33.33 %
_OpenWriteFile(string)	0	0.00 %	3	100.00 %
TLProjectFolder	173	93.01 %	13	6.99 %
TLProjectPicker	205	64.47 %	113	35.53 %
TLQueryFolder	102	87.18 %	15	12.82 %
TLReconnecting	3	4.48 %	64	95.52 %
TLServerFolder	225	94.94 %	12	5.06 %
TLSettingProject	27	81.82 %	6	18.18 %

Code Coverage Results
v-jperez@PERSONIF-IHITS3 2006-01-24 23:12:

Figure 7.15   Code coverage is the second main meaning of "coverage." Here you see the test results viewer expanded to show the coverage statistics against the source code.

From this view, you can also paint the source code under test to see exactly which lines were and were not exercised, as shown previously in Figure 6.9.

Tracking Code Coverage from Testing

Code coverage settings in VSTS are specified in the test run configuration. Whenever you choose to collect code coverage as part of the test run configuration, you see the coverage statistics at the end of the test run. To promote the test results and the coverage results to the metrics warehouse, you need to "Publish" the test results from the Test Results Viewer. BVT results are published automatically, but for other runs you choose whether to accumulate the metrics.

As discussed in Chapter 4, "Project Management," use these metrics descriptively, not prescriptively. Coverage metrics against code and requirements are very useful, but they are only two dimensions. Do not let coverage statistics lull you into a false sense of confidence. "100% coverage" merely means that this metric does not reveal any more gaps. It does not tell you anything about the extent to which you have tested conditions for which no code or no requirements have been written. Indeed, the fastest way to increase a code coverage measure is usually to remove error-handling source code, which is probably the last behavior you want to encourage.

Assume that there are gaps in more dimensions that these coverage measures don't reveal.

Risks

In Chapter 2, "Value-Up Processes," I described the MSF views of constituency-based and event-driven risk management. Both sets of risk need to be considered for testing.

Most risk testing is negative testing, that is, "tests aimed at showing that the software does not work."[8] These tests attempt to do things that should not be possible to do, such as spending money beyond a credit limit, revealing someone else's credit card number, or raising an airplane's landing gear before takeoff.

Note that coverage testing does *not* provide any clue about the amount of negative testing that has been done, and requirements-based coverage helps only to the extent that QoS requirements capture error prevention, which is usually at much too cursory a level. In testing for risks, you are typically looking for errors of omission, such as an unwritten error handler (no code to cover) or an implicit (and hence untraceable) requirement.

To design effective negative tests, you need a good idea of what could go wrong. This is sometimes called a "fault model." You can derive your fault model from any number of knowledge sources. Example sources of a fault model illustrating constituency-based knowledge are listed in Table 7.2.

Table 7.2   Typical Sources and Examples for a Fault Model

Source	Sample Fault to Test For
Business Rules	Customers can't spend over their credit limits.
Technical Architecture	The authentication server could be down.
Domain Knowledge	This spending pattern, although legal, could indicate a stolen credit card.
User Understanding	If there's no rapid confirmation, a user could push the Submit button many times.
Bug Databases	Under this pattern of usage, the server times out.

VSTS lets you capture these potential faults in the work item database as risks. Typically, you would start during early test planning, and you would review and update the risk list in planning every iteration and probably more frequently. The same traceability that tracks test cases to scenario work items enables you to trace tests to risk work items so that you can report on testing against risks in the same way (see Figures 7.16 and 7.17).

Figure 7.16   Risks are captured as work items so that they can be managed in the same backlog, tracked to test cases, and reported in the same way as other work item types.

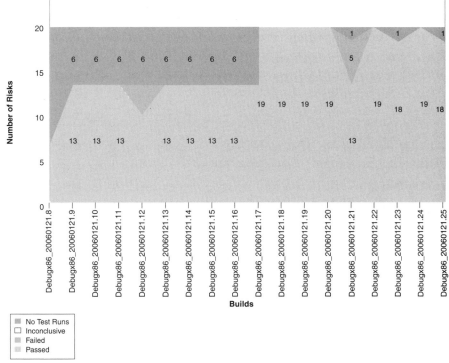

Figure 7.17   Because risks are a type of work item, you can measure test coverage against risks in a manner similar to the coverage against scenarios.

Does It Work in Production as Well as in the Lab?

Have you ever filed a bug and heard the response, "But it works on my machine"? Or have you ever heard the datacenter complain about the cost of staging because the software as tested never works without reconfiguration for the production environment?

These are symptoms of inadequate configuration testing. Configuration testing is critical in three cases:

1. Datacenters lock down their servers with very specific settings and often have a defined number of managed configurations. It's essential that the settings of the test environment match the datacenter environment in all applicable ways.

2. Software vendors and other organizations that cannot precisely control customers' configurations need to be able to validate their software across the breadth of configurations that will actually be used.

3. Software that is used internationally will encounter different operating system settings in different countries, including different character sets, hardware, and input methods, which will require specific testing.

Fortunately, VSTS supports explicit configuration testing in two ways: by enabling you to set up test labs with virtual machines and by explicitly tracking *test run configurations* and recording all test results against them.

Test Lab Setup

When you have combinations to test, cycling test lab machines among them can be a huge drain on time. Normally, you must clean each machine after a previous installation by restoring it to the base operating system, install the components, and then configure them. If you are rotating many configurations, this preparation time can dwarf the actual time available for testing.

An alternative is to set up the configurations on "virtual machines" using Microsoft Virtual Server, included in VSTS (see Figure 7.18). Rather than installing and configuring physical machines, you install and configure a virtual machine. When the virtual machine is running, it appears to the software and network to be identical to a physical machine, but you can save the entire machine image as a disk file and reload it on command.

Setting up a library of virtual machines means that you will go through the setup and configuration time once, not with every test cycle.

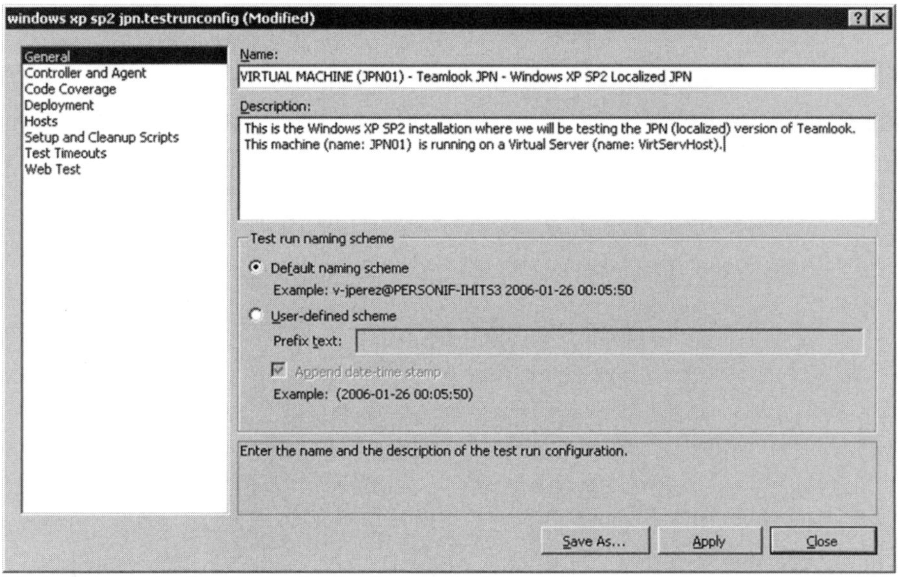

Figure 7.18 Your solution may need to run in different target environments. These might be different localized versions of the OS, different versions of supporting components, such as databases and web servers, or different configurations of your solution. Virtual machines are a low-overhead way of capturing the environments in software so that you can run tests in a self-contained image for the specified configuration.

Reporting

The other major issue with testing configurations is tracking and reporting what has been tested so that you can identify gaps in configuration coverage and prioritize your next testing appropriately. Fortunately, VSTS tracks the configuration used on every test run (see Figure 7.19). Reports make it easy to track the configurations that have been used and those that lack good test coverage.

It's usually a good idea to vary the configurations with every round of testing so that you cycle through the different configurations as a matter of course. Because the test results are always tracked against the test run configuration, you will also have the information for reproducing any results, and you will improve your coverage of configurations this way.

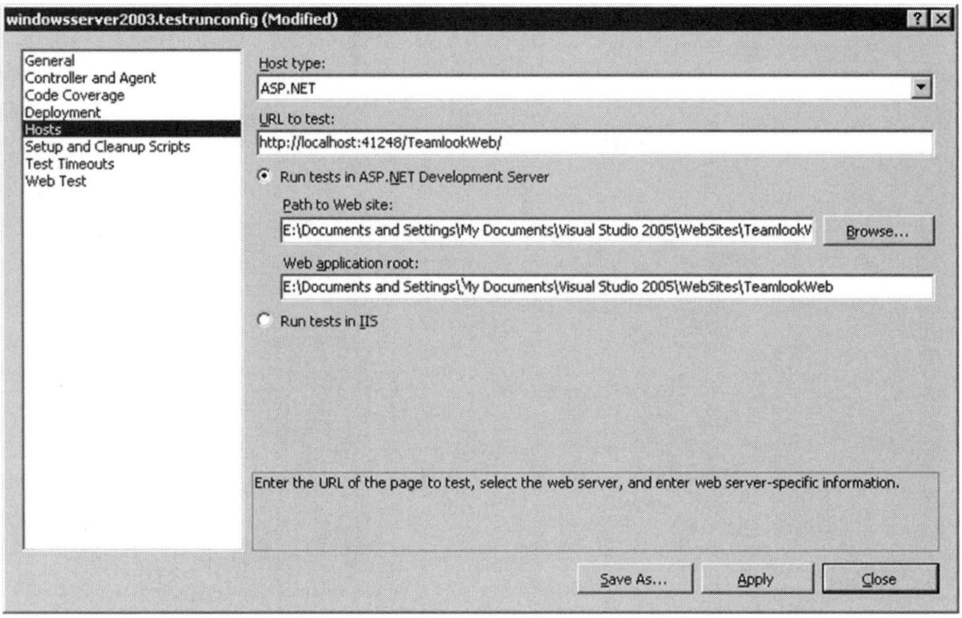

Figure 7.19   Run configurations can capture the representative target environments of the systems under test. The metrics warehouse accumulates test results by configuration so that you can build a picture over time of the test coverage against configurations.

Are We Testing Enough?

Defining "Good Enough"

In Chapter 3, I presented Kano Analysis as a technique for thinking holistically in terms of satisfiers and dissatisfiers for a project, and in Chapter 4, I discussed planning an iteration. The iteration's objectives should determine the test objectives.

Although it may be hard to determine what constitutes "good enough" testing for a project as a whole, it's not that hard for the iteration. The whole team should know what "good enough" means for the current iteration, and that should be captured in the scenarios, QoS that are planned to be implemented, and risks to be addressed in the iteration. Testing should verify the accomplishment of that target through the course of the iteration.[9]

A value-up practice for planning "good enough" is to keep the bug backlog as close to zero as possible. Every time you defer resolving or closing a bug, you impose additional future liability on the project for three reasons: The bug itself will have to be handled multiple times, someone (usually a developer) will have a longer lag before returning to the code for analysis and fixing, and you'll create a "Broken Windows" effect. The Broken Windows theory holds that in neighborhoods where small details, such as broken windows, go unaddressed, other acts of crime are more likely to be ignored. Cem Kaner, a software testing professor and former public prosecutor, describes this well:[10]

> The challenge with graffiti and broken windows is that they identify a community standard. If the community can't even keep itself moderately clean, then: (1) Problems like these are not worth reporting, and so citizens will stop reporting them. (We also see the converse of this, as a well-established phenomenon. In communities that start actually prosecuting domestic violence or rape, the reported incidence of these crimes rises substantially—presumably, the visible enforcement causes a higher probability of a report of a crime, rather than more crime). In software, many bugs are kept off the lists as not worth reporting. (2) People will be less likely to clean these bugs up on their own because their small effort won't make much of a difference. (3) Some people will feel it is acceptable (socially tolerated in this community) to commit more graffiti or to break more windows. (4) Many people will feel that if these are tolerated, there probably isn't much bandwidth available to enforce laws against more serious street crimes.

Similarly, in projects with large bug backlogs, overall attention to quality issues may decline. This is one of many reasons to keep the bug backlog as close to zero as possible.

Set Iteration Test Objectives by Assigning Work Items to the Iteration

In VSTS, all work items, including scenarios, QoS, bugs, and risks, can be assigned to an iteration. This assignment creates a test target list for that iteration, or in other words, a visible bar defining good enough testing for that iteration. You can, of course, add more to that list or reschedule items to future iterations, but there is always a visible, agreed definition of the iteration test goals, and changes to it are tracked in an auditable manner.

Exploratory Testing

Most testing I've discussed so far is either automated or highly scripted manual testing. These are good for finding the things that you know to look for but weak for finding bugs or issues where you don't know to look. Exploratory testing, also called ad hoc testing, is an important mindset to bring to all of the testing that you do. In exploratory testing, the tester assumes the persona of the user and exercises the software as that persona would. Kaner, Bach, and Pettichord describe exploratory testing this way:

> By exploration, we mean purposeful wandering; navigating through a space with a general mission, but without a prescripted route. Exploration involves continuous learning and experimenting. There's a lot of backtracking, repetition, and other processes that look like waste to the untrained eye.[11]

Exploratory testing can be a very important source of discovery, not just of bugs but also of unforeseen (or not yet described) scenarios and QoS requirements. Capture these in the backlog of the work item database so that you can use them in planning the current and future iterations. As a manager, plan for a certain level of exploratory testing in every iteration. Define charters for these testing sessions according to the goals of the iteration. Tune the charters and the resource level according to the value you get from these sessions. In short, plan capacity for exploratory testing.

Testing as Discovery

Embrace testing that discovers new scenarios, QoS requirements, and risks in addition of course to finding bugs. Capture the new scenarios, QoS, and risks as work items in the product backlog. This is vital information. It makes the quantitative coverage measurement a little harder in that you're increasing the denominator, but that's a small price to pay for helping the project deliver more customer value.

A particular type of scenario test is the "soap opera." Hans Buwalda describes the technique in his article "Soap Opera Testing" as follows:

> Soap operas are dramatic daytime television shows that were originally sponsored by soap vendors. They depict life in a way that viewers can relate to, but the situations portrayed are typically condensed and exaggerated. In one episode, more things happen to the characters than

most of us will experience in a lifetime. Opinions may differ about whether soap operas are fun to watch, but it must be great fun to write them. Soap opera testing is similar to a soap opera in that tests are based on real life, exaggerated, and condensed.[12]

Soap operas are harsh, complex tests—they test many features using intricate and perhaps unforeseen sequences. The essence of soap operas is that they present cases that are relevant to the domain and important to the stakeholders but that cannot be tested in isolation. They are a good test of robustness in iterations where the software is mature enough to handle long test sequences.

False Confidence

When you have automated or highly scripted testing, and you do not balance it with exploration, you run the risk of what Boris Beizer coined as the "Pesticide Paradox":[13]

Every method you use to prevent or find bugs leaves a residue of subtler bugs against which those methods are ineffectual.

In other words, you can make your software immune to the tests that you already have. This pattern is especially a concern when the only testing being done is regression testing, and the test pool is very stable. There are three ways to mitigate the Pesticide Paradox:

1. Make sure that the tests the software faces continually include fresh ones, including good negative tests.
2. Look at gaps in test coverage against scenarios, QoS, risks, and code. Prioritize the gaps and think about tests that can close them.
3. Use progressively harsher tests, notably soap operas and exploratory testing, to confirm, from a knowledgeable domain expert's perspective, that the software doesn't have undiscovered vulnerabilities.

Exploratory testing, soap operas, and risk identification all mitigate against a false sense of confidence.

When Should We Test?

In principle, it seems obvious that at any time in development project, you should test the functionality that needs to be tested at that time. In practice, however, teams historically experience tremendous churn because testers do not know when to test. In these cases, testers claim they're blocked, developers feel the testers are wasting their time, and collaboration quickly disintegrates.

VSTS alleviates this issue in three ways:

1. The iteration structure makes clear what functionality is planned when, and course corrections are frequent enough to enable plans to be fine-tuned (refer to Chapter 4).
2. The common product backlog makes clear what scenarios and QoS have actually been resolved and are therefore ready for test at a particular time.
3. The build report makes clear for every daily build what tasks and scenarios have actually been delivered and integrated in the build and whether the build itself has passed BVTs and is ready for further testing (see Figure 7.20).

In addition to using the transparency provided by VSTS, a test manager should carefully think about which tests are appropriate for which cycles (see Figure 7.21).

Check-In Cycle

The atomic programming cycle is the set of activities leading to checking in source code. In VSTS, source should be delivered with unit tests and resolution of the corresponding work items. As a developer, before checking in, you should run the unit tests for any functionality that you deliver and any that is dependent on your delivery. Depending on the software project, it might be appropriate to supplement unit tests with component integration tests. (You should also run static code analysis.) Check-in policy can enforce this practice.

Daily Build Cycle

BVTs run with the nightly build automation, as discussed in the previous chapter. For BVTs, it is best to have lots of tests, each for relatively fine-grained scenarios, rather than a few, more complex tests. Typically, these are a superset of the pre-check-in unit tests that the individual team members ran before delivering new source code, plus resilient scenario tests that other team members have delivered. Having small, self-contained tests makes it possible to quickly isolate the failure cases and drill into them. It also makes it possible to update the tests when the corresponding scenarios change.

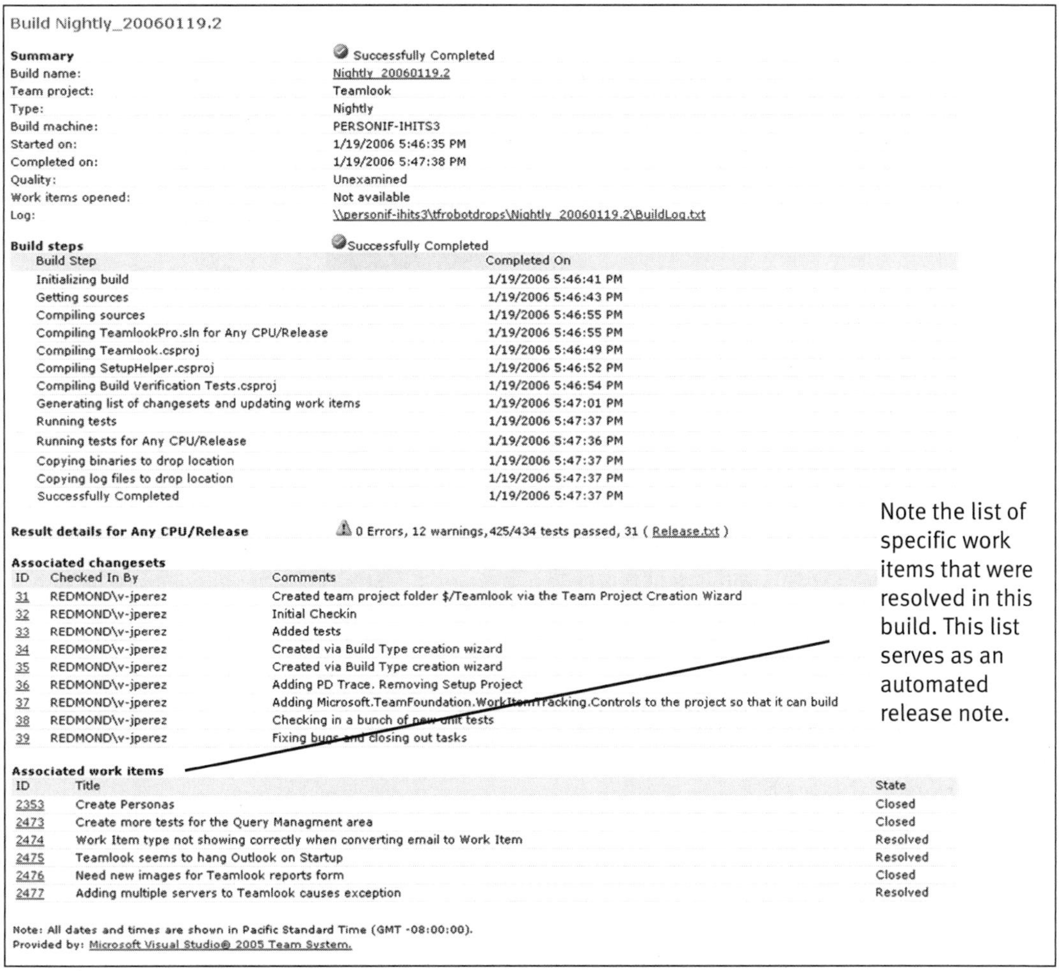

Note the list of specific work items that were resolved in this build. This list serves as an automated release note.

Figure 7.20   The daily build produces an automated report that includes the work items that have been resolved in the build. In other words, the report accumulates all the items that were marked resolved when code was checked in. This lets you see immediately whether intended functionality can be expected to work in the build and correspondingly which tests can now be run.

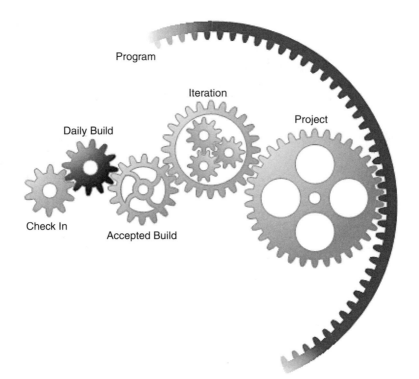

Figure 7.21   MSF uses the concept of interlocking cycles to group activities to the appropriate frequency and to allow the right things to happen first. Testing activities vary according to these cycles.

It is important that the suite of BVTs grow from iteration to iteration. As the software functionality matures, completed work from every prior iteration should be verified continually with BVTs.

Accepted Build Cycle

After a software build has passed the BVTs, it is ready for further testing. Now you can test the new scenarios and QoS that have been implemented in the current iteration. This list should be obvious from both the work items of the product backlog and the build reports. As scenarios and QoS first become available, you should run supportive tests. As these easier tests pass, you should run ever more challenging tests.

Which builds should be promoted for further testing? The answer depends on the goals of the iteration and the length of time it takes to test a build thoroughly. When there is significant new functionality from one nightly build to the next, the new work should be tested and feedback should be given to the developers as soon as practical. This prioritization is a "Last In, First Out" stack, and it ensures that the developer receives bugs on recent work while it is still fresh in mind.

On the other hand, some testing cycles for broad business functionality or many configurations take days or (unfortunately) weeks to complete. Setup requirements, such as configuring and loading a database, can make changing builds disruptive during a test cycle. If (and only if) that's true, and the particular testing is not dependent on the new work, it may be worth delaying the acceptance of the new build into test. Even better is to find a way to shorten the amount of time needed to run the full test pass.

Iteration Cycle

The scenarios and QoS scheduled for an iteration should be considered exit criteria that need to be verified by testing. The work items that track these scenarios and QoS should not be closed until the corresponding functionality has passed testing in the software as a whole. If you reach the end of an iteration and discover that you have not completed the planned scenarios and QoS, this is essential information for planning the next iterations. (See the discussion of project velocity in Chapter 4.)

However, you should not let an exit criterion be declared satisfied until testing has confirmed that the expected code works. This makes the iteration cycle the most visible testing cycle. In a well run project, where testing happens concurrently with development, there will not be a large testing bottleneck at the end of the iteration. On the other hand, if testing is not kept in lockstep with development, there may be a big bulge. This growing bulge will be visible during the iteration in the Remaining Work chart. It is undesirable, creates a significant risk, and will disrupt the rhythm of the project substantially. As a test manager or project manager, you should keep your eye on this chart daily to avoid becoming trapped at iteration end (see Figure 7.22).

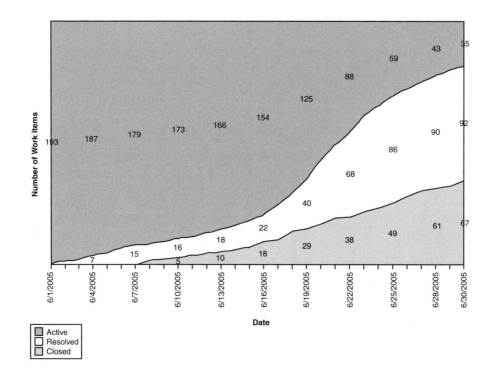

Figure 7.22   The bulge in this Remaining Work chart indicates that although the coding of scenarios is progressing well, there is a bottleneck in testing. This may be due to inadequate testing resources or inadequate quality of scenarios delivered in the builds. (You would check the Reactivations report next if you suspected poor quality.)

Project Cycle

At the end of an iteration, the software should be passing the tests planned for that iteration, and in subsequent iterations, it should continue to pass them. When the software keeps passing the tests put to it, you develop great momentum. The more automated the tests, the more frequently they are run, and the more frequently this confidence is reinforced.

Of course, the more mature the project, the harsher the tests should be. Continue to use soap operas, negative tests, and exploration to check for blind spots. Use configuration testing to make sure that production constraints have been addressed. Check trends on coverage against code, requirements, and risk.

Which Tests Should Be Automated?

In the last ten years, a lot has been written about the pitfalls and benefits of test automation.[14] I will simplify the arguments here. Automation is useful when it achieves high coverage and when the tests will be used many times across changes in the software under test (SUT). However, automation is expensive and hard to maintain, especially if based on the SUT's user interface. Moreover, automation often leads to a false sense of security, especially when its results are not balanced against views of coverage and when its test cases are not balanced with harsh exploratory and negative testing.

These considerations lead to some guidelines:

1. Automate tests that support programming, such as unit tests, component/service integration tests, and BVTs, and make sure that they achieve very high code coverage, as discussed in Chapter 6, "Development."

2. Automate configuration tests whenever you can.

If you expect your software to be long-lived, then

3. Automate scenario tests when possible, but expect that they will need maintenance. Where possible, do not rely on the UI for testing and instead code more durable tests against the appropriate APIs.

4. Automate load tests, but again, expect that they will need maintenance.

And . . .

5. Guard against a false sense of confidence with exploratory testing, negative tests, soap operas, and tests against risks. Most of these will be manual because you will be more interested in maximizing the diversity of your testing than repeating the same tests every time.

How Efficient Is Our Team, Or Our Outsourced Team?

Together, the reports from the metrics warehouse answer the question of team effectiveness and efficiency. Specific patterns of problems are covered in Chapter 9, "Troubleshooting the Project," but here is a general guide to using the reports to answer this question.

The Remaining Work report, as illustrated previously in Figure 4.4, shows you the cumulative flow of intended work through testing. The middle band, from Resolved to Closed, is the work in process of testing. If you see a relatively consistent width, as in Figure 4.4, then you know that you have a smooth flow. The smooth flow gives you a clear indication of the match of your resources to capacity. (This contrasts with the bottleneck shown in Figure 7.22, indicating a resource mismatch or problem with quality at the time of resolution.) Velocity (Figure 4.5) in the Resolved series drills into the details of the capacity and its variance.

Requirements Test History (Figure 7.14) shows the progression of the testing against scenarios and QoS, while Quality Indicators (Figure 4.7) puts test results, bugs, and code coverage together. By putting these series together, you can make sure that the independent dimensions are progressing as expected.

Of course, in judging testing, you need to look at upstream quality that is being passed into testing. The Build History report (Figure 9.11) shows the status of daily builds, which should be completing successfully and passing their BVTs with rare exceptions. Quality Indicators provides two series that should be watched together—code churn, the indicator of how much new code needs to be tested, and code coverage, the measure of how much of it actually is being tested. Reactivations (Figure 4.9) are bugs that have been reopened after being resolved, that is, reported fixed. If these are high or rising, it's a clear indicator of upstream problems.

Summary

This chapter has covered testing in a value-up paradigm. I started with an exercise to illustrate the importance of testing as a key source of information and its tenets of creating information fast, addressing risk, and maximizing diversity.

Next, I went through basic questions that testing should answer and illustrated how to use VSTS to help answer them:

- Are we delivering the customer value?
- Are the qualities of service, such as performance and security, fit for use?
- Have we tested the changes?
- What haven't we tested?
- Does it work in production as well as in the lab?

- Are we testing enough?
- When should we be running the tests?
- Which tests should be automated?
- How efficient is our team, or our outsourced team?

These are the simple value-up questions that testing needs to address.

Endnotes

1. Cem Kaner, James Bach, and Bret Pettichord, *Lessons Learned in Software Testing* (New York: Wiley, 2002), 1.

2. The root of many of these is IEEE STD 829-1983.

3. For example, Beck 2000, op. cit.

4. Adapted from Brian Marick, "Classic Testing Mistakes," 1997, available at http://www.testing.com/writings/classic/mistakes.pdf.

5. Originally called context-driven testing by Kaner, Bach, and Pettichord (257), I've included it as part of the Value-Up Paradigm.

6. [Kaner 2003] "Cem Kaner on Scenario Testing," *STQE Magazine*, September/October 2003, 22, available at www.stickyminds.com. For a detailed view of Kaner's course on this subject, see http://www.testingeducation.org/BBST/ScenarioTesting.html.

7. James A. Whittaker and Herbert H. Thompson, *How to Break Software Security: Effective Techniques for Security Testing* (Boston: Addison-Wesley, 2004). Whittaker and Thompson have identified 19 attack patterns that are standard approaches to hacking systems.

8. Boris Beizer, *Software Testing Techniques* (Boston: International Thomson Computer Press, 1990), 535.

9. James Bach has written extensively on the heuristics for defining when our software is good enough for its purpose. See http://www.satisfice.com/articles.shtml for a collection of his essays.

10. Cem Kaner, private email. Malcolm Gladwell, *The Tipping Point* (Little Brown & Co., 2000), 141, has popularized the discussion, based on Mayor Giulini's use in New York City. The statistical evidence supporting the theory is disputable; see Steven D. Levitt and Stephen J. Dubner, *Freakonomics: A Rogue Economist Explores the Hidden Side of Everything* (New York: HarperCollins, 2005). Nonetheless, the psychological argument that communities, including software teams, can become habituated to conditions of disrepair is widely consistent with experience.

11. Kaner, Bach, and Pettichord 2002, 18.

12. Hans Buwalda, "Soap Opera Testing," *Better Software*, February 2004, 30–37, available at www.stickyminds.com.

13. Boris Beizer, *Software Testing Techniques* (Boston: International Thomson Computer Press, 1990), 9.

14. For a classic discussion of the risks of bad automation, see James Bach, "Test Automation Snake Oil," originally published in *Windows Tech Journal* (November 1996), available at http://www.satisfice.com/articles/test_automation_snake_oil.pdf.

8. Reporting Bugs

 **Everyone**

"A group of programmers were presenting a report to the Emperor. "What was the greatest achievement of the year?" the Emperor asked. The programmers spoke among themselves and then replied, "We fixed 50% more bugs this year than we fixed last year." The Emperor looked on them in confusion. It was clear he did not know what a "bug" was. After conferring in low undertones with his chief minister, he turned to the programmers, his face red with anger. "You are guilty of poor quality control. Next year there will be no bugs!" he demanded. And sure enough, when the programmers presented their report to the Emperor the next year, there was no mention of bugs."[1]

—Geoffrey James, *The Zen of Programming*

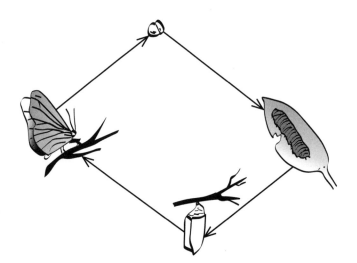

Figure 8.1   Lifecycle of a (real) bug. Real bugs have a well-defined lifecycle, according to their
species. Their metamorphosis is a good metaphor for software bugs, which often start
with a simple observation of a probable source of customer dissatisfaction (the egg) and
proceed to a well-defined report of the observed symptoms, steps to reproduce, and a
technical investigation (the larva), to a fix for the problem (the chrysalis), and finally to a
working build with the fix verified (the adult). Like real bugs, not all software bugs survive
to adulthood. Of course, unlike real bugs, software bugs can retreat back to their larval
state when the fixes are unsuccessful. Those are the reactivations.

In a value-up paradigm, quality is everyone's business all the time. Prevention of
errors is one of the most important aspects to every activity. So why do I have a separate chapter on bugs—isn't that antiquated thinking? In most organizational cul-
tures I have seen, bugs take on such an important life that they should be addressed
head on. And despite the best-known lifecycle and development practices, bugs still
occur, although their nature changes. Hence this chapter. MSF for Agile Software
Development defines this principle:

> **Quality is everyone's job every day.** Quality requires both bug preven-
> tion and solution verification. Utilize practices such as code analysis
> and peer reviews to prevent bugs as well as maximize the testing to find
> bugs. All roles are responsible for prevention and verification of bugs.[2]

Consistent with MSF, I call bugs "bugs" and not "defects." "Defect" often has connotations of blame and nonconformance to spec, both of which are red herrings. For value-up purposes, anything that diminishes perceived value is a bug and should be considered for triage and potential change. For the same reason, I do not distinguish here between bugs and change requests, although in certain processes, they would be treated differently. Take them all to triage the same way.

> **Implicit and Explicit Change Requests**
>
> Consistent with the Agile value of embracing change, MSF for Agile Software Development does not have a change request work item type. Changes may be captured as bugs or new scenarios, depending on the scope.
>
> On the other hand, MSF for CMMI Process Improvement has an explicit Change Request work item type to support the Configuration Management Process Area of the CMMI.

A Cautionary Tale

Let's revisit the practices of two testers on our project, Caliban and Ariel. At the end of the project, Caliban had reported 100 bugs; Ariel had reported 74. (Assume that they were all equal priority and severity.) Prospero, who is their manager, must pick one of the two testers for a key new project. Whom should Prospero pick? Based on this information alone, he'd probably pick Caliban.

Before choosing, however, Prospero took a look at the state of their bugs at the end of the project (see Table 8.1).

Table 8.1   Breakdown of Reasons Given for Closure of the Bugs

	Caliban	Ariel
Fixed and Validated	10	40
Works as Planned	15	2
No Plan to Fix	20	6
Duplicate	15	6
Deferred	40	20

Prospero noted that *80%* of the bug fixes customers received were the result of Ariel's work, and only 20% were the result of Caliban's efforts. As a result, he picked Ariel.

The point of this exercise is to raise the significance of the bug's lifecycle, not just its initial state as an ovum on a leaf. A lot can happen between the time when you report a bug and the time (if ever) when the customer receives software with the fix. It's important that you create that ovum with the right material to mature on the right path.

A (Software) Bug's Life

Not unlike biological bugs, software bugs go through a very precise set of states (see Figure 8.2). In VSTS, the default states and transitions that are allowed depend on the process template that you choose for the project. The selection and timing of permissible states, the groups who authorize advancing a bug to the next state, and the allowable reasons for the transition are governed by a set of rules in the chosen process. If you have the permission, you can customize the rules further to match your team's workflow.

> **With VSTS**
> - In MSF for CMMI Process Improvement, bugs have four states, starting with Proposed. They need to become accepted before becoming Active.
> - In MSF for Agile Software Development, bugs only have three states, starting with Active.

Anyone can *propose* a bug, that is, request that it be queued for fixing.

A project manager can *activate* the bug and assign it to a developer.

After investigating and fixing the code, the developer marks the bug as *resolved* with the next check-in (see Figure 8.3). The developer is not allowed to close the bug directly.

The check-in process automatically *resolves* the bug when the corresponding source code is checked-in.

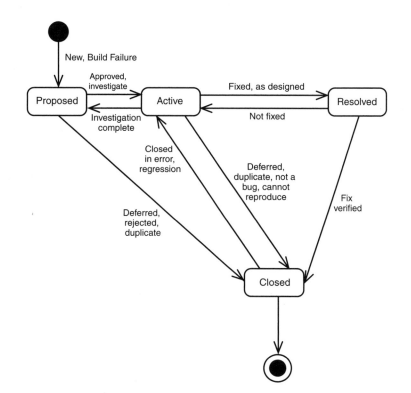

Figure 8.2   This state chart is the lifecycle of a software bug in MSF for CMMI Process Improvement.

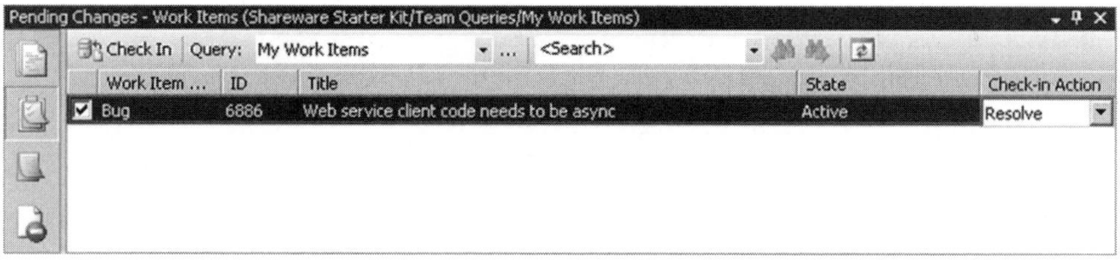

Figure 8.3   In VSTS, merely by checking off the bug in the check-in dialog, the developer associates the changeset being delivered with the bug being fixed. The association is permanent and is used to populate the build report and the metrics warehouse.

A tester can see the resolved bug in the corresponding query. Only the tester *closes* the bug after verifying that it passes the tests to prove the fix. (Of course, if the test fails, then the tester would *reactivate* the bug.)

In practice, workflows can be simpler or more complex. MSF Agile, for example, does not require a proposed state before activation, does not enforce different permissions, and instead relies on trust. On the other hand, some processes, especially in late iterations, do not allow check-in until the code has been reviewed. Work items can enforce this rule through another state or a separate field, and check-in policy can enforce the workflow.

Whatever they are, these rules are the tangible form of the process for your current project.

Bug Reporting Is Like Journalism

Caliban has an anecdote about his favorite bug. It goes something like this:

> I found this bug in the lab months ago and reported it. No one paid attention; so they triaged it out and marked it deferred. Last week our biggest customer found it too and all of a sudden it's a crisis. Now we need to ship a service release, which means that I'll be in the lab all weekend checking the fix. Why couldn't they have paid attention when I reported it the first time?

Why indeed? Very often the answer is that the bug report was not clear enough to communicate the impact to the triage committee, and the reported bug was closed. Prospero, Caliban's manager, has a different view of Caliban's story: "Why can't Caliban make his bug reports clear enough for the team to act on them?" (And, as before, Prospero did not choose Caliban for his next project.)

The lesson from Caliban's experience is well summarized in this quote from Kaner, Bach, and Pettichord:

> **Your advocacy drives the repair of the bugs you report.**
>
> Any bug report that you write is an advocacy document that calls for the repair of the bug.
>
> Some bugs will never be fixed. Your responsibility is not to make sure that all the bugs are fixed. Your responsibility is to report bugs accurately and in a way that allows the reader to understand the full impact of the problem.

How well you research and write the report will often have a substantial effect on the probability that the bug will be fixed.[3]

Writing up a bug well is like writing newspaper (or web page) copy. It is journalism. The title is like the headline, and you should expect most readers never to look "below the fold." The journalist's six basic questions—*what, where, how, who, why, and when*—need to be covered in a summary sentence or two.

Know Your Audience

The first audience for your bug reports is the triage committee. (Triage is discussed in Chapter 4, "Project Management.") They will see a query that looks something like Figure 8.4.

The triage committee includes the busiest people on the project. It is common for them to spend *less than one minute* reviewing each bug. (An important reason for daily triage is to keep the length of the list down so that individual work items get the attention they deserve.) In that minute, the fate of your bug report will be decided, as was the fate of Caliban's bugs. If Caliban had spent a little more time on the quality of his bug reports, the value of his work (and his performance rating) might have been considerably higher.

Active Bugs [Results]

Query Results: 10 results found (1 currently selected). The query has been modified. You must re-run the query to see the changes.

ID	Work Item Type	Assigned To	Priority	Title	State
10535	Bug	Juan Perez (Personify Design)	1	Credit Card payment form doesn't use HTTPS/SSL	Active
10537	Bug	Juan Perez (Personify Design)	1	Application hangs during splash screen	Active
10538	Bug	Juan Perez (Personify Design)	1	Not all application users required to register upon downloading application	Active
10539	Bug	Juan Perez (Personify Design)	1	Possible security vulnerability with payment backend	Active
10533	Bug	Juan Perez (Personify Design)	2	Password text box doesn't hide text	Active
10542	Bug	Juan Perez (Personify Design)	2	Registration Web Service causing incorrect Log	Active
10534	Bug	Juan Perez (Personify Design)	3	Delay while submitting exception report via web service	Active
10536	Bug	Juan Perez (Personify Design)	3	FAQ #4 is incorrect	Active
10540	Bug	Juan Perez (Personify Design)	3	Sample UI should be isolated into a different assembly	Active
10541	Bug	Juan Perez (Personify Design)	3	Documentation states incorrect system requirements	Active

Note that there may be many more records here than fit on the screen at once.

The most important information here is the title, which is truncated to 60 characters average. Which bugs do you understand from these titles?

Figure 8.4 Keep in mind what your readers will see during triage. It's not all the detail, just what fits on the query results list. You should write bugs to be viewed in this format.

Learn from History

Reading bug reports, especially after they have been triaged, is a good way to learn about your project and your audience. Auditing triage meetings is another—you learn what is important to stakeholders in practice. Here are some tips on using your bug database:

- Execute the repro steps on interesting bugs. It's a good way to learn the software under test in its more interesting cases (and a good way to learn how to write clear steps).

- Read the commentary to see how other team members answer bug reports to learn both what they think is important and how to improve your reporting style.

- Study closed bug reports to see which bugs have and have not been fixed, based on the way they were reported. If you want yours fixed, report them like the ones that historically do get fixed.

- If you're working on an existing solution, read tech support logs for errors to check and stories to support your bugs.

SOAP: An Analogy from Medicine

The software world borrowed the term "triage" from medical practice, so it's appropriate to look at the context of its use in medicine. Medical personnel learn the acronym SOAP (nothing to do with web services) to describe clinical reporting. Here is an excerpt from a medical syllabus from the University of Maryland School of Pharmacy:[4]

For each patient . . . care problem (one or more), write a progress note (in the SOAP format) to include:

Subjective information that supports the problem identified;

Objective information that supports the problem identified;

Assessment of the problem including etiology, severity, effectiveness/toxicity of current treatment, list of therapeutic alternatives with discussion of advantages and disadvantages of each (therapeutic and economic), rationale for recommendations; and

Plan for managing the identified problem including a specific outline for implementation and continued monitoring of the problem and therapeutic response.

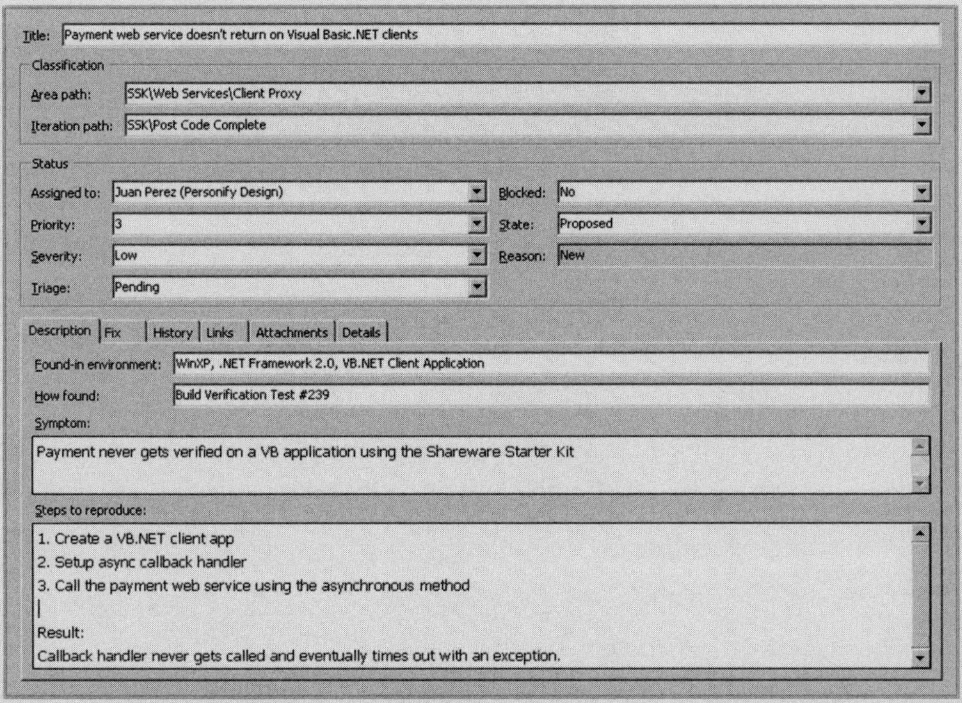

Figure 8.5   The SOAP mnemonic is a useful way to think of the fields of the form and a healthy conversation history. The Title and Symptom are **s**ubjective; the fields such as Found In [Build], Found-in Environment, and Steps to Reproduce are **o**bjective; Priority, Severity, Area Path, and Root Cause are **a**ssessment, and Iteration and Fix are the **p**lan.

Good craftsmen watch what other good craftsmen do, including those in other disciplines. SOAP is a good model to use when you report bugs and review bug reports. Let's take a look at the standard bug reporting form that VSTS provides with MSF for CMMI Process Improvement.

Subjective Data

The most important question for the readers of your report is: *What's the impact on the user?* Most of the time, the answer requires some thought. Ask yourself questions like the following:

- What will the customer say to Product Support when she sees this?
- What will the customer expect from experience with other software (including competitors' products)?
- What will sales reps or trainers say if they hit this in a demo?
- What scenarios will be affected by this bug?
- What is the downstream impact of this bug?
- How many users will care and how often?
- Is this an isolated occurrence?
- Is there a security risk here?
- Are other qualities of service affected?

Write this story first. How you answer these questions will influence both how much time you should spend researching the bug and what data you should collect with the report.

Titles Matter

As you can see in Figure 8.4, the title is often the only information that the reader sees. If the title is unclear, when truncated to fit the column width, the rest of the information may never be read.

Descriptions Stick

The persistent next level of information about the bug is the description. History changes can get very long, but the description should be the succinct detail about the bug.

One Report Per Bug

If you have two bugs, then write two reports. Keeping each observed bug in its own report will make all the reports easier to understand.

Objective Data

After you have written the subjective data about the bug, it is time to gather objective data.

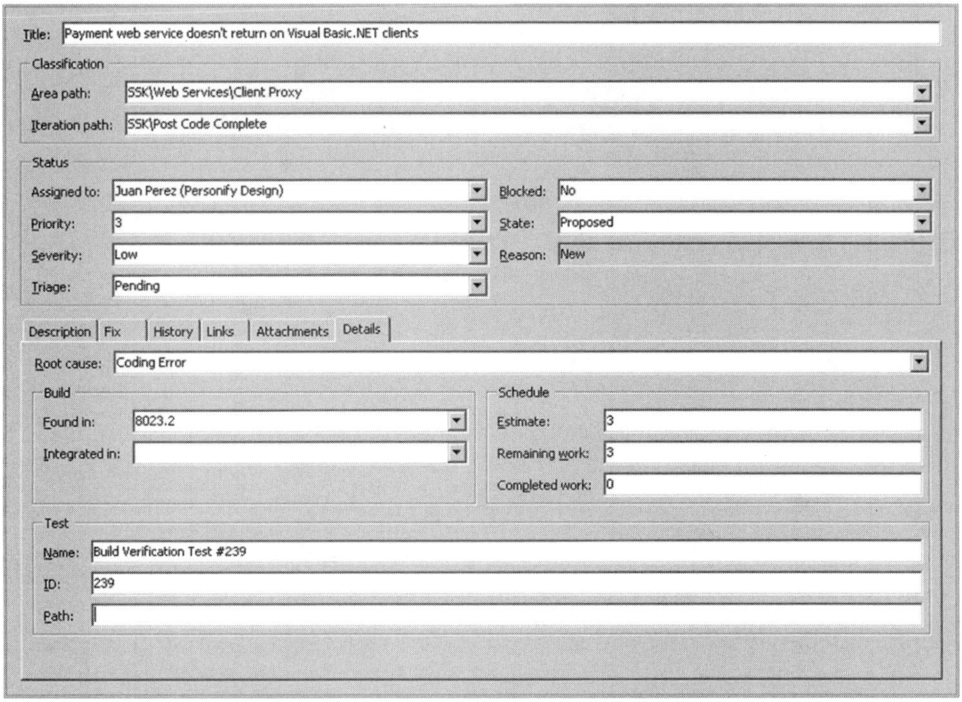

Figure 8.6   The bug work item type, here from MSF for CMMI Process Improvement, captures the information that all its users need to query, track, and analyze the bug.

Quality of Service

Be clear about the type of issue that you are reporting—what QoS is affected.

Related Feature or Code

If you can relate the bug to a specified feature that you are testing or to specific areas of the code under test, then do so.

Test to Reproduce

If you have a test to reproduce the bug, identify it.

Attachments

What data can you attach to the bug report to demonstrate the conditions in which the bug occurs? All these can be useful, where applicable:

- Screenshots
- Data files
- Configuration files
- Trace files
- Server logs
- Dr. Watson logs

Reproduction Steps

How do you reproduce the bug in the minimum number of steps with the least setup? Eighty percent of the developer's effort in working on a bug is often in the reproduction—how well can you streamline that process? Anything unnecessary is clearly wasteful. Make the repro steps accurate and clear. Check them before submitting the bug.

Preconditions

Is special setup needed to reproduce the error, such as loading a particular database? If the problem can be demonstrated with production data or customer data, it's particularly compelling.

Assessment Data

The assessment will change a lot through the bug's life as people refine the diagnosis and observation, debug the source, try and test fixes, study related bugs, and so on. It is your job to keep the bug history accurate and thorough as you learn more about the bug and its conditions.

Some of the assessment you can do on the initial report, and more of it will evolve with the bug history and conversation.

Is It a Duplicate?

Spend a little bit of time looking through the database to determine whether this is more information about an existing bug or something new, but don't go crazy. It's easy enough for someone to mark your bug as a duplicate later. Obviously, if you have discovered more about an existing bug, update the existing one with your findings.

How General Is It?

Uncorner your corner cases.[5] Frequently, you will discover bugs using extreme values, unusual configurations, or long entry sequences. Essential to understanding the importance of the bug is to know how specific or general the conditions must be. Here are some tips:

- **Vary the data.** If you discover the bug with a particular set of input values, try different ones. Especially try different equivalence classes. How dependent is the bug's appearance on specific values or classes?
- **Vary the configurations.** If you find the bug in a particular configuration of hardware and software components, try it on a very different set of machines.
- **Vary the flows.** If the bug appeared under a particular sequence of actions (especially if it is a long one), see whether there are other (preferably shorter) paths that lead to the same result.
- **Look for suspect interactions.** If something seems to be a strange side effect, but you're not sure, keep poking. For example, after you use one program, another might suddenly seem slower. Perhaps they rely on some common component, data, or OS service.
- **Are there more?** Hypothesize where similar bugs may be lurking. Look for them.

How Severe Is It?

When you first find a bug, there is a great temptation to be satisfied and to report it. In fact, you might be at the tip of a much worse problem. Note the initial symptom but also keep using the software under test. You are likely to discover poorly handled error paths and exceptions, unforeseen interactions, and other problems that would baffle a user (and tech support).

Plan

At initial reporting, the primary planning tools you have are priority and ownership. Depending on your process, these may be settable only by the triage committee, or in less formal organizations, the submitter may fill these in directly. Priority should be handled in the same way as it is for project management.

Iteration

Think carefully about the planned iteration. Often in early iterations, bugs are filed appropriately against functionality that won't work until later. A purpose of triage is to remove this noise from developers' immediate queues.

Summary

This chapter focused on bug reporting. Obviously, as all previous chapters discussed, it is far better to prevent bugs from occurring with good requirements, architecture, and development practices than to discover them and incur the rework necessary to fix them. Nonetheless, they happen, and their details should be captured by everyone who finds them.

When you write up a bug, be conscious of your audience. Most of your readers will only see the title, perhaps in truncated form. Work hard to make the title summarize the impact and importance of the bug clearly; otherwise, the rest of the information might be overlooked.

A useful mnemonic for completing the rest of the report is SOAP (subjective-objective-assessment-plan), borrowed from the world of hospitals. In particular, the medical analogy can help you think hard about the assessment and plan, and it can help move you away from thinking of bugs as a numbers game.

Endnotes

1. Geoffrey James, *The Zen of Programming* (Santa Monica: Infobooks, 1988), 59–60. Quoted in Weinberg *Systems Thinking* 1992, 33.

2. MSF for Agile Software Development.

3. Kaner, Bach, and Pettichord, *op. cit.*, 65–6.

4. http://www.pharmacy.umaryland.edu/courses/syllabi/PDF/PHNT534.pdf

5. Kaner, Bach, and Pettichord, *op. cit.*, 73.

9.
Troubleshooting the Project

Program Manager
Project Manager

"Happy families are all alike; every unhappy family is unhappy in its own way."

—Leo Tolstoy, *Anna Karenina*[1]

Figure 9.1
Leo Nikolayevich Tolstoy.

Tolstoy's aphorism applies to software projects, too. There are many patterns of unhappiness in a software project, which are usually manifested in a couple dozen symptoms.

This chapter focuses on these patterns, the symptoms, and how to recognize them. By now, I hope you are convinced of the value-up paradigm, which asserts that we apply systems to look continually for ways to improve the flow of value. In Chapter 1, "A Value-Up Paradigm," I contrasted this to the "iron triangle" view of the work-down paradigm, which assumes fixed capacity and reduces problems to time, resources, functionality, and quality.[2]

The metrics warehouse, like the work item database, enables you to run a project based on trust and transparency. Everyone on the team gets to see the same data, ask the same questions, look for the answers, and be part of finding the solution. This chapter might be criticized for being unnecessarily quantitative. By no means do I mean to suggest that you always need numbers to grasp problems or that solutions and improvements should be numeric. As discussed in Chapter 4, "Project Management," the metrics need to be descriptive, not prescriptive.

Pride of workmanship, one of the MSF mindsets, is assumed for everyone, and the metrics are a tool to reinforce that pride, not supplant it. You win at sports by playing well and keeping your eye on the ball, not on the scoreboard. The scoreboard just keeps count so that you don't have to be distracted by arguing about whose numbers are right.

Many symptoms require no metrics warehouse. A well-known example is the *Inverse Dilbert Correlation Factor*: The more Dilbert cartoons there are pasted on office doors and bulletin boards, the less well off the project is.[3] (Of course, an absence of cartoons might be a warning sign of a certain company policy, too.) Another example is the morale of the team, which is visible in the energy level and enthusiasm. If team members are losing sleep over project problems, they should be able to tell you what's bothering them. And if you aren't seeing it, then you're not spending enough time with the rest of your team.

On the other hand, we are all susceptible to blind spots. Trends and drilldowns are great for identifying possible risks and oversights, and the health charts are a great starting point. They give you the data to ask the right questions, but only the team can find the answers. The greatest benefit of the metrics charts is their capability to complement what you sense or suspect from interacting with your fellow team members, trying current builds of the software, reviewing code, researching bugs, planning iterations, and so on. The charts give you indicators of the overall health of the project and, when you suspect a problem, the ability to look at the data to confirm or deny the suspicion.

For the rest of this chapter, I catalog a series of potential problems, many of which you may recognize from personal experience, and how they can show up in the VSTS project health charts. The goal here is to show how VSTS, with its daily reporting, can provide early warnings and help you with continuous course correction to improve capacity.

Using Excel with the Metrics Warehouse

In addition to the standard reports that are installed with the process template in VSTS, you can access all the metrics warehouse data from Microsoft Excel. See the MSDN topic:

Development Tools and Technologies

   Visual Studio Team System

      Team Foundation

         Team Foundation Project Leads

            Using Reporting and Metrics

               Team Foundation Server Reporting

                  Using Team Reports

                     Using Microsoft Excel for Team Foundation Server Reporting

---

Underestimating

One of the most frequently reported problem symptoms is underestimation. When progress falls short of the plan and effort is greater than estimated, project members are underestimating the resources, difficulty, time, or other factors (see Figure 9.2).

If you see this pattern, you will, of course, want to drill down into the root causes. There are several possible reasons for underestimating, covered in Figures 9.3–9.10.

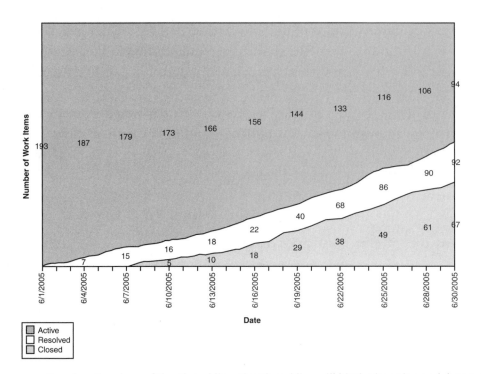

Figure 9.2   Based on the slope of the Closed line, the Closed line will hit the iteration end date well below the planned level, meaning that not all the scenarios planned for this iteration will be completed before iteration exit.

Uneven Task Decomposition

Check the degree of variation in the task definition and the size range of the task granularity. You would hope to see tasks planned to the scale of one to three days (see Figures 9.3 and 9.4).

Architectural Blind Spots

Sometimes the team discovers a need for an architectural change. This could be the need to focus more heavily on integration, reconsider QoS, change the component structure, introduce new common services, change the planned deployment environment, or otherwise make extensive architectural changes.

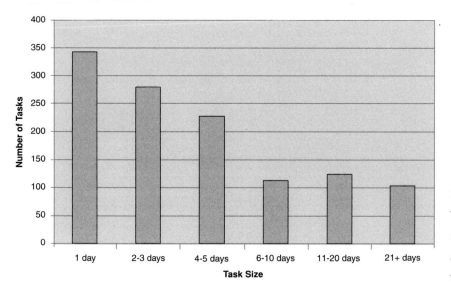

Figure 9.3
This histogram of
number of tasks
against size shows
that task size varies
significantly.

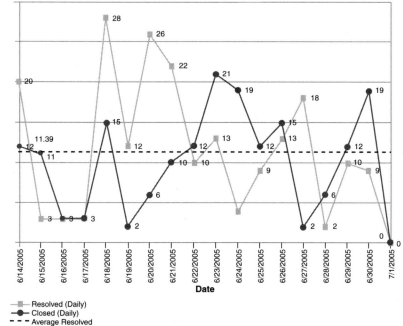

Figure 9.4
Correspondingly, the
Project Velocity chart
shows a high variance
in the number of
tasks closed per day.

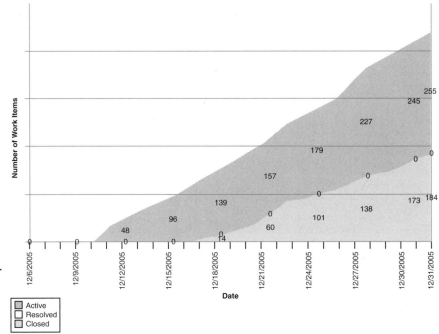

Figure 9.5
This Remaining
Work chart, filtered
for tasks, shows sig-
nificant growth in
tasks being added
to the backlog.

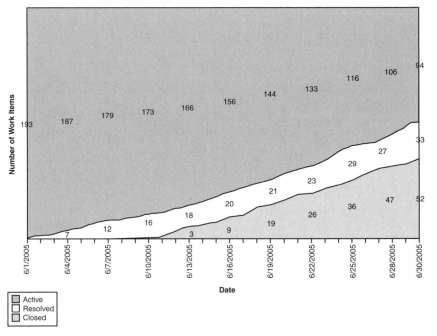

Figure 9.6
Simultaneously, when
filtered for scenarios,
the Remaining Work
chart shows the sce-
narios stuck in the
active state, and the
total number planned
for the iteration is
declining.

Examining the Remaining Work charts in Figures 9.5 and 9.6 shows the pattern. Scenarios and QoS requirements are staying active longer than expected (in fact, some need to be cut from the iteration), while development tasks are rising significantly. This late discovery of tasks may indicate undiscovered architectural work.

Scope Creep

"Scope creep," depending on your perspective, is the usual term for the late piling on of requirements or the inability of the project manager to keep the current iteration focused on its initial target. In other words, at the start of an iteration, you normally know which scenarios are chosen for the iteration. If this list shifts, the team can be seriously disrupted (see Figure 9.7).

On the other hand, it is entirely appropriate to rethink the future *between* iterations. A purpose of iteration chunking is to give you the opportunity to correct your course based on new learning and new information.

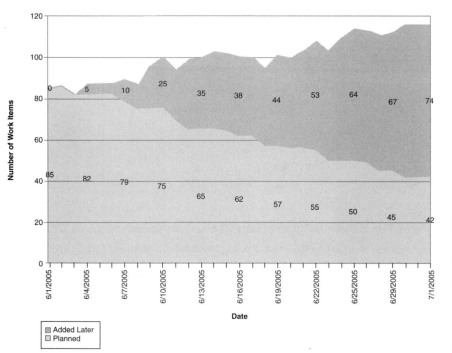

Figure 9.7
The Unplanned Work chart, filtered for scenarios, shows a significant climb in the Added Later area.

	ID	Iteration Path	Assigned To	State	Title
	2481	Shareware Starter Kit	Juan Perez (Personify Design)	Proposed	Need to identify a localization vendor for JPN
	2482	Shareware Starter Kit	Juan Perez (Personify Design)	Active	Payment vendor hasn't approved the Payment Web Service account
	2483	Shareware Starter Kit	Juan Perez (Personify Design)	Active	Need to hire two more Testers
	2484	Shareware Starter Kit	Juan Perez (Personify Design)	Proposed	Need to contract an IIS Hoster than can hardware load balance
	2485	Shareware Starter Kit	Juan Perez (Personify Design)	Active	Haven't signed contracts with government agencies involved
	2486	Shareware Starter Kit	Juan Perez (Personify Design)	Active	Need new logo from design firm
	2487	Shareware Starter Kit	Juan Perez (Personify Design)	Proposed	Security firm hasn't returned security review results

Issues [Results]
Query Results: 7 results found (1 currently selected).

Figure 9.8 Trying to bluff the schedule shows up in an accumulating list of issues that aren't being resolved.

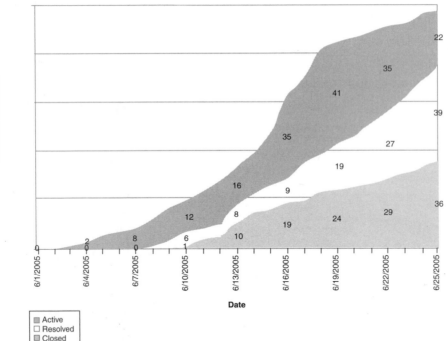

Figure 9.9 This cumulative flow diagram for bugs shows a steeply rising top line because most bugs are not known at the start of the iteration. The widening *Active* band indicates a find rate higher than the current fix rate, growing the bug backlog. This could happen for a variety of reasons, such as newly integrated functionality being available for test, a bug bash, new reports from beta users, and so on. On the other hand, the bubble in the *Resolved* band shows a period when testers cannot verify the number of bug resolutions as quickly as they are being delivered.

Inadequate Bug Allotment

If you plan tasks that consume 100% of your available resources, then you have no capacity left to handle unplanned work. It is necessary to schedule time for handling bugs and other work that will arise but that might not be known at iteration start.

Sometimes, especially in feature-boxed planning, this pattern is a sign of political dysfunction. One example is "schedule chicken," where competing teams bluff the schedule because they expect someone else to miss the dates by a larger margin than they will (see Figures 9.8 and 9.9).

Resource Leaks

In some environments, a team does not fully control its own time. For example, developers might be pulled off new development to fix bugs on production releases, or people might be pulled into someone's pet project. ("Can you set up this demo for me?") These are resource leaks because the resources you scheduled are being reallocated to unplanned work that does not benefit your project. To spot resource leaks, look for unusual variations in the Project Velocity graph (see Figure 9.10) or flat spots in the Remaining Work chart.

Development Practices Too Loose

It is a development responsibility to deliver working software for testing. If the software isn't passing the build verification tests (BVTs), or the BVTs and unit tests are inadequate, then fix the problem at its source. Ordinarily, the team will know if these are problems, but if you are a manager and therefore are one step removed, you might first see signs in these reports.

Build Failures

A nightly build is the heartbeat of your project (refer to Chapter 6, "Development"). If your builds are not completing successfully or are not passing BVTs, as shown in Figure 9.11, then you need to do what is necessary to fix the problem immediately. Usually the team will self-correct and restore the working build without much management intervention.

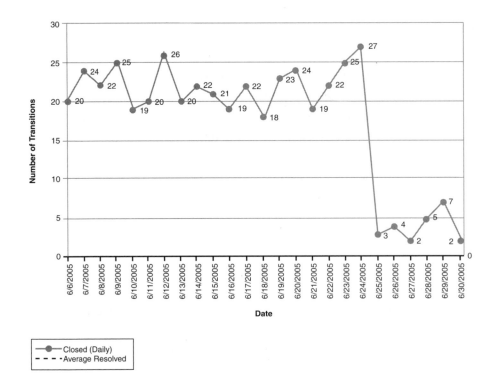

Figure 9.10   On this Project Velocity graph, the number of development tasks closed takes a sudden dip in week 4. There may be a known reason (vacation, scheduled training, illness, and so on), or it may be a sign that something is interfering with the expected work. It's a good question for your standup meetings.

Builds

What are the details for the builds?

Build Name ⇕	Flavor ⇕	Platform ⇕	Build Quality ⇕	% Tests Passed	% Code Coverage	% Code Churn
BVT_20060119.1	Release	Any CPU	Rejected	8.489 %	86.489 %	104.986 %
BVT_20060118.2	Release	Any CPU	Released	4.286 %	44.286 %	101.429 %
BVT_20060118.1	Release	Any CPU	Rejected	1.429 %	84.489 %	102.189 %
BVT_20060116.1	Release	Any CPU	Rejected	6.489 %	82.189 %	106.489 %
Nightly_20060112.1	Release	Any CPU	Ready for Initial Test	84.286 %	2.189 %	101.429 %

Figure 9.11   This build summary shows that some builds are not completing and others are failing BVTs.

Inadequate Unit Testing

Code should be delivered with adequate unit tests—that's pretty well accepted nowadays. The best automated approximation for the breadth of the unit tests is code coverage (refer to Chapter 7, "Testing," on the use and misuse of code coverage). If you are practicing Test Driven Development or similar techniques, then your code coverage should approach 100%, except where you have good reasons for exclusions. If your unit tests are reused as BVTs, then the coverage should be visible with the Quality Indicators and Build reports (see Figures 9.12 and 9.13).

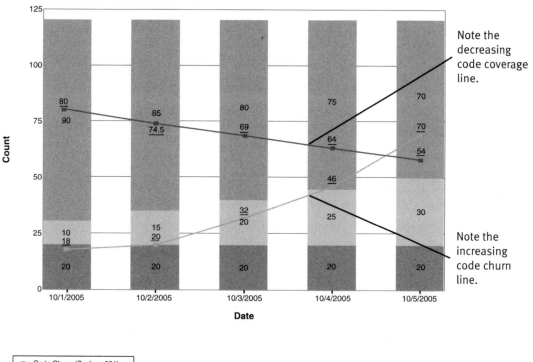

Figure 9.12   This Quality Indicators report shows a decrease in code coverage and an increase in code churn over the five days. This is a clear warning that new code is being checked in without corresponding unit tests to cover it.

Builds

What are the details for the builds?

Build Name	Flavor	Platform	Build Quality	% Tests Passed	% Code Coverage	% Code Churn
Teamlook Beta 20060126.1	Release	Any CPU	Released	89.247 %	86.489 %	104.286 %
SSK Admin 20060126.1	Release	Any CPU	Under Investigation	4.286 %	44.286 %	108.489 %
Shareware Starter Kit 20060126.1	Release	Any CPU	Rejected	68.489 %	84.489 %	104.986 %
Personal Build 20060126.1	Release	Any CPU	Released	74.286 %	82.189 %	101.429 %
Nightly 20060118.1	Release	Any CPU	Released	91.429 %	68.489 %	102.189 %
Nightly 20060116.1	Release	Any CPU	Ready for Initial Test	86.489 %	64.286 %	106.489 %
BVT 20060116.1	Release	x86	Rejected	68.489 %	91.429 %	100.013 %

Figure 9.13   This Build Details report shows that code coverage varies widely across the different source projects. This indicates uneven unit testing or at least uneven coverage from the BVTs.

Reactivations

Another warning sign is a high reactivation rate, sometimes called a "fault feedback ratio." Reactivation rate counts the number of supposedly fixed bugs whose fixes don't work (see Figure 9.14). These reactivations create a vicious cycle of rework that crowds out planned tasks.

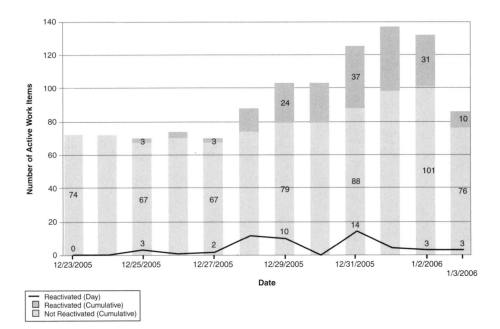

Figure 9.14   This Reactivations graph shows a high and rising rate of bug fixes that were rejected in testing. This trend is clearly digging a hole that will consume resources for no visible customer benefit.

Note that if you encounter high reactivations, it's worth looking into the root causes. Although sloppy development practice is an obvious possibility, other potential causes include poor bug reporting, poor test lab management, and overly aggressive triage.

Bluffing

Bluffing, that is, reporting work as complete when it isn't, is hard to achieve when you have the transparency of a value-up process with VSTS. If someone is bluffing, you would expect to see a combination of the patterns shown previously—build breaks, high reactivations, rising code churn, and decreasing code coverage from unit testing and BVTs. There will be enough anomalies that the behavior might correct itself through pride of workmanship and peer pressure. Of course, if it doesn't, you need to intervene.

Tests Passing; Solution Doesn't Work

One of the more frustrating project situations is to find that tests are reported as passing but the solution under the test still doesn't work for observers outside the test team. In these cases, you want to identify why the tests do not seem to find the same issues that other users do. Figures 9.15–9.18 are examples of this case.

High Bug Find Rate

Frequently you see a high test pass rate but still see a large incoming bug rate (or worse, customers or beta users are reporting lots of bugs that testing seems to be missing).

This can occur for several reasons:

- The tests might be too gentle for this stage of the solution. In early iterations, gentle tests are good, but as the solution matures, tests should exercise broader scenarios and integrations. These tests might be missing.

- Tests might be stale or be testing the wrong functionality.
- It might be time to switch test techniques. (See Chapter 7.)

Consider Figures 9.15, 9.16, and 9.17.

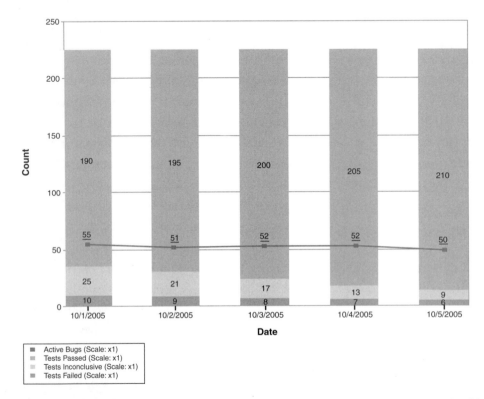

Figure 9.15   On the Quality Indicators chart, the test pass rate is high, but active bugs are also high.

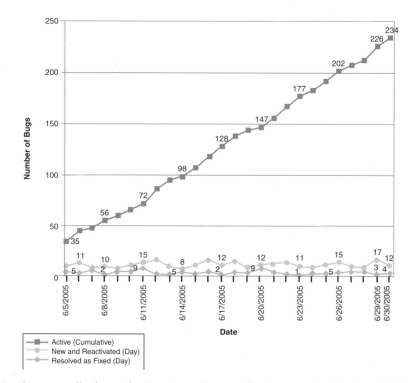

Figure 9.16 Correspondingly, on the Bug Rates chart, active bugs are high because find rate stays high.

Bugs Found Without Corresponding Tests

Were there bugs found without corresponding tests?

ID ⇕	State ⇕	Priority ⇕	Title	Created By ⇕
56	Active	1	Payment web service doesn't return on Visual Basic.NET clients	Juan Perez (Personify Design)
80	Active	1	All DateTime fields should be ReadOnly by default	Juan Perez (Personify Design)
81	Active	2	Close timeout when checking in add of 4947 and 164 dirs	Juan Perez (Personify Design)
82	Active	2	Update unshelve to use pend methods to resolve issues correctly	Juan Perez (Personify Design)
83	Active	2	MS Project: Not picking up title/cannot sync	Juan Perez (Personify Design)
84	Proposed	3	Build failure in build: Nightly Build_20060111.1	tfssvc

Figure 9.17 Tests aren't finding the bugs. On this report, many of the bugs found have no corresponding test. This might be a sign that testing is looking elsewhere. And, if you are expecting regression testing to prevent their undiscovered recurrence, you will need regression tests that you don't have yet.

Tests Are Stale

Tests do not necessarily evolve at the same rate as the code under test. This risk is present especially when tests are heavily automated. In this situation, you see high test pass rates with ongoing code churn and diminishing code coverage (see Figure 9.18).

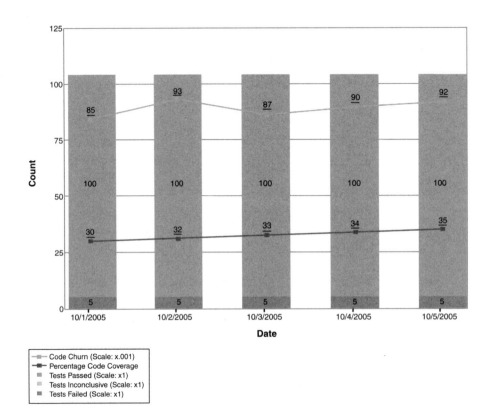

Figure 9.18   This Quality Indicators chart shows a high rate of code churn and a low rate of code coverage from testing, yet test pass rates remain high. This suggests that the tests being run are not exercising the new code. Don't be lulled by the high test pass rate—these tests are clearly not testing all the new development work.

Solution Stuck in Testing

Sometimes it appears that there is a bottleneck in testing, as indicated by the Remaining Work chart (see Figure 9.19).

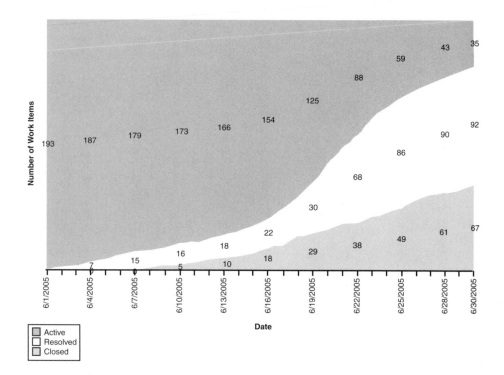

Figure 9.19   This Remaining Work chart shows a bulging line in *Resolved*, meaning that the developers are reporting work items resolved, but testers haven't closed them. Further drilldown is warranted.

This bulge in testing can happen for very different reasons. It always merits further drilldown.

Tests Failing

One case is that lots of tests are failing, requiring effort to diagnose the failures and report the bugs. This should prompt you to investigate why the software is failing so often. Note that code churn is stuck at a high level as well, indicating that lots of new code is being written (see Figure 9.20). The next patterns to look for are the ones shown previously in this chapter under "Development Practices Too Loose" (see Figures 9.12 through 9.14).

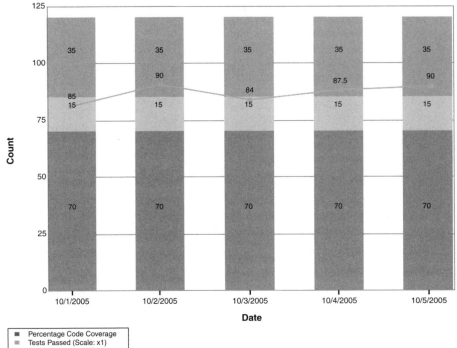

Figure 9.20   The Quality Indicators chart shows that lots of tests are being run with reasonable code coverage, but the tests are failing. This is probably an indicator of loose development practices, although in early iterations, it might be an indicator that the tests are too harsh for this stage of the solution.

It's also possible that tests are failing because the team discovered an unexpected need to refactor the code. This might be entirely healthy and foreseen—it is exactly the kind of answer that the metrics alone cannot tell you.

Too Little Testing

On the other hand, the problem might be that not enough testing is being done to process the incoming work quickly enough (see Figures 9.21 and 9.22). This could be a limitation of resources, planning, or logistics.

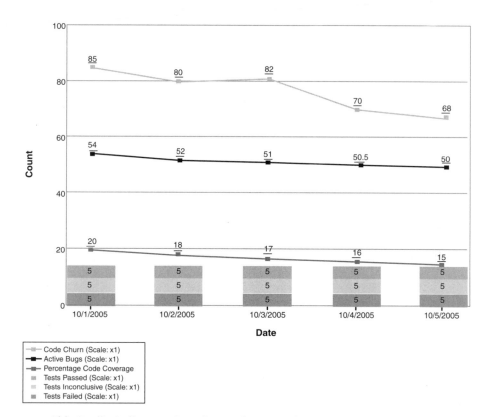

Figure 9.21   This Quality Indicators chart shows a low rate of tests being run. This would probably mean that too little testing has been happening. This could be due to inadequate resource allocation for testing, or it could be that testers are doing something else, such as writing test automation rather than testing the current functionality. In either case, resource balancing may be warranted.

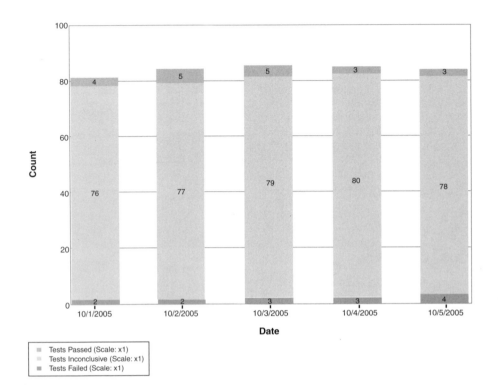

Figure 9.22   A variant pattern that occurs with automated test generation is that the developers have generated tests, but no one has finished the logic, so the tests are inconclusive.

Summary

In this chapter, I showed a large number of antipatterns that projects experience, using examples from the VSTS metrics warehouse. None of these are direct prescriptions for a cure, but they are illustrations of data that allow you to ask the right questions of the team.

When everyone on the team can see the same metrics across all the dimensions, discussions shift from trying to determine the data to trying to answer the questions posed by the data. With trust and transparency, it becomes possible for everyone to participate in identifying and executing solutions.

Endnotes

1. Tolstoy, *Anna Karenina*.
2. Anderson 2005, op. cit.
3. Edward Yourdon, *Death March: The Complete Software Developer's Guide to Surviving 'Mission Impossible' Projects* (Upper Saddle River, NJ: Prentice Hall, 1997).

10

Conclusion

"It is true that we have really in Flatland a Third unrecognized Dimension called 'height,' just as it also is true that you have really in Spaceland a Fourth unrecognized Dimension, called by no name at present, but which I will call 'extra-height.' But we can no more take cognizance of our 'height' than you can of your 'extra-height.' Even I—who have been in Spaceland, and have had the privilege of understanding for twenty-four hours the meaning of 'height'—even I cannot now comprehend it, nor realize it by the sense of sight or by any process of reason; I can but apprehend it by faith."

—Edwin Abbott, *Flatland: A Romance of Many Dimensions*[1]

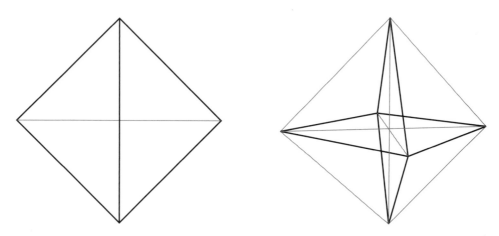

Figure 10.1 These two figures are both two-dimensional views of the same octahedron. If you cover the right-hand image, however, you will probably see the left image as a square with two diagonals. Only when you see the two together do the diagonals appear as edges of a three-dimensional shape.

In this book, I've described how a team of peers can apply a value-up approach and apply Visual Studio Team System (VSTS) to improve their capacity for creating customer value through their work. I've done this from the various qualitative viewpoints of the disciplines and from the quantitative metrics that get captured in the process. Both are multidimensional approaches.

I have frequently used the two instances of MSF (Microsoft Solutions Framework) as references because they are the process guidance that ships with VSTS and because they are the processes that, as far as I know, most closely represent value-up thinking. I have tried, wherever possible, to give credit to the intellectual sources of the ideas.

Expected Criticisms

At the time I am writing this book, Team System has just shipped. I've made a number of claims, and I expect a fair amount of criticism for them, so let me plead guilty to five major indictments right now:

1. **This book is not Agile enough.** In particular, I expect to be dinged for not following the Agile Manifesto tenets closely enough.[2] For example, I write more about processes and tools than individuals and interactions, and more about change in the context of a plan than responding to change without a plan. Actually, I think that a huge strength of the Agile community has been the effervescent tooling that has emerged for unit testing and change management. And processes such as XP have demonstrated the great value of discipline. With VSTS, we are trying to make tools and practices like these easier and more approachable to a much wider community than they have been before.

2. **This book is not prescriptive enough.** A value-up tenet is the importance of situationally specific strategies. I've tried to focus on recognizing and understanding the situation, trusting that if the whole team can see the same data, the team can work on the prescriptions. There is certainly a book waiting to be written on situationally specific management patterns.

3. **There is not enough depth for each of the disciplines.** I've written this as the introductory book to a series. A book targeted specifically to development practices with VSTS will be available shortly after this one is released. I hope

many authors will join me over the next few years. And I realize that I stopped short on the vital topics of user experience, release management, and operations.

4. **I don't have enough data to support my claims.** Not yet. Microsoft is certainly going to accumulate case studies around VSTS, and you will be able to find them on http://msdn.microsoft.com/teamsystem. I hope that they reveal enough insight into the processes used and enough data to illustrate the values that I discuss here.

5. **The sources are too random.** Software engineering is not new and does not occur independently of its business context. I've tried hard to bring in the threads of both the valuable work of the community and the business environment of the twenty-first century. I often find software debates to be very black-and-white, but I see the situation as much more multi-colored. I hope that you too may come to prefer the color and gradation over the absolute black or white projection.

I also might be accused of making too much of a product sales pitch. I have tried to argue the design ideas that led to the creation of VSTS with as many examples as I could fit. I've tried wherever possible to distinguish the ideas from the implementation, but I have used the product to illustrate them. I hope you found the presentation balanced.

Value-Up, Again

The core idea of this book is that a new paradigm is emerging for software development, which I've called the value-up approach. The early intellectual roots of value-up lie in the work of Deming, Weinberg, and Goldratt, and the Agile, Lean Manufacturing, and Theory of Constraints communities. The central tenet of value-up is to maximize the flow of customer value.

Consistent with these roots, value-up espouses these ideas:

1. **Embrace change.** Invest in just enough planning and design to understand risk and to manage the next small increment.

2. **Measure only those deliverables that the customer values.** View all interim measures skeptically.

3. **Understand quality as value to the customer.** The customer's perception may change, so keep options open and plan for frequent delivery.

4. **Accept variance as a part of all processes.** Distinguish special-cause from common-cause variance. Treat them differently.

5. **Use intermediate work products only insofar as they improve the flow of value.** Use them to reduce uncertainty and variation, not measure progress.

6. **Increase capacity by attacking bottlenecks in the flow of value.** Tune resources and time only after removing the bottlenecks.

7. **Be transparent and trusting.** Assume that the team takes pride in its workmanship and wants it to be seen.

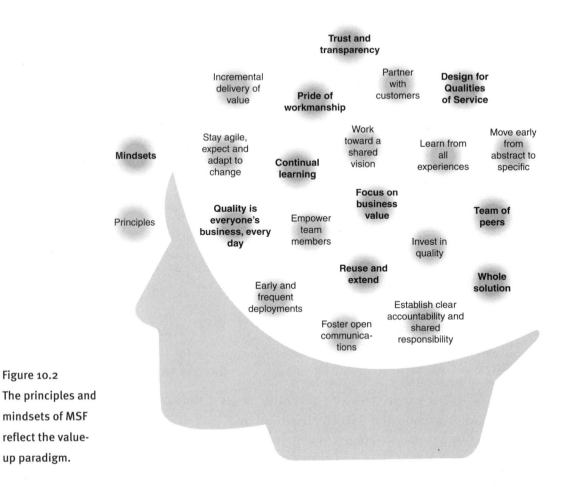

Figure 10.2

The principles and mindsets of MSF reflect the value-up paradigm.

If you consider this list to be motherhood and apple pie, then I've achieved half my purpose.

The second half of my purpose is to convince you that tooling can make a large, positive difference. VSTS is not the first product to address the software lifecycle, and it won't be the last. However, I believe that it is the first that attempts to offer a comprehensive value-up approach for the whole team in a simple, productive, integrated, and extensible manner. Free trials of the product are available, and you can judge its suitability for yourself. Of course, VSTS is a new product, and there will be a large number of requests to take it further. I welcome the dialogue.

VSTS, by instrumenting the software process, enables trustworthy transparency. The metrics warehouse gives the whole team a common view of the facts and a common base of historical performance. This common view changes the discussion from "Whose numbers are right?" to "What should we do next?"

I hope that VSTS spawns similar innovations across the industry. Improving the capacity of IT and the software industry is one of the great economic challenges and opportunities of the coming decades. I believe that this requires both a value-up approach and the tooling to support it.

Endnotes

1. Edwin Abbott, *Flatland: A Romance of Many Dimensions, by A Square* (Boston, Roberts Brothers, 1885), Preface to Second Edition.

2. www.agilemanifesto.org

Index

A

accepted build cycle, testing during, 198-199
accessibility, as QoS (quality of service), 69
actors, personas versus, 65-66
Actual Quality versus Planned Velocity graph, 97-98
ad hoc testing. *See* exploratory testing
adapting process (iterative development), 35
adaptive approach, plan-driven approach versus, 38-39
adaptive projects, 51
advocacy groups, viewpoints of risk, 36-37
Agile Alliance, 2, 29
Agile Manifesto, 2
agility, 3
AIB (Applied Integration Baseline), 122
Anderson, David J., 8, 32
Application Designer, 124
Applied Integration Baseline (AIB), 122
architecture, 116
  baseline architecture, 119-122
  citizenship, 128
  Design for Operations, 128-131
  QoS mindset and, 126-128
  reference architectures, 122-123
  SOA (service-oriented architecture), 116-119
    VSTS and, 124-127
  troubleshooting, 224-226
  validating, 121
  value-up approach, 116, 119
  in VSTS, 116
assessment data in bug reports, 216-218
attractiveness, as QoS (quality of service), 69

audit trails, 109-111
auditability, 41
auditors, 41
Austin, Robert, 83
automated build system, 156-161
automated code analysis, 138-139
automated scenario testing, 172-175
automated testing, 201
availability, as QoS (quality of service), 70

B

baseline architecture, 119-120
  reference architectures, 122-123
  refining, 121-122
batch sizes, 32
Beizer, Boris, 195
bluffing, 233
Boehm, Barry, 28
bottom-up estimation, 100
branching (source control), 156
Broken Windows theory, 193
Brooks, Fred, 30
bug find rate, 233-235
Bug Rates graph, 93-94
bugs. *See also* prioritizing bugs; testing
  capacity to handle, 228-229
  lifecycle of, 206-210
  reactivation rate, troubleshooting, 232
  writing bug reports, 210-212
    assessment data in, 216-218
    objective data in, 214-216
    plans in, 218
    SOAP analogy, 212-213
    subjective data in, 213-214

inform**IT**